Access 2003
FOR
DUMMIES®

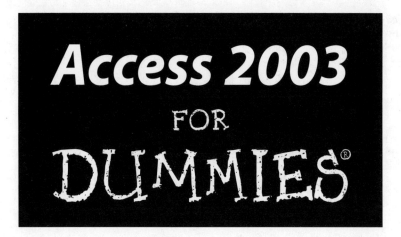

by **John Kaufeld**

WILEY

Wiley Publishing, Inc.

Access 2003 For Dummies®

Published by
Wiley Publishing, Inc.
111 River Street
Hoboken, NJ 07030
www.wiley.com

Copyright © 2003 by Wiley Publishing, Inc., Indianapolis, Indiana

Published by Wiley Publishing, Inc., Indianapolis, Indiana

Published simultaneously in Canada

For general information on our other products and services or to obtain technical support, please contact our Customer Care Department within the U.S. at 800-762-2974, outside the U.S. at 317-572-3993, or fax 317-572-4002.

Wiley also publishes its books in a variety of electronic formats. Some content that appears in print may not be available in electronic books.

Library of Congress Control Number: 2003101916

ISBN: 0-7645-3881-0

Manufactured in the United States of America

10 9 8 7 6 5 4 3 2

About the Author

John Kaufeld got hooked on computers a long time ago. Somewhere along the way, he discovered that he really enjoyed helping people resolve computer problems. John finally achieved his B.S. degree in management information systems from Ball State University and he became the first PC support technician for what was then Westinghouse near Cincinnati, Ohio.

Since then, he has logged nearly a decade of experience working with normal people who were stuck with a "friendly" PC that turned on them. He's also trained more than 1000 people in many different PC and Macintosh applications. Today, John conducts media skills and promotion seminars for up-and-coming entrepreneurs and writes in his free moments. His other ventures include More Than Games, an amazingly cool board and card game store (www.morethangames.com); ShipperTools.com, a shipping system that helps small businesses and eBay sellers save money with the US Postal Service (www.shippertools.com); and his Feed the News Beast small-business seminars (www.feedthenewsbeast.com).

His other titles include the best-selling *AOL For Dummies*, plus too many other database and Internet books to leave him emotionally unscarred. John lives with his wife, two children, and two gerbils in Fort Wayne, Indiana.

Dedication

To Jenny, because without you, I'd be completely nuts.

To J.B. and the Pooz for reminding Daddy to smile when all he could do was write.

To John Wiley & Sons for the opportunity of a lifetime.

My sincere thanks to you, one and all.

Author's Acknowledgments

As with any good magic trick, there's more to putting out a book than meets the eye. Granted, writing a book like this demands long periods of intense sitting, but it actually takes a team of intense sitters to complete the finished product you hold in your hands.

Kudos upon kudos go to my project editor, Susan "Spink" Pink for her diligent efforts to make my ramblings follow commonly accepted semantic guidelines. As an extra added bonus, she even laughs at my jokes. Sometimes. Equally significant thanks go to technical editor Allen Wyatt for verifying that I didn't make most of this stuff up.

More gratitude than I can express here goes to Senior Acquisitions Editor Steve Hayes and to the King of Acquisitions (or whatever his real title is), Andy Cummings. This year, they both proved that there's more to working relationships than meets the eye. If it wasn't for you two . . . well . . . I don't even want to think about it. You both mean more to me than you'll ever know.

Finally, ten years worth of sincere thanks go to Diane Steele for her support, encouragement, and willingness to take a chance on a proven geek (but an unproven writer).

Publisher's Acknowledgments

We're proud of this book; please send us your comments through our online registration form located at www.dummies.com/register/.

Some of the people who helped bring this book to market include the following:

Acquisitions, Editorial, and Media Development

Project Editor: Susan Pink

Acquisitions Editor: Steven H. Hayes

Technical Editor: Allen Wyatt, Discovery Computing Inc.

Editorial Manager: Carol Sheehan

Media Development Supervisor: Richard Graves

Editorial Assistant: Amanda Foxworth

Cartoons: Rich Tennant (www.the5thwave.com)

Production

Project Coordinator: Maridee Ennis

Layout and Graphics: Seth Conley, Lynsey Osborn, Shae Wilson

Proofreaders: Carl William Pierce, Toni Settle

Indexer: TECHBOOKS Production Services

Publishing and Editorial for Technology Dummies

> **Richard Swadley,** Vice President and Executive Group Publisher

> **Andy Cummings,** Vice President and Publisher

> **Mary C. Corder,** Editorial Director

Publishing for Consumer Dummies

> **Diane Graves Steele,** Vice President and Publisher

> **Joyce Pepple,** Acquisitions Director

Composition Services

> **Gerry Fahey,** Vice President of Production Services

> **Debbie Stailey,** Director of Composition Services

Contents at a Glance

Table of Contents

Introduction

· ·

*B*eing a normal human being, you probably have work to do. In fact, you
may have *lots* of work piled precariously around your office or even
stretching onto the Internet. Someone, possibly your boss (or, if you work at
home, your Significant Other), suggested that Access may help you do more
in less time, eliminate the piles, and generally make the safety inspector
happy.

So you picked up Access, and here you are. Whee!

About This Book

If you feel confused instead of organized, befuddled instead of productive,
or just completely lost on the whole database thing, *Access 2003 For Dummies*
is the book for you. And don't worry — you aren't alone in those feelings.
Unlike word processors and presentation programs, few people catch on to
databases by themselves. (Those few who manage the feat usually turn into
computer support people as a way of working through the trauma.)

This book has a simple purpose: to show you how Access works, what to do
with it, and why you might actually care, while carefully *not* turning you into
a world-class nerd in the process. What more could you want?

Conventions Used in This Book

Every now and then, you need to tell Access to do something or other.
Likewise, there are moments when the program wants to toss its own comments and messages back to you (so be nice — communication is a two-way
street). To easily show the difference between a human-to-computer message
and vice-versa, I format the commands differently.

Here are examples of both kinds of messages as they appear in the book.

This is something you type into the computer.

```
This is how the computer responds to your command.
```

Because Access *is* a Windows program, you don't just type all day — you also
mouse around quite a bit. Although I don't use a cool font for mouse actions,

I *do* assume that you already know the basics. Here are the mouse movements necessary to make Access (and any other Windows program) work:

- ✔ **Click:** Position the tip of the mouse pointer (the end of the arrow) on the menu item, button, check box, or whatever else you happen to be aiming at, and then quickly press and release the left mouse button.

- ✔ **Double-click:** Position the mouse pointer as though you're going to click, but fool it at the last minute by clicking twice in rapid succession.

- ✔ **Click and drag (highlight):** Put the tip of the mouse pointer at the place you want to start highlighting and then press and hold the left mouse button. While holding down the mouse button, drag the pointer across whatever you want to highlight. When you reach the end of what you're highlighting, release the mouse button.

- ✔ **Right-click:** Right-clicking works just like clicking, except that you're exercising the right instead of the left mouse button.

Of course, the Access menu comes in handy, too. When I want you to choose something from the main menu bar, the instruction looks like this:

Choose File➪Open Database.

If you think that mice belong in holes, you can use the underlined letters as shortcut keys to control Access from the keyboard. To use the keyboard shortcut, hold down the Alt key and press the appropriate underlined letter. In the example above, the keyboard shortcuts are Alt+F, then Alt+O. Press them one right after the other, with the Alt key down the whole time.

If you aren't familiar with all these rodent gymnastics, or if you want to know more about Windows in general, pick up a copy of one of the many *Windows For Dummies* titles. Every version of Windows has one!

What You Don't Have to Read

Must you completely ingest this entire tome before understanding Access? Goodness, no! (Besides, I don't think the book ingests well — at least not without a trip or two through the shredder.) Certain stuff made it into the book simply because I couldn't find any way to leave it out.

For one thing, feel free to ignore anything marked by the Technical Stuff icon, like the one next to this paragraph. You don't need to know the stuff marked by these little signposts to make Access function helpfully in your world. If you *feel* like going deeper into the uncharted depths of the program, you can always start the trip with a glance at the Technical Stuff texts.

If you use Access only for working with your company's big corporately designed databases, don't worry about the database design chapter. Your Information Systems department probably won't let you mess around with the database structure anyway, so why worry with design details in the meantime?

Foolish Assumptions

You need to know only a few things about your computer and Windows to get the most out of *Access 2003 For Dummies*. (Turning yourself into a full-bore computer nerd is totally out of the question.) In the following pages, I presume that you

- ✔ Know the basics of whichever flavor of Windows you're using.
- ✔ Want to work with databases that other people have created.
- ✔ Want to use and create queries, reports, and an occasional form.
- ✔ Want to make your own databases from scratch every now and then.
- ✔ Have Microsoft Windows 98, 98 SE, ME, 2000, NT 4, or any flavor of XP, and Access for Windows on your computer (if you have the entire Office suite, that's fine, too). If your computer still uses Windows 95, spend some quiet time with the machine. After that, give it a decent burial and go splurge on a new computer. Your old one deserves a well-earned rest (and you deserve a gold star for putting up with an old machine for that long).

The good news is that you don't have to know (or even care) about table design, field types, relational databases, or any of that other database stuff to make Access work for you. Everything you need to know is right here, just waiting for you to read it.

How This Book Is Organized

To give you an idea of what's ahead, here's a breakdown of the six parts in this book. Each part covers a general topic of Access. The part's individual chapters dig into the details.

Part 1: Which Came First, the Data or the Base?

Right off the bat, this book answers the lyrical question "It's a data-*what?*" By starting with an overview of both database concepts in general and Access in particular, this book provides the information you need to make sense of the whole database concept. This part also contains suggestions about solving problems with (or even *without*) Access. If you're about to design a new Access database to fix some pesky problem, read this section first — it may change your mind.

Part II: Truly Tempting Tables

Arguably, tables (where the data lives) are at the center of this whole database hubbub. After all, without tables, you wouldn't have any data to bully around. This part gives you the information you need to know about designing, building, using, changing, and generally coexisting in the same room with Access tables.

Part III: Finding the Ultimate Answer to Almost Everything

If tables are at the center of the Access universe, then queries are the first ring of planets. In Access, queries ask the power questions; they unearth the answers you *know* are hiding somewhere in your data. In addition to covering queries, this part also explains how to answer smaller questions using Find, Filter, and Sort — Query's little siblings.

Part IV: Turning Your Table into a Book

Seeing your data on-screen just isn't enough, sometimes. To make your work *really* shine, you have to commit it to paper. Part IV covers the Access report system, a portion of the software entirely dedicated both to getting your information onto the printed page and to driving you nuts in the process.

Part V: Wizards, Forms, and Other Mystical Stuff

At some point, technology approaches magic (one look at the control panel for a modern microwave oven is proof of that). This part explores some of the mystical areas in Access, helping you do stuff faster, seek assistance from the wizards, get your computer to do what you want just by talking to it, and even venture into a bit of programming. If the Internet's limitless possibilities pique your online fancy, look in this part for info about the new Web connectivity features in Access. They're really amazing!

Part VI: The Part of Tens

The words *For Dummies book* immediately bring to mind the snappy, irreverent Part of Tens. This section dumps a load of tips and cool ideas onto, and hopefully *into,* your head. You can find a little bit of everything here, including timesaving tips and the solutions to the most common problems awaiting you in Access.

Icons Used in This Book

When something in this book is particularly valuable, I go out of my way to make sure that it stands out. I use these cool icons to mark text that (for one reason or another) *really* needs your attention. Here's a quick preview of the ones waiting for you in this book and what they mean:

Tips are *really* helpful words of wisdom that promise to save you time, energy, and perhaps some hair. Whenever you see a tip, take a second to check it out.

Some things are too important to forget, so the Remember icon points them out. These items are critical steps in a process — points that you don't want to miss.

Despite my best efforts, sometimes I give in to the nerdy side and slip some technical twaddle into the book. The Technical Stuff icon protects you from obscure details by making them easy to avoid. If you're in an adventuresome mood, check out the technical stuff. You may find it interesting.

The Warning icon says it all: *Skipping this information may be hazardous to your data's health.* Pay attention to these icons and follow their instructions to keep your databases happy and intact.

Where to Go from Here

Now nothing's left to hold you back from the wonders of Access. Cleave tightly to *Access 2003 For Dummies* and dive into Access.

- ✔ If you're brand new to the program and don't know which way to turn, start with the general overview in Chapter 1.

- ✔ If you're about to design a database, I salute you — and recommend flipping through Chapter 4 for some helpful design and development tips.

- ✔ Looking for something specific? Try the Table of Contents or the Index, or just flip through the book until you find something interesting.

Bon voyage!

Part I

Which Came First, the Data or the Base?

The 5th Wave   By Rich Tennant

"Our classroom PCs have created a challenging atmosphere where critical analyzing, synthesizing, and problem-solving skills are honed. I think the students have gotten a lot out of them, too."

In this part . . .

Everything starts somewhere. It's that way with nature, with science, and with meatballs that roll down your tie. So what more fitting way to begin this book than with a look at where databases start — as a glimmer in someone's mind.

This part opens with a heretical look at problem solving, and then moves along to cover the highlights of Access itself. A little later in this part, you discover the secrets of good data organization and where to find help when the world of Access gets you down.

All in all, this part is a pretty good place to start — whether you're new to the database concept or just to Access. Either way, welcome aboard!

Chapter 1

The 37-Minute Overview

*I*t's confession time. This chapter probably takes longer than 37 minutes to finish. Then again, you may spend *less* time than that if you're somewhat familiar with the program or if you're a speed-reader. Either way, the chapter *does* give you a good overview of Access 2003 from start to finish (and I mean that literally).

Because the best way to get into Access is to literally *get into* it, this chapter leads you on a wild, galloping tour of the software, covering the highlights of what you and Access will probably do together on a daily basis. Think of the chapter as a "Day in the Life" story, designed to show you the important stuff.

If you're new to Access 2003, this chapter makes a good starting point. If you're familiar with older versions of Access, I recommend that you skim this chapter anyway to see the changes introduced in this new version. Enjoy the trip!

In the Beginning, There Was Access 2003

To start Access, click the Start button and choose Microsoft Access 2003 from the Start menu (see Figure 1-1). If Access is hiding from you, look for a program group with a name such as Office or Microsoft.

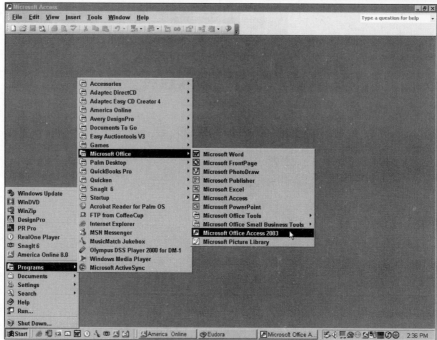

Figure 1-1:
For a smart program, Access 2003 doesn't hide very well.

If you still can't find Access on the Start menu, you have to create your own shortcut (egads!). Follow these steps to create a shortcut:

1. **Click the Start button. Then, depending on which version of Windows you use, choose F̲ind⇨F̲iles or Folders or choose Sear̲ch⇨F̲or files and folders.**

   The Find: All Files dialog box appears.

2. **For the file name, type** msaccess.exe, **and then click Find Now.**

   Windows finds the program file.

TECHNICAL STUFF

If Windows finds two copies of the program (as Figure 1-2 shows), that usually means your system has both an older *and* a newer version of Access installed. To tell the two programs apart, right-click the first entry, and choose Properties from the pop-up menu. A little window appears, sharing all kinds of nifty information about the file. Click the Version tab along the top of the little window. For Access 2003, the file version number should start with 11. If it begins with something smaller than 11, close the window and repeat the process with the other file. If *neither* file shows the right version number, Access 2003 apparently isn't installed on your machine (or at least Windows can't find it). In that case, haul out the CD-ROMs and install the little fellow.

3. **Right-click (hold down the right mouse button) and drag the file from the Search Results window to the Start button.**

   The Start menu opens.

4. **Drag the file to Programs and release the mouse button where you want Access to appear (see Figure 1-2).**

   A pop-up menu appears, asking you what you want to do.

5. **Choose Create Shortcut Here.**

   Congratulations. You just added a shortcut to the Start menu!

Granted, the shortcut's name needs some help (something called *shortcut to msaccess.exe* looks pretty geeky on your menu), but you can correct that with just another click or two. To rename the shortcut in your menu, right-click and choose Rename. Type a clever new name in the Rename dialog box, and then click OK.

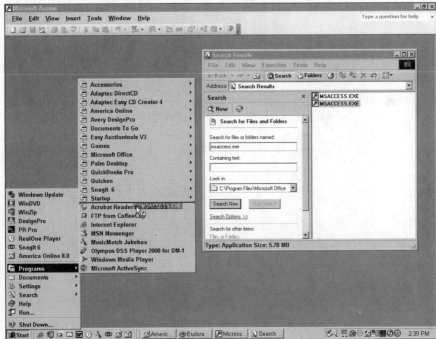

Figure 1-2:
Drag the Access icon onto the Start menu to add it to the computer's program list.

Opening an Existing Database

Access without a database file is like a CD player without a CD: Nice to look at, but you can't dance to it.

Database files fall into two distinct categories:

- **Database files that exist:** Odds are good that you're working with an existing database (after all, you build a database once, but use it forever). If so, read on — this section is for you.

- **Database files that don't exist:** If you're bound and determined to create a database, flip to Chapter 4 for detailed help on design and creation.

If you just started Access 2003, your screen looks like Figure 1-3. By default, Access opens with the task pane displayed. The task pane sits on your screen, looking quite handsome, waiting for you to open an existing database, create a new one, and so on. Opening an existing database takes only a moment — simply select it from the list in the Open section.

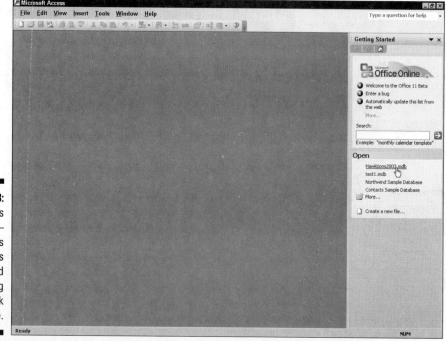

Figure 1-3:
Success at last — Access 2003 is running and displaying the task pane.

If you don't see the database you're looking for, follow these steps:

1. In the Open list, click More.

The Open dialog box appears, as shown in Figure 1-4.

2. Double-click the database you're interested in.

The database loads, and you're ready to work.

If you still can't find the database you want, it's probably in another directory folder. Skip to the sidebar in Chapter 6 for help with tracking down the database in your hard driveor network.

If you've worked with Access for a while (printing reports, checking out a form or two, and generally keeping yourself busy) and now want to open another database, follow these steps:

1. Choose File➪Open or click the Open button on the toolbar.

The Open dialog box (still appearing for your viewing pleasure in Figure 1-4) pops onto the screen.

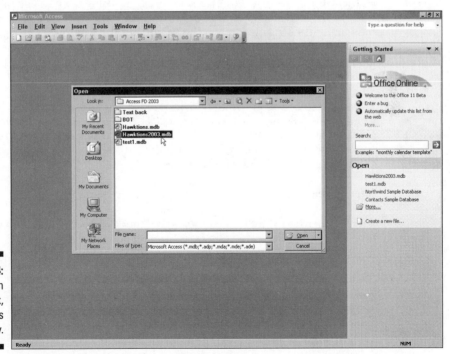

Figure 1-4:
The Open dialog box, in all its glory.

2. **Double-click the name of the database you want to use.**

   If the database isn't listed, it's probably in some other folder. Skip to the sidebar in Chapter 6 for help with tracking down the database in your hard drive or network.

If you see an ominous-looking message asking whether you want to *convert* or merely *open* your file, it means that the database file you want to use came from an older version of Access. Access 2003 wants to convert your existing files to the current database file format — and you probably want it to do that, too. Follow the on-screen instructions for turning the database into a cool, new Access 2003 table, and everything should turn out just fine. Remember to back up the file before converting it (just in case something goes wrong)!

Touring the Database Window

When a database opens, it usually looks like Figure 1-5. Although Access stores all the parts of your database in one big file, it organizes them inside that file by what they are: tables, queries, forms, and so on. Access refers to all these things as *objects,* because it just can't bring itself to use the term *stuff.* To list a particular kind of object in your database, click one of the buttons under the Objects bar (on the left side of the window). The right side of the window changes to show all the stuff — er, objects — in the category, along with a few extra entries for making new objects and fiddling with the ones already there.

The top of the database window tells you the file format. In Figure 1-5, the format is Access 2000. You can use Access 2003 to open prior file versions (such as Access 2000 or Access 97), but you can't use anything older than Access 2000 to open an Access 2003 file. That's why everyone you work with should use the same software version!

After opening the database, you can fiddle with its parts:

- ✔ To open a table, click the Tables item under Objects, and then double-click the table you want to see.

- ✔ To run a report, query, or form, click the appropriate item in the Objects section and then double-click the item you want to work with.

- ✔ When you get tired of a database, close it by clicking the Close button (the X box in the upper-right corner of the window) or by choosing File➪Close. If you're a keyboard fan, Ctrl+W does the deed without disturbing the mouse. (No, I don't know how they got Ctrl+W from the word *Close* either. I guess all of the good letters were taken.)

If you want to know more about working with the cool Access 2003 interface, check out Chapter 2.

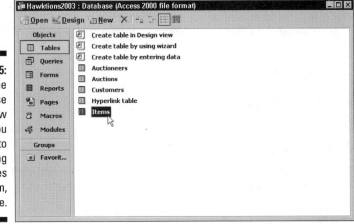

Figure 1-5:
The
database
window
gives you
access to
everything
that makes
up your, um,
database.

If some kind soul invested the time to make your life a little easier, a startup screen (or *switchboard*) resembling Figure 1-6 appears automatically when you open the database. The switchboard is basically a glorified menu of things to do with the database. Chapter 4 has more information about startup screens.

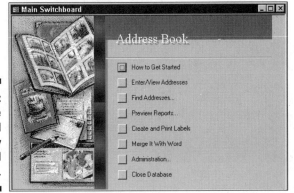

Figure 1-6:
A database
fronted
by a fancy
switchboard
screen.

Finding Information Amongst the Grass Clippings

If you want preschoolers to eat something, just let them take it outside and drop it into the yard first, preferably right after you cut the lawn with a mulching mower. Finding specific information in your Access table is a little like a toddler's method of sifting through sticky grass in search of candy. Whether you're looking for last names, first names, part numbers, or postal codes, Access makes finding your target records a whole lot easier — and infinitely less messy.

Here's one way to find records:

1. **Open the table that you want to search.**

   If you don't know how to open a table, go back to the preceding section.

2. **Click the column you want to search.**

   The blinking toothpick cursor leaps into the column, showing that Access really heard you.

3. **Choose Edit➪Find or click the Find toolbar button.**

   The Find and Replace dialog box appears, as shown in Figure 1-7. Access displays the name of the current field in the Look In section of the dialog box. To look in the entire table, click the down arrow next to the field name, and then choose the table entry from the drop-down list.

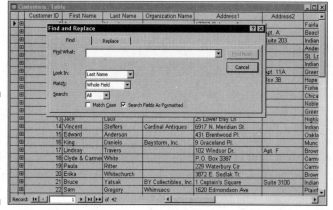

Figure 1-7: The Find and Replace dialog box, at your service.

4. **In the appropriately named Find What text box, type the text you want to find.**

   Spell carefully because Access looks for *exactly* what you type!

5. **To start the search, press Enter or click the Find Next button.**

   The search begins — and probably ends before you know it. If the program finds a matching record, Access highlights the data, as shown in Figure 1-8.

   If no record matches your criteria, a big, officious dialog box informs you that Microsoft Access finished searching the records but found no matches. (If the Office Assistant is on the screen, you are quietly told the search results rather than whacked by the big dialog box.) Click OK and smile as the dialog box disappears; then double-check what you typed in the Find What text box. You probably just mistyped something. If so, correct it and try the search again.

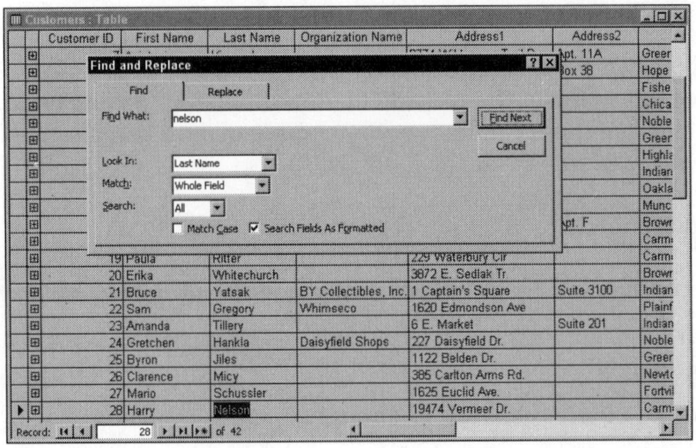

Figure 1-8:
Customer
Nelson is
found!

Access automatically tries to match an entire field in the table with what you typed. So, if you type *Kaufeld* in the Find dialog box, Access *won't* find a record containing *Kaufeld School of Creative Writing*. Why? Because that entry is not an exact match for *Kaufeld* — it's only a partial match. To make Access accept partial matches as well as full ones, change the Match setting in the Find and Replace dialog box from Whole Field to Any Part of Field.

If you *still* can't find the record, Chapter 10 provides more details about the Find dialog box.

6. **When you're finished, click Cancel or press Esc to close the Find dialog box.**

The right mouse button also provides some devious ways to find records, but I'm saving those tricks for Chapter 10.

Making a Few Changes

Unfortunately for fruit growers and dairy farmers, life isn't always peaches and cream. Your customers move, the phone company changes an area code, or the digital gremlins mess up your typing skills. Whatever the cause, your job probably includes correcting the various problems in your database. Lucky you.

Changing the stuff in your tables isn't hard. In fact, making changes is almost too easy. The follow list outlines the precise steps you need. Keep in mind that Access 2003 *automatically* saves your changes. When you finish working on a record, Access writes the new information to the database *right then.* If you make a mistake, *immediately* press Ctrl+Z to undo your changes — don't put it off until later.

Here's a quick word from the Society of the Perpetually Nervous: Be *very* careful when changing the records in your database. Making changes is easy; recovering from them can be tough. Access can help you undo only the *last change you made.*

When you're ready to change a record, follow these steps:

1. **Open the table by double-clicking it in the database window.**

   Your table appears, with its data hanging out on the screen and generally looking cool.

2. **Click the field you want to change.**

   A flashing toothpick cursor appears in the field, and the mouse pointer changes to an I-beam.

3. **Perform whatever repairs the field needs.**

   All the standard editing keys (Home, End, Backspace, and Delete) work when you're changing the contents of a field in Access. See Chapter 6 for the key-by-key details.

4. **When the field looks *just right,* press Return to save the changes.**

   As soon as you press Return, the data is saved — and I do mean *saved.* If you immediately decide that you like the old data better, press Ctrl+Z or choose Edit⇨Undo Saved Record.

Reporting the Results

Capturing all those wonderful details in your tables is nice, but seeing those records fill a printed page looks even nicer. That's where the Access report system comes into play.

Making your database look wonderful on paper is a cinch with Access. The program has all kinds of report options, plus a reasonably strong report wizard to walk you through the hard stuff. Part IV tells you all you could ever want to know about the really cool report features.

Because printing a report is one of the most common things people do with database programs, here's a quick look at how it works in Access:

TIP

Help is always just a few clicks away

No matter where you are in Access, help is always nearby. Chapter 3 covers all your help options in gory detail, but here's one to get you started.

If you're stumped for what to do next, press the F1 key; this is the Windows universal *help me* key. The F1 key displays a task pane that's jam-packed with help topics ranging from an overview of the newest, coolest features of

Access 2003 to phenomenally trivial explorations of macros. If your computer has a live Internet connection, the Help task pane also connects you a multitude of online Office assistance, too.

Unless you're in the mood to browse, pose your question to the Office Assistant or type your search topic into the box at the top of the window and see what the Help system offers. Either way, your answer is only a moment away!

1. In the database window, click the Reports button.

Access lists all of the reports available in this database, as shown in Figure 1-9. If the list shows only the two Create report options, no reports exist yet. In that case, flip ahead to Part IV for help building and using reports.

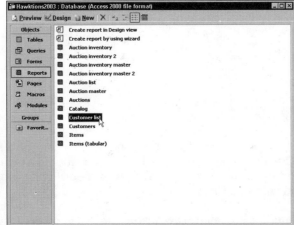

Figure 1-9: Click the Reports button to access your reports.

2. Right-click the report you want to print.

A menu pops up next to your mouse pointer.

3. **Choose Print from the pop-up menu, as shown in Figure 1-10.**

   Access puts a little dialog box in the middle of the screen to tell you how the print job is going. When the print job is finished, the dialog box vanishes without a trace.

   If you change your mind while the report is printing, click Cancel in the Print dialog box to stop the process.

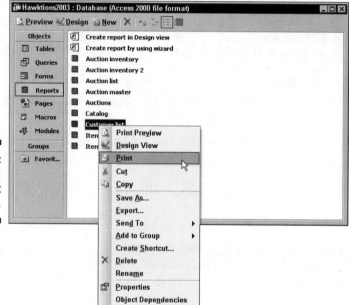

Figure 1-10:
Voila!
An instant
Print menu.

Saving Your Hard Work

The Access 2003 automatic save feature is good because it's one less detail left lying around to clutter up your life. Whether you entered a bunch of new records or simply corrected a couple that were ever-so-slightly wrong, your work is automatically safe and sound.

On the other hand, the automatic save feature *isn't* so good because Access doesn't pay any attention to what it saves — it just saves everything in the database file. If you accidentally wipe out 237 records and then make a few errant clicks, you can say *good-bye records, hello backups.*

I said it before, but it bears repeating: When you change the records in your tables, *please* be careful. Messing up a record takes only a second. Don't let this tragedy happen to you.

The Great Backup Lecture

I know you've probably heard this before, but the PC support nerd in me won't let the chapter close without a few words about backing up your databases. Although I joke about it, regular backups are a *vital* part of using Access (or any program, for that matter).

Why is backing up so important? Take a minute and imagine life without your computer. Don't reminisce about business in the Good Old Days of the 1970s — think about what would happen if you walked in one morning and found *no* computer awaiting your arrival. None. Zippo. The desk is empty — no business letters, no receivables, no customer list, nothing. Everything was on the computer, but now the computer is history.

Unless you want to wave good-bye to your business, you need a formal backup plan. Even if it's just you and your computer, make some notes about how your backup process works:

  ✔ **How often is the computer backed up?** A better question is "How much data can you afford to lose?" If your information changes daily (an accounting system, for example), you need to make backups every day or two. If you mainly play adventure games on your machine and use Access as infrequently as possible, back up every week or two. No universal rule is right for everyone.

  ✔ **Where are the backup disks or tapes stored?** If the backups are conveniently stored right next to the computer, they'll be conveniently destroyed along with the computer in the event of a fire, tornado, or hurricane. Keep your backups in another building, if possible, or at least in another room.

  ✔ **How do you back up the data?** Write down a step-by-step procedure, along with a method for figuring out what tape or disk set to use in the backup process.

  ✔ **How do you *restore* the data?** Again, create a step-by-step process. Your mind won't be particularly clear if tragedy strikes and you have to restore destroyed data, so make the steps simple and understandable.

After you settle into the backup routine, try restoring your data once to make sure that your system works. You're *much* better off finding out before the disk dies rather than afterward. Set aside a few hours to ensure that your efforts pay off on that fateful day when the disk drive dies. You'll thank me later.

If you're in a corporate environment, it's possible that your local Department of Computer People automatically backs up your data. To find out for sure, give them a call.

Making a Graceful Exit

When it's time to shut down for the day, do so the right way:

1. **If you have a database open, choose File⇨Close or click the Close button in the upper-right corner of the database window.**

   I'm old-fashioned enough not to trust my program to close everything by itself without screwing something up. Whenever possible, I save and close my work manually before shutting down the program.

2. **Close Access by choosing File⇨Exit.**

Go ahead and shut down Windows as well if you're finished for the night. To do so, click the Start button and then click Shut Down. When Windows asks whether you're serious about this shutdown, click Yes. After Windows does whatever it is that software does just before bedtime, turn off your computer and make your escape to freedom.

Chapter 2

Finding Your Way Around like a Native

In This Chapter

▶ Peering around the interface

▶ Looking at the pretty windows

▶ Checking out the toolbars

▶ Ordering from the menu

▶ Performing tricks with the right mouse button

Cruising around an unfamiliar city is fun, exciting, and frustrating. Seeing the sights, recognizing famous landmarks, and discovering new places to exercise your credit card make it fun. Finding yourself lost deep within a neighborhood that's "in transition" makes it, uh, exciting. And getting lost on the trip back adds that special air of frustration to the jaunt.

If you're comfortable with earlier versions of Access, then driving your mouse through Access 2003 feels much like driving through your hometown — 20 years later. The terrain looks somewhat familiar, but you're in for some surprises — "Where'd they move that menu item? It used to be right over, um . . . oh geez, half of the menu's gone — no, wait, it's back. Eeesh . . . I need more coffee."

Nothing feels worse than watching your work pile up while deciphering a new program. This chapter springs you out of that trap with a tour of the sights and sounds of Access 2003. It covers the common features you see and deal with on the screen, from the main window to the toolbar and beyond. Kick back and enjoy the jaunt — it's a great way to get comfortable with Access 2003.

Making Sense of the Sights

Because Access is, after all, a Windows program, the first stop on this merry visual trip is the program's main window. Figure 2-1 shows Access in a common pose, displaying a database window (which I cover later in this chapter).

To make the most of Access, you need to be familiar with nine parts of the main window. I describe each part briefly in the paragraphs that follow. If you're *really* new to Windows, consider picking up a copy of the appropriate *Windows* Whatever *For Dummies* by Andy Rathbone (published by Wiley Publishing, Inc.).

- **Control menu button:** Click the icon (the Access key) in the upper-left corner to open the Control menu. Double-click the icon to close Access.

- **Title bar:** Every window comes complete with a space along the top for the title. This space has a second purpose, too: It changes color to let you know which program is currently active in Windows. Double-clicking the title bar alternately maximizes and restores Access.

- **Main menu:** Between the title bar and the toolbar sits the Main menu. Aside from preventing fights between the two bars, this menu is also your main stopping point for Access commands and functions.

- **Toolbar:** Think of the toolbar as an electronic version of Lon Chaney, the Man of a Thousand Faces. Just about every time you do something in Access, this bar does a quick change to serve up the tools you need. I tell you more about this slippery character later in this chapter.

- **Utility buttons:** These three buttons appear on every window. From left to right, they

   - Reduce the current program to a button on the taskbar

   - Make the current program either fit in a window or take up the entire screen (one button, two tasks)

   - Close the current window

- **Status bar:** Access is a talkative system, with words of wisdom to share about every little feature. Whenever Access wants to tell you something, a message appears on the status bar. On the far right of the status bar are indicators for keyboard settings such as Caps Lock.

- **Database window:** In the midst of this maelstrom sits a serene database window, explained in the next section.

✔ **Task pane:** Filling the right side of the Access screen is the new and improved *task pane*. This massive part of your on-screen world appears and disappears at your command, by choosing View➪Task Pane from the main menu. Think of this pane as your one-stop information source. Access uses the task pane for everything from opening existing database files to working with the Help system.

✔ **Office Assistant:** This annoying little fellow shows up in all Microsoft Office products, including Access. When you have a question or want some help, give him a click and ask away. (And when boredom sets in, right-click the Assistant and select Animate for some brief entertainment.)

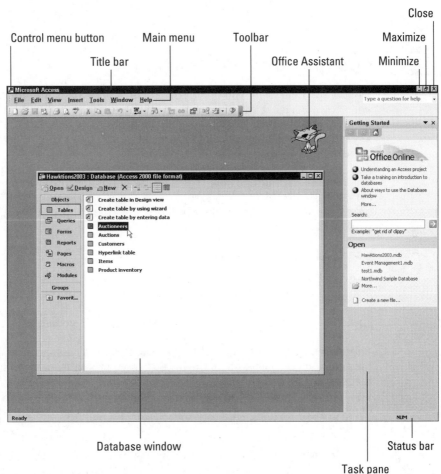

Figure 2-1:
Access in
all its glory.

Windows Shopping for Fun and Understanding

There's more to Access 2003 than the big picture window. The program is chock-full of little windows for every need and occasion. This section looks at four of the most common windows: the database, datasheet, form, and query windows.

To see how these windows work, what to do with them, and why you should even care, keep trekking through this book. Databases and datasheets appear in Part II, queries star in Part III, and forms have a supporting role in Part V.

The database window

Most of the time when you open a database, it appears in a window like the one shown in Figure 2-2. This window gives you access to all the stuff in your database, provides tools to change displays or create new items, and generally helps you manage your database stuff. And it looks cool. Who can ask for more?

The Objects bar buttons down the left side of the window switch between lists of *objects* (tables, queries, reports, and so on) that make up the database. Four toolbar buttons sit at the top of the database window to help you work with the database's objects:

- ✔ Open displays the current object
- ✔ Design lets you change the object
- ✔ New creates a new object
- ✔ The X deletes the current object (kiss that table good-bye!)

The View buttons sit to the right of the big Delete (X) button. The View buttons change how Access lists the objects in your database. Your choices run the gamut from colorful, friendly icons to detailed mini-dossiers. In fact, the View buttons probably look familiar — the same ones appear in Windows Explorer. Feel free to try the settings yourself — you can't hurt anything! (Just don't accidentally click the X, okay?)

Your database *may* start up looking like Figure 2-3. Don't let the pretty face fool you, though — this window is just a fancier front hung onto Figure 2-2's database. Seeing something like this window is a clue that you're working with a formal Access application. Most likely, the form was created by one of your in-house nerds. This special form is called a *switchboard*.

View buttons

Toolbar buttons

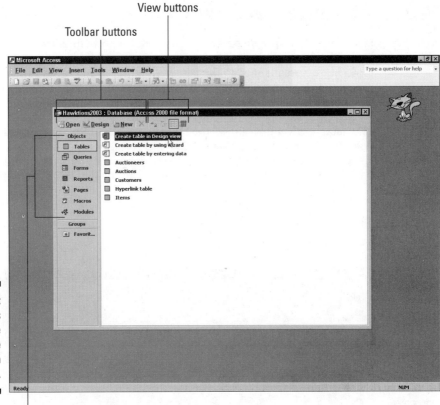

Figure 2-2:
Well, this is
another fine
database
I've gotten
myself into.

Objects bar

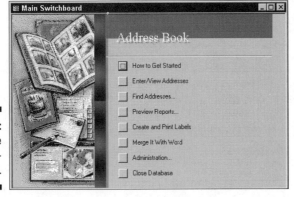

Figure 2-3:
An example
of a switch-
board.

The datasheet window

Is it a table or a spreadsheet? Only its owner knows for sure! Looking at Figure 2-4, it's easy to see why you may confuse the two. It's a table, but it looks like a spreadsheet. In datasheet view, an Access table appears (and arguably acts) like a simple spreadsheet. The resemblance is only skin-deep, though. This table is really a different animal.

The datasheet window shows the table name across its top, just as it should. Below that, the table's *fields* are arrayed across the window. The table's *records* are laid out in rows. Don't worry if you're not exactly sure about the difference between a record and a field. Chapter 4 has all the details about that.

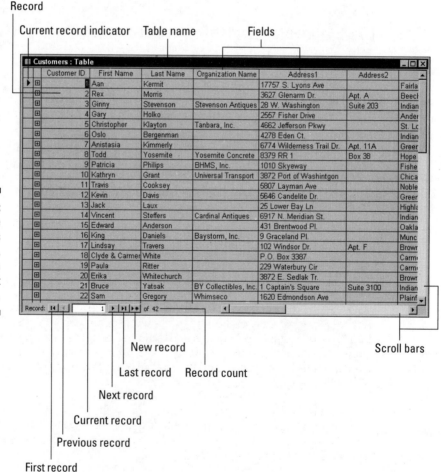

Figure 2-4:
The
Customers
table,
dressed in
spreadsheet
drag.

On the right side and lower-right corner are a pair of *scroll bars* that make moving through the table a real breeze. The *navigation buttons* hang out in the window's lower-left side. These buttons are a lot like the controls on a compact disc player or VCR. The buttons that have arrows pointing to a bar take you to the first or last record of the table. The arrow-only buttons move you to the next or preceding record. Clicking the arrow-and-asterisk button adds a new record to the table.

If Access displays a little plus sign to the left of each record in a table, the table is related to at least one other table in your database. (Chapters 4 and 5 explain what you need to know about creating and using relationships between tables.) When you click the plus sign next to a particular record, Access displays the related data from the related tables. For example, Figure 2-5 displays all the items that Kevin Davis ordered.

Figure 2-5:
Click the
plus sign
next to a
record to
drill down to
related
information.
Kevin sure
is a good
customer!

	Customer ID	First Name	Last Name	Organization Name	Address1	Address2	
	1	Aan	Kermit		17757 S. Lyons Ave		Fairla
	2	Rex	Morris		3627 Glenarm Dr.	Apt. A	Beech
	3	Ginny	Stevenson	Stevenson Antiques	28 W. Washington	Suite 203	Indian
	4	Gary	Holko		2557 Fisher Drive		Ander
	5	Christopher	Klayton	Tanbara, Inc.	4662 Jefferson Pkwy		St. Lo
	6	Oslo	Bergenman		4276 Eden Ct.		Indian
	7	Anistasia	Kimmerly		6774 Wilderness Trail Dr.	Apt. 11A	Greer
	8	Todd	Yosemite	Yosemite Concrete	8379 RR 1	Box 38	Hope
	9	Patricia	Philips	BHMS, Inc.	1010 Skyeway		Fishe
	10	Kathryn	Grant	Universal Transport	3872 Port of Washintgon		Chica
	11	Travis	Cooksey		5807 Layman Ave		Noble
	12	Kevin	Davis		5646 Candelite Dr.		Greer

	Item ID	ItemName	MinimumBid	Description	DateIn	DateO
	17	Notebook computer	$760.00	486DX/2 notebook computer. 16mb F	2/1/98	
	18	Portable printer	$100.00	Portable ink-jet printer. Handles both	2/1/98	

	13	Jack	Laux		25 Lower Bay Ln		Highla
	14	Vincent	Steffers	Cardinal Antiques	6917 N. Meridian St.		Indian
	15	Edward	Anderson		431 Brentwood Pl.		Oakla
	16	King	Daniels	Baystorm, Inc.	9 Graceland Pl.		Munc
	17	Lindsay	Travers		102 Windsor Dr.	Apt. F	Browr
	18	Clyde & Carmen	White		P.O. Box 3387		Carm

Record: 1 of 2

The form window

Form view is the other popular way to look at Access tables. With forms, the data looks more, well, traditional — none of that sissy spreadsheet-style stuff. A form usually shows the data in a table at the blinding rate of one record per screen, the same way that the nerds of the 1970s worked with their data, using million-dollar computers that had all the intelligence of today's microwave ovens.

Figure 2-6 is a simple but classic example of an Access form. Along the top is the ever-anticipated title bar. The table's fields take up the middle of the form. In the lower-left corner are the same navigation buttons you saw and fiddled with in the datasheet window.

If forms pique your interest, check out Chapter 22 for more information.

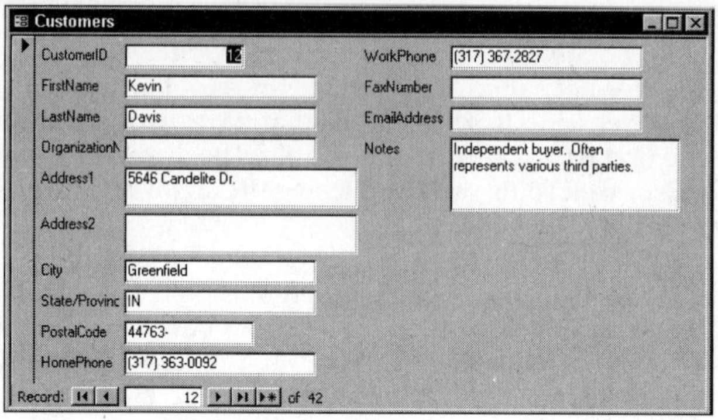

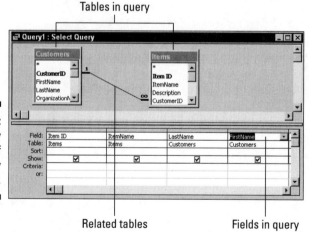

Figure 2-6:
There's
Kevin
again —
what a ham!

The query window

The heart of any database program is its capability of organizing and searching for information. In particular, the heart of Access is the query system. And sitting at the heart of the query system is the *query window,* lovingly reproduced in Figure 2-7.

Tables in query

Figure 2-7:
The key
elements of
the query
window.

Related tables   Fields in query

Here are the key pieces of the query window:

> ✔ **Title bar:** The title bar displays the query's given name at the top of the window.

> ✔ **Tables:** Any tables involved in the query appear in the window's upper half. If the query uses more than one table, this section also shows how the tables are linked (or *joined*).

> ✔ **Query criteria:** These are the instructions that make the query work. They appear in the lower half of the window.
>
> ✔ **Scroll bars:** The scroll bars move the window around to show your query clearly.

When you run a query, Access usually displays the results in a datasheet.

Belly Up to the Toolbar, Folks!

Toolbars are the Microsoft Office equivalent of sliced bread — they're *that* useful. Access has a bunch of them, too. You can't find yourself without a toolbar around to help.

So what *is* a toolbar? It's that row of cool buttons just below the menu at the top of the screen. Figure 2-8 shows the Database toolbar in action (as much action as any inanimate object ever shows).

Figure 2-8:
The
Database
toolbar.

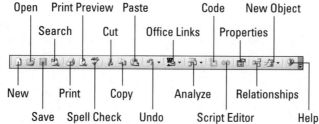

The toolbars give you single-click access to the best features of Access. The engineers designed the toolbars to contain the most common functions you need when working with data. The Datasheet toolbar, for example, includes three buttons that control the Filter tools (tools that help you quickly find information in your database). Instead of working your way through a menu to find these Filter tools, they're out in the open, just a mouse click away.

Because a toolbar exists for literally every occasion, you find toolbar descriptions scattered throughout the book. Don't worry if you can't remember what all the buttons do — neither can I. If you're button-challenged, just pause the mouse pointer over a button. After a moment, the button gets tired of that heavy pointer and, hoping that you'll go away, displays a *screen tip* — a small box with some text that describes the purpose of the button.

If you wait a decent amount of time (like two seconds) and no quick help pops up, it has probably been turned off. Right-click the toolbar and choose Customize. On the Options tab, make sure that Show ScreenTips on Toolbars is checked. While you're on the Options tab, check or uncheck the Large Icons check box to make the buttons large or small.

Menus, Menus Everywhere

Truth be told, there isn't a lot to say about the Access 2003 menus. Access continues carrying the banner of Microsoft's *context-sensitive* menus that show different options depending on what you're doing at the moment.

Some features never change, though. Here's a brief rundown of generic menu truisms:

 ✔ If your mouse dies, you can get to the menu items from the keyboard. Just hold down the Alt key and press the underlined letter of the menu item you want. For example, press Alt+F to open the File menu.

 ✔ Some menu items are assigned a specific key. The Copy command (Edit➪Copy on the menu) also works without the menu by pressing Ctrl+C. If an item has a keyboard equivalent, Access lists that key combination right next to the item in the pull-down menu.

Playing with the Other Mouse Button

Your mother probably told you to never play with your right mouse button. Well, she was wrong. In days of yore, Windows 95 introduced us to the raison d'etre for the right mouse button: to display a pop-up or context menu of things you can do with or to the item you just clicked. For example, Figure 2-9 shows the Customers table after it was right-clicked. Access responds by offering a list of common processes for tables. Instead of working through the main menu to copy the current table, for instance, I can right-click and select Copy from the pop-up menu. Talk about a time-saver!

No matter what Windows application you work with, experiment with the right mouse button. If in doubt, right-click. Try right-clicking everything in sight and see what happens.

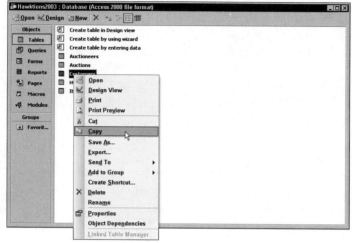

Figure 2-9:
Too cool —
an instant
menu!

Chapter 3

Calling the Online St. Bernard and Other Forms of Help

*G*etting in over your head is easy sometimes. For example, mountains are *much* taller after you start climbing them than they were when you looked up from the ground. Plus, your equipment *never* seems to fail when you're packing it. Instead, your trusty gear waits until you're in the middle of nowhere, dangling precariously from the crumbling edge of a craggy peak. Then and only then does your gear remember its mortal fear of heights and have heart failure.

That's what Saint Bernards are for. When you're lost in the Alpine wilderness — cold, wet, and alone — it's reassuring to know that a Saint Bernard will be along soon. I'm a little unclear about precisely what the dog *does* when it finds you, but at that point, I'd probably settle for the companionship alone. In the spirit of Alpine Saint Bernards everywhere, Access offers its own built-in Saint Bernard: the Office Assistant and the rest of the online Help system. Although they look more like a few dialog boxes than a husky canine, they still come through when you need 'em.

This chapter explores several different ways to find answers to your Access questions. Knowing where to look for information is as important as knowing the information itself, so browse ahead and discover your options.

Finding Help Here, There, and Waaaay Over There

No matter where you are in Access, the Help system waits nearby, ready to throw in a helpful tip, offer a handy reminder, or lead you through a painfully confusing set of obtuse steps. In fact, the Help system inside Access 2003 takes assistance to a whole new level by linking you with the help information stored on your computer *and* with the massive Help databases at Microsoft's Web site.

Because the new Help system relies so much on Web-based information, it works best if your computer links to the Internet through an always-on, high-speed connection such as DSL, cable, or a corporate network at the office. With those connections, the Access Help system can always find the best, most recent tidbits to answer your questions.

If your computer gets to the Net through a dial-up connection (or if you ask a question of the Help system without an Internet link running), Access still responds, thanks to the excellent files stored right there on your computer. By providing two parallel Help systems, the Access developers made sure that you could get assistance no matter where or when you need it, whether your computer is online or not.

Asking Questions of the Software

Access 2003 gives you three ways to ask for help. Figure 3-1 shows them in action all at once, which is overkill for anybody except slightly geeky computer book authors trying to come up with clever screen shots for their books.

To use the Help system, choose whichever one of the three methods described next feels the most comfortable and matches your work style. After you get past the "ask your question" step in the help process, all three of these little guys feed into the same behind-the-scenes help information, and they all display their results in the same big Search Results task pane on your screen. Only the system's questioning methods were changed to confuse the innocent.

Following are your three question-asking options in the new version of Access:

> ✔ **The *Type a Question for Help* box:** This little text box always sits at the upper-right corner of your Access window, just below the Close and Restore buttons. To use it, click in the box, type your question, and press Enter.

✔ **The Office Assistant:** Yes, the friendly, lovable Office Assistant appears again in this version of Access. It works a bit differently than previous Office Assistants, though. Instead of both asking the question and displaying possible solutions, the new Office Assistant merely handles the question. Answers appear in the task pane, not in the Office Assistant's little thought bubble. To ask a question through the Office Assistant, click once on the Assistant. When its thought bubble appears, type your question and press Enter.

✔ **F1, the classic Windows Help button:** For years and years, the F1 button dutifully called forth help from pretty much any program you used. It does the same thing with Access 2003, so those many years of training still come in handy. Pressing F1 displays the Access Help task pane, filled with all kinds of links leading to helpful destinations across the Net. Atop the task pane sits the Search box, where you pose your question. To ask something, click in the Search text box, type your question, and press Enter.

Office Assistant   Question box

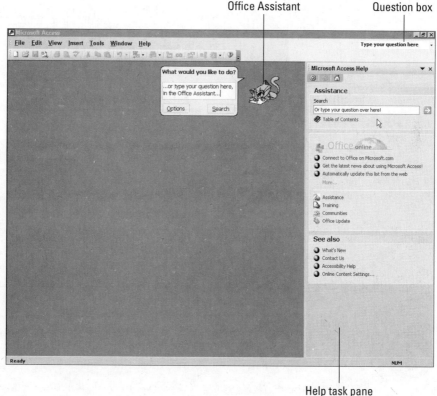

Figure 3-1:
Whether you use the box, the Office Assistant's bubble, or the big Help task pane, Access 2003 collects your questions.

Help task pane

Figure 3-1 shows the various question-asking areas in action. Although all three options lead you to the same set of results, pressing F1 offers the most information. Because it displays the Help task pane, you get not only a chance to ask a question, but also links for training, general assistance on business tasks, connections to Microsoft's online communities, and easy software updating. With all those options, it pays to invest a few minutes with the Help task pane's options about once a month. You never know what you might uncover!

Your Internet Connection Knows More Than You May Think

If you have access (pardon the pun) to the Internet or an account on America Online, a world of database answers waits at your modem.

Microsoft maintains official support areas on the major online services, plus a complete Web page for the Internet crowd. A host of informal question-and-answer areas cover Microsoft products as well. Table 3-1 explains how to find the support areas in your favorite online haunts.

Table 3-1	Microsoft Support Online	
System	*Access Command*	*Notes*
America Online	keyword **Home and Office**	Look for *MS Access* in the message boards
Usenet	`microsoft.public.access.gettingstarted`	Requires access to Internet newsgroups
Usenet	`comp.databases.ms-access`	Requires access to Internet newsgroups
Web		Requires Web access

A slew of *For Dummies* books can help you navigate the online world. Among them are *AOL For Dummies* (written by yours truly) and *The Internet For Dummies,* 8th Edition (by John Levine, Carol Baroudi, and Margaret Levine Young). Wiley Publishing, Inc. brings these fine books to you.

TIP

Drinking at the never-empty well of a mailing list

If you have an e-mail account, consider signing up for the Access mailing list to join a never-ending discussion of Access at all levels, from novice to nerd. Aside from filling your mailbox with important-looking messages, the list gives you a way to get answers quickly at any time.

To join the mailing list, send a message to LISTSERV@peach.ease.lsoft.com. You can write anything as the subject of your message (the computer on the other end doesn't care). In

the body of the message, type **SUBSCRIBE ACCESS-L** followed by your real name, *not* your e-mail address. The mailing list computer automatically picks up your e-mail address from the message itself.

After you subscribe, your first message explains how the list works, how to send messages to it, and how to get off the list when you decide you've had enough. Give it a try — mailing lists are great tools!

Talking to a Human

Sometimes, you've had it up to *here* with computers and automation in general. At that point, you just want to talk to a human — any human — who can help solve your problem. Microsoft provides a variety of phone numbers for just such occasions.

Answers about basic installation questions come to you free from Microsoft as a thank-you gift for purchasing its product. Asking about anything else costs money, so choose your questions wisely. After choosing those questions, select the right number from the following list:

- ✔ **For basic installation phone support,** call 425-635-7056 from the United States. Human beings are available from 5 a.m. to 9 p.m. Pacific time, Monday through Friday (except holidays), and 6 a.m. to 3 p.m. Saturday and Sunday.

- ✔ **For answers to all other Access problems,** call 800-936-5700 from the United States or Canada. Unless your company purchased an annual support contract from Microsoft, solutions from this number cost a flat $35 *per incident.* So what's an incident? According to Microsoft, an *incident* is *all the calls related to the same problem* (or something close to that). The bottom line is that if you call several times trying to solve the same problem, you pay for only one call. This number runs with the same hours as the basic installation support group: 5 a.m. to 9 p.m. Pacific time, Monday through Friday (except holidays), and 6 a.m. to 3 p.m. Saturday and Sunday.

✔ **If you have a light, fluffy question,** such as "What's the current version number of Microsoft Access?" (or "What's the weather like in Redmond, Washington?"), call the Microsoft sales department at 800-426-9400. These folks are at the phones, waiting for your call, from 6:30 a.m. to 5:30 p.m. Pacific time, Monday through Friday.

✔ **If you are deaf or hearing-impaired and have a TDD or TT modem,** call 800-892-5234 between 5 a.m. and 9 p.m. Pacific time, Monday through Friday, and 6 a.m. to 3 p.m. Saturday and Sunday. You can use this number for questions about all Microsoft products (Word, Excel, PowerPoint, and the others).

Part II
Truly Tempting Tables

In this part . . .

With Access well in hand, you begin a life of storing, managing, organizing, and reorganizing data. (By the way, welcome to your new life. I hope you enjoy your stay here.) Because data hangs out in tables, you need to know how to do the whole table thing if you have any hope of making your data do tricks.

This part eases you into the role of Commander of All Tables by covering the basics. You go from creating tables to using tables to maintaining and repairing tables. Heck, if you're not careful, you may find yourself tackling that wobbly leg on the dining room table by the end of Chapter 9.

Chapter 4

Designing and Building a Home for Your Data

In This Chapter

▶ Reviewing database terms

▶ Simplifying your day with sample fields

▶ Uncovering flat files and relational databases

▶ Designing your tables

▶ Creating a database

▶ Building a table with the Table Wizard

▶ Assembling a table by hand

*T*his may be the single most important chapter in this book. Why? Because useful databases grow from carefully considered plans. The problem is that nobody ever explains stuff like how to successfully string a bunch of fields together and make a table out of them. For some unknown reason, they think you already know how to do it — that it's instinct, like birds flying south for the winter or my wife finding the best sales in the mall.

If you didn't pop from the womb muttering, "Phone numbers and postal codes are treated as text even though they're numbers" (and I worry for you if you did!), this chapter is for you. The following pages divulge the secrets of fields, tables, and databases in full Technicolor glory. The chapter covers the database terms you need to know, tips for choosing fields and designing tables, and details on assembling the pieces into great databases.

Although I hate making a big deal out of techie terminology, this time I must. Please, for your own sanity, get a good grip on the information in the first section of this chapter. The database terms described there appear *everywhere* in Access. Whenever you build a query, design a form, or create a report, the terms stealthily await you, ready to leap out and befuddle the ill-prepared. Steel yourself for their attack by spending time in the terms section that follows.

Database Terms to Know and Tolerate

Wait! Don't skip this section just because it's about terminology. I keep the technoweenie content of this book to a minimum, but you simply *must* know a few magic words before your foray into database development.

If you just felt faint because you didn't realize that you are developing a database, put the book down for a moment, take a few deep breaths, and remember that it's *only* a computer, not something really important like kids, kites, or chocolate mousse.

The following sections list the few terms you really, really need to know. There's a brief explanation of each one, plus a translation guide for people who have worked with other database software such as FileMaker, FoxPro, Oracle, and Paradox.

The terms appear in order, starting with the smallest piece of a database (the data) and advancing to the largest (the entire database). It's much like a backward version of that "flea on the wart on the frog on the bump on the log in the hole in the bottom of the sea" song that my kids sing incessantly some days. The definitions kind of build on each other, so it makes the most sense if you start with *data* and work your way to *database*.

Data (your stuff)

Data is the stuff that Access stores, shuffles, and stacks for you. Every time you write your name on a form (last name first, of course), you create data. In a database program's skewed approach to the world, Your Name may be stored as one piece of data (your entire name, with or without the middle initial), two pieces (first and last name), or even more pieces (title, first name, middle initial, last name, and suffix). The details depend on how the database designer set up the database's fields (that's covered in the next section, so don't worry about it right now). Here are a couple of tidbits about data:

- Almost all database programs agree that data should be called data. Don't expect this degree of cooperation to continue much beyond the term data, because that's where it ends.

- Database programs view data differently than you and I do. When you see 16773, you know it's a number — that's intuitive to you. Access and the other database programs see 16773 as either a number or a group of characters (a *1*, followed by a *6*, a *7*, and so on), depending on what type of field it's stored in. There's more about this peculiar behavior in the "Frolicking through the Fields" section, later in the chapter. For the sake of your sanity, please make sure you're comfortable with this little oddity because it can throw you for a loop sometimes.

Fields (the rooms for your stuff)

Because people don't want their data to wander around homeless, the technical wizards created *fields* — places for your data to live. Each field holds one kind of data. For example, to track information about a baseball card collection, your fields might include Manufacturer, Player Name, Position, Year, Team, Condition, and so on. Each of those items is a unique *field* in your database.

When thinking about fields, remember these things:

✔ As with the term *data,* programs such as FoxPro and FileMaker all agree what a field is. However, larger database packages, such as Oracle and Microsoft SQL Server, use the term *column* instead of *field.*

✔ The programs mostly disagree when you talk about the specific types of fields available. Just because you *always used to do it this way in FileMaker* doesn't mean the same method works in Access. For more details, look at the "Frolicking through the Fields" section, later in this chapter.

Records (the rooms in one house)

Having fields is a good start, but if you stop there, how do you know which last name works with which first name? Something needs to keep those unruly fields in order — something like a *record.* All the fields for one baseball card, one accounting entry, or one of whatever it is you're tracking with Access are collectively known as a *record.* If you have two baseball cards in your collection, you have two records in your database, one for each card. (Of course, you *also* have a mighty small card collection.)

For a little more about records, check out the following:

✔ FoxPro and FileMaker concur on the term *record.* Oracle and Microsoft SQL Server use the term *row* instead.

✔ Each record in a *table* contains the same fields but (usually) different data in those fields.

✔ A single record contains all the information you need about a single item (accounting entry, recipe, or whatever) in your table.

Table (the houses of a neighborhood)

A *table* is a collection of records that describe similar data. The key phrase to remember in that last sentence is *similar data.* All the records in a single table contain fields of similar data. The information about that baseball card collection may fit into a single table. So would the accounting data. However, a single table would *not* handle both baseball cards *and* accounting entries. Combining the two is a novel concept (and may even make accounting fun), but it doesn't work in Access.

Top off your new knowledge with a couple more table tidbits:

- FileMaker and FoxPro basically agree with Access about what a table is, as do Oracle and Microsoft SQL Server.

- Did you notice that I said the baseball card collection *may* fit in one table? You often use a few *related* tables to hold the data instead of a single big honking table. That's all you need to know for now, but understanding this topic is important. Be sure to peek at the "Flat Files versus Relational Databases: Let the Contest Begin!" section, later in this chapter, for the whole scoop.

Database (a community of neighborhoods)

An Access *database,* or *database file* (the terms are interchangeable), is a collection of everything relating to a particular set of information. The database contains all the tables, queries, reports, and forms that Access helps you create to manage and work with your stuff. Instead of storing all those items *individually* on the disk drive, where they can become lost, misplaced, or accidentally erased, they're grouped into a single collective file.

Frolicking through the Fields

A field, you remember, is the place where your data lives; each field holds one piece of data such as Year or Team.

Because there are so many different kinds of stuff in the world, Access offers a variety of field types for *stuff storage.* In fact, Access puts ten field types at your disposal. At first blush, ten choices may not seem like much flexibility but, believe me, it is. And, thanks to the field options, you also can customize how the fields look and work to precisely suit your needs. All this and it makes popcorn, too.

Each field offers a number of options to make customizing incredibly useful. You can ask for some information, test the entry to see whether it's what you're looking for, and automatically format the field just the way you want. Everything you need to know about this cool stuff awaits your attention in Chapter 7.

All the field types appear in the following list. They're in the same order as they appear on the screen in Access. Don't worry if you can't figure out why *anyone* would want to use one type or another. Just focus on the ones you need, make a mental note about the others, and go on with your work:

- ✔ **Text:** Stores text — letters, numbers, and any combination thereof — up to 255 characters.

  Numbers in a text field aren't numbers; they're just a bunch of digits hanging out together in a field. Be careful of this fact when you design the tables in your database.

  Text fields have one setting you need to know about: size. When you create a text field, Access wants to know how many characters the field holds. That's the field *size.* If you create a field called First Name and make its size 6, *Joseph* fits into the field but not *Jennifer.* This rstriction can be a problem. A good general rule is to make the field a little larger than you think you need. It's easy to make the field even larger if you need to, but it's potentially dangerous to make it smaller. Surgery on fields is covered in Chapter 9.

- ✔ **Memo:** Holds up to 64,000 characters of information — that's almost 18 pages of text. This is a *really big* text field. It's great for general notes, detailed descriptions, and anything else that requires a lot of space.

- ✔ **Number:** Holds real, for-sure numbers. You can add, subtract, and calculate your way to fame and fortune with number fields. If you're working with dollars and cents (or pounds and pence), use a currency field.

- ✔ **Date/Time:** Stores time, date, or a combination of the two, depending on which format you use. Use a date/time field to track the whens of life. Pretty versatile, eh?

- ✔ **Currency:** Tracks money, prices, invoice amounts, and so on. In an Access database, the bucks stop here. For that matter, so do the lira, marks, and yen. If you're in the mood for some *other* kind of number, check out the number field.

- ✔ **AutoNumber:** Does just what it says: It fills itself with an automatically generated number every time you make a new record. AutoNumber is cool. Just think, when you add a customer to your table, Access generates the customer number automatically! Microsoft SQL Server has something similar, but the poor people who use Oracle have to jump through hoops to generate customer (or other types of) numbers.

✔ **Yes/No:** Holds Yes/No, True/False, and On/Off, depending on the format you choose. When you need a simple yes or no, this is the field to use.

✔ **OLE object:** OLE Stands for Object Linking and Embedding — a powerful, nerdy technology — and is pronounced "o-lay." An OLE object is something like a Word document, an Excel spreadsheet, a Windows bitmap (a picture), or even a MIDI song. By embedding an OLE object in your table, your database will automatically "know" how to edit a Word document or an Excel spreadsheet, play a MIDI song, and so on.

✔ **Hyperlink:** Thanks to this field type (and a little bit of Net magic provided by Microsoft Internet Explorer), Access now understands and stores the special link language that makes the Internet such a cool place. If you use Access on your company's network or use the Internet extensively, this field type is for you. I show you more about hyperlinks and other neat Internet tricks in Chapter 21.

✔ **Lookup Wizard:** One of a database program's most powerful features is the *lookup.* It makes data entry go faster (and with fewer errors) by letting you choose a field's correct value from a preset list. No typing, no worry, no problem — it's quite a helpful trick. In some database programs, adding a lookup to a table is hard. Luckily, the Access Lookup Wizard makes the process much less painful. Ask the Office Assistant for all the details about the Lookup Wizard.

To give you a head start in the database race, Table 4-1 lists fields starring in databases around the world. Some oldies but goodies are in here, plus some examples especially for the new millennium.

Table 4-1	A Field for Every Occasion		
Name	*Type*	*Size*	*Contents*
Title	Text	4	Mr., Ms., Mrs., Mme., Sir
First Name	Text	15	Person's first name
Middle Initial	Text	4	Person's middle initial; allows for two initials and punctuation
Last Name	Text	20	Person's last name
Suffix	Text	10	Jr., Sr., II, Ph.D., and so on
Job	Text	25	Job title or position

Name	Type	Size	Contents
Company	Text	25	Company name
Address 1, Address 2	Text	30	Include two fields for the address because some corporate locations are pretty complicated these days
City	Text	20	City name
State, Province	Text	4	State or province; apply the name appropriately for the data you're storing
Zip Code, Postal Code	Text	10	Zip or postal code; note that it's stored as text characters, not as a number
Country	Text	15	Not needed if you work within a single country
Office Phone	Text	12	Voice telephone number; increase the size to 17 for an extension
Fax Number	Text	12	Fax number
Home Phone	Text	12	Home telephone number
Cellular Phone	Text	12	Cell phone or car phone
E-mail Address	Text	30	Internet e-mail address
Web Site	Hyperlink		Web page address; Access automatically sets the field size
Telex	Text	12	Standard Telex number; increase the size to 22 to include answer back service
SSN	Text	11	U.S. Social Security number, including dashes
Comments	Memo		A freeform space for notes; Access automatically chooses a field size

All these samples are *text* fields, even the ones for phone numbers. That's because Access sees most of the stuff you want to pack a database with as *text*. Remember that computers think there's a difference between a *number* and a string of digits, such as the digits that make up a phone number or government ID number.

Playing the (field) name game

Of all the Windows database programs out there, I think Access has the simplest field-naming rules. Just remember these guidelines to make your field names perfect every time:

✔ **Start with a letter or a number.** After the first character, you're free to use any letter or number. You can include spaces in field names, too!

✔ **Make the field name short and easy to understand.** You have up to 64 characters for a field name, but don't even think about

using all that space. However, don't get stingy and create names like N1 or AZ773 unless they mean something particular to your company or organization.

✔ **Use letters, numbers, and an occasional space in your field names.**

Although Access lets you include all kinds of crazy punctuation marks in field names, don't do it. Keep it simple so that the solution you develop with Access doesn't turn into a problem on its own.

Here's an easy trick to figure out what type of field to use for a number: When creating a field, ask yourself, "Will I ever do *math* with this number?" If so, it goes in a number field. Otherwise, stuff it in a text field.

For an easier trip through table creation, check out the Table Wizard section, called "Creating Tables at the Wave of a Wand" later in this chapter. The wizard knows a slew of ready-made fields to use in your tables.

Flat Files versus Relational Databases: Let the Contest Begin!

Unlike ice cream, cars, and summer days, the tables in your database come in only two basic flavors: flat and relational.

A database is either flat file or relational — it can't be both.

These two escapees from the *Nerd Term of the Month Club* explain how tables store information in your database. And now for the cool part: When you build a new database, *you* get to choose which organizational style your database uses! Don't let it worry you, though — you're not on your own in making the decision. The following paragraphs tell you a little about each kind of organization. (Chapter 5 goes into lots of detail on the subject, too.)

Flat files: Simple answers for simple needs

In a *flat* system (also known as *flat file*), all the data is lumped into a single table. A phone directory is a good example of a flat file database: Names, addresses, and phone numbers (the data) are crammed into a single place (the database). Some duplication occurs — if one person has three phone lines at home, his or her name and address are listed three times in the directory — but that's not a big problem. Overall, the database works just fine.

Relational databases: Complex solutions to bigger problems

The *relational* system (or *relational database*) uses as little storage space as possible by cutting down on the duplicated (the nerds call it *redundant*) data in the database. To accomplish this, a relational database splits your data into several tables, with each table holding some portion of the total data.

Borrowing the preceding phone book example, one table in a relational database can contain the customer name and address information, while another can hold the phone numbers. Thanks to this approach, the mythical person with three phone lines only has *one* entry in the "customer" table (after all, it's *still* just one customer) but has *three* distinct entries in the "phone number" table (one for each phone line). By using a relational database, the system stores the customer's personal information only once, thus saving some space on the computer's disk drive (see Figure 4-1).

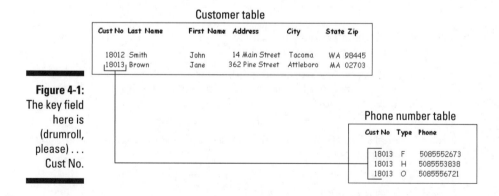

Figure 4-1:
The key field here is (drumroll, please) . . . Cust No.

Customer table

Cust No	Last Name	First Name	Address	City	State	Zip
18012	Smith	John	14 Main Street	Tacoma	WA	98445
18013	Brown	Jane	362 Pine Street	Attleboro	MA	02703

Phone number table

Cust No	Type	Phone
18013	F	5085552673
18013	H	5085553838
18013	O	5085556721

The *key field* (or *linking field*) is the key to this advanced technology. All related tables in a relational database system contain this special field. The key field's data identifies matching records from different tables. The key field works just like the claim stub you receive when you drop off film for processing at the local store. To join up with your film again, you present the claim check, complete with its little claim number. That number identifies (or *links*) you and your film so that the clerk can find it.

Likewise, in the phone book example, each customer can have a unique customer ID. The "phone number" table stores the customer ID with each phone number. To find out who owns a phone number, you look up the customer ID in the "customer name" table. Granted, it takes more steps to find someone's phone number than it does in the plain flat file system, but the relational system saves storage space (no more duplicate names) and reduces the chance of errors at the same time.

If this process seems complicated, don't feel bad. Relational databases *are* complicated! (Even some computer geeks don't understand them.) That's why Chapter 5 explains the concept in infinitely more detail, complete with examples of how the process works and warning signs to watch for lest you turn into a full-fledged database nerd. For your own sanity, be patient with yourself when wrestling with relational databases. There's no shame in asking for some help from your friendly neighborhood computer jockey, either.

Figuring out what all this means

Now you at least have an idea of the difference between flat file and relational databases. But do you care? Yes, you do. Each approach has its unique pluses and minuses for your database:

- ✔ Flat file systems are easy to build and maintain. (A Microsoft Excel spreadsheet is a good example.)

  Anyone can create a workable flat database system — and I *do* mean anyone. They're great for simple listings such as mailing lists, phone directories, and video collections. Flat systems are simple solutions for simple problems.

- ✔ Relational systems shine in big business applications such as invoicing, accounting, or inventory.

  If you have a small project (such as a mailing list or membership database), a relational approach may be more solution than you need. Developing a solid relational database takes skill and practice (and, in some countries, a nerd license).

Your company probably has a lot of information stored in relational database systems. Understanding how to use relational systems is important for you, so that's covered just about everywhere you turn in this book. Specifically, check out Chapter 5 to find out about dealing with the relationships between tables.

I don't recommend that you set off to build a relational database system by yourself. If you're sure that you need one, enlist the Database Wizard or a friendly guru to help you bring the database to life. There's a lot to understand about how fields work together to form relations. Get some help the first time and then try it on your own later.

Although Access is a relational database program, it does flat systems quite nicely. Whether you choose flat file or relational for your database project, Access is the right program!

Great Tables Start with Great Designs

You're *almost* ready to start the computer and run Access — but not quite. You need to design the tables for your database. I know this seems like a lot of paperwork, but it's absolutely necessary to build good databases. When I create systems for my clients, this is exactly how I do it:

1. **Get out a clean pad of paper and something to write with.**

   Despite the wonders of PCs and Windows, some jobs are easier on paper. Besides, if the database design work isn't going well, you can always doodle.

2. **Write brief descriptions of the reports, lists, and other outputs you want from the system.**

   Why start with the stuff that comes out? Because these reports and such are the *real* reason you're creating the database.

   Don't worry about making this a perfect and complete list. Settle for an *includes most everything* list, because you can always go back later and add new stuff to it.

3. **On another sheet of paper, sketch some samples of the reports, lists, and other outputs you listed in Step 2.**

   You needn't create detailed report designs at this point — that's not the goal. Right now, you're figuring out what you need to build the stuff that ultimately comes from your database (the reports, lists, mailing labels, and everything else). Just get a rough idea of what you want the most important reports to look like and write down the stuff that's on them. This list becomes the road map to your database's fields. (After all, you can't print a mailing label if your database doesn't store addresses somewhere.)

4. **For each field in your list, write a name and field type. For text fields, include a size.**

You need to do this step even if you're planning to use the Database Wizard or Table Wizard when you build the table. Although those wizards automatically size and name the fields you create, you can still customize the fields to your liking.

5. **Organize the fields into tables.**

Look for data that naturally goes together, such as name, address, and phone number for a contact database, or product ID, description, distributor, cost, and selling price for an inventory system.

If you have a lot of fields or if you run out of ideas for putting them together, get help from your friendly guru.

This last part is the hardest, but it gets easier with practice. To build your experience, create some sample databases with the Database Wizard and look at how the database's tables fit together. Choose a topic you know about (accounting, event scheduling, or compact disc collecting) and see how the pros at Microsoft designed their tables. Open the various tables in design view (in the database window, right-click the table name and choose Design from the pop-up menu). Which fields went in each table? Why are tables organized that way? Get a big-picture view of how the tables interact in the database by clicking the Relationships button on the toolbar. Access displays the Relationships window (see Figure 4-2), which graphically shows how all the tables in the database are linked. Follow the lines between the tables to unravel the connections.

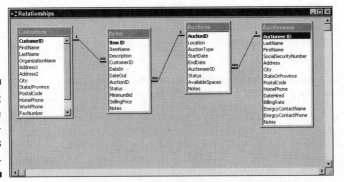

Figure 4-2:
The Relationships window.

Building a Database

After reading page after page of this book, writing reams of notes, and sucking down two or three cans of pop, the moment is finally here — it's time to build the database! Here's where you create the master holding file for your tables, reports, forms, and other stuff. Plus, if you use a Database Wizard, this step also creates all the tables, reports, and forms for you — it's one-stop shopping!

Without further ado, here's how to create a database:

1. **If Access is not already running, take a moment to start it.**

2. **Choose File⇨New from the main menu (as shown in Figure 4-3) or click the New toolbar button.**

   The New File task pane appears on the right side of the screen.

3. **Click the <u>On My Computer</u> link in the Templates section (about halfway down the New File task pane).**

   The Templates window finally appears.

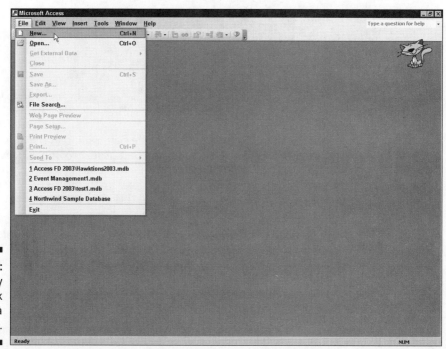

Figure 4-3:
It takes only
a quick click
to create a
database.

4. **In the Templates window, click the Databases tab.**

   A list of database template wizards appears, as shown in Figure 4-4. If none of the templates meets your needs, you can select Templates on Office Online from the New File task pane to see more templates.

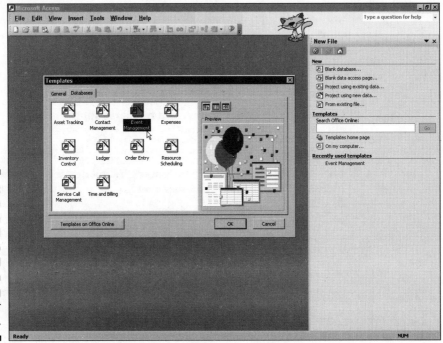

Figure 4-4:
Choose one of the wizard templates to get a head start on creating your database.

To create a database by hand, click the General tab in the Templates window, and then double-click Blank Database. Provide a file name for your database — and voilà! One blank database is awaiting your command. Skip the rest of the steps here, and instead turn to "Creating Tables at the Wave of a Wand" later in this chapter for guidance on adding tables to your blank database.

5. **Look through the list until you find a database wizard template that seems most like what you want to do, and then double-click it.**

   The oddly-named File New Database dialog box appears.

6. **Type a name for your database and then click Create (as shown in Figure 4-5).**

To store the database somewhere other than in the default location (usually the My Documents folder), choose a different folder by clicking the down arrow beside Save In and work through the directory tree until you find the folder you're looking for.

Figure 4-5:
Type a name
for the
database,
click Create,
and you're
on your
way.

If a dialog box pops up and asks whether you want to replace an existing file, Access is saying that a database with the name you entered is already on the disk. If this is news to you, click No and then come up with a different name for your new database. On the other hand, if you *intended* to replace that old database with a new one, click Yes and proceed.

7. **The Database Wizard starts by telling you about the type of database you selected. Read its description, and then click Next to continue.**

Access displays a list of tables and fields that it plans to include in your new database (see Figure 4-6). The left section shows all the tables. The right section shows the fields in the currently selected table. Check marks appear next to the fields slated to appear in the table.

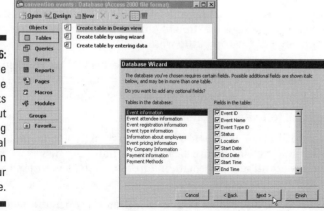

Figure 4-6:
The
Database
Wizard asks
you about
adding
optional
fields in
your
database.

If you just want the wizard to get on with things and build the database, click the Finish button instead of Next. That gives the Wizard a green light to create your database automatically. Use this option on your first couple of tries with the wizard. It saves time and presents you with a nicely finished product. You can always change the fields and other options later with the design tools in Access.

8. **If you want to add or remove any standard fields in the database, click the check box next to the field. View the fields in another table by clicking the table name. When you finish prowling through the fields, click <u>N</u>ext.**

   Usually, you stick with the fields Access suggests. To add new fields not offered by the wizard, let the wizard finish its steps and then take the completed table into design view. For more about that, see Chapter 9.

   Congratulations — that completes the hardest part of building your database with the wizard. It's all easy stuff from here. After clicking the Next button, Access offers you some screen style options.

9. **Click the visual style that best meets your needs, and then click Next.**

   Unless you feel a driving need for a visually stunning database, stick with the Standard display option. The others look pretty, but most of them make your database load more slowly. If you simply *must* add some visual diversity, try the International, Sumi Painting, or SandStone options. With your main visual choices in place, Access suggests options for your report designs.

10. **Choose the style for your reports (at last), and then click <u>N</u>ext.**

    Single-click the options for a quick preview of the available possibilities.

11. **Name your masterpiece, choose a picture, and then click <u>N</u>ext.**

    Take heart — the database is almost finished! The wizard kindly offers its own lame name, but feel free to change it by simply typing something new in the box at the top of the window.

To add a picture to your reports, check the Yes I'd Like to Include a Picture check box and then click the Picture button to choose the graphic you want to feature on the database's reports.

12. **Click <u>F</u>inish to build the database.**

    The wizard clunks and thunks for a while, giving you constant updates on how it's doing (see Figure 4-7). When it finishes, the wizard prompts you for any additional information it needs, such as your company name, address, and such.

13. **When the wizard prompts you for additional information, such as your company name, address, and such, oblige it by providing it.**

The Database Wizard completes the job by automatically creating a friendly switchboard screen like the one shown in Figure 4-8.

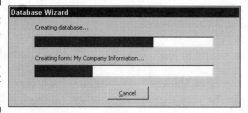

Figure 4-7:
The Database Wizard, hard at work.

Now that the database is ready, flip through Chapters 6 and 7 for information on entering data, customizing the tables, and getting comfy with your new addition.

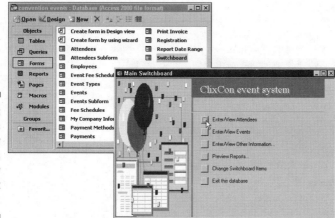

Figure 4-8:
Access proudly displays the new database it built for you.

Creating Tables at the Wave of a Wand

Adding a new table to an existing database is easy with the Access Table Wizard. The Table Wizard offers a variety of ready-made fields to choose from, plus it does all the dirty work of table creation behind the scenes, so you can focus on important stuff.

With the Table Wizard, you don't so much *build* a table as *assemble* it. The wizard brings lots of pieces and parts — you choose what you want and go from there.

The assembly approach is helpful when you're not familiar with building tables. Instead of worrying about details such as field types and sizes, you get to worry about bigger stuff, such as field names and purposes. After you build a few tables, you probably won't use the Table Wizard. Instead of helping, the wizard starts getting in the way because you already know what fields you want and how to make them.

Without further ado, here's how to ask the wizard to help you build a table:

1. **Choose File⇨Open or click the Open Database button on the toolbar to open the database file that needs a new table.**

   The database pops into its window.

2. **On the left side of the database window, click the Tables button to tell Access that you want to work with tables. Double-click the Create Table by Using Wizard entry in the database window to start the creation process.**

   If everything works right, the Table Wizard dialog box shown in Figure 4-9 appears. If some other bizarre window appears, close that window and repeat this step.

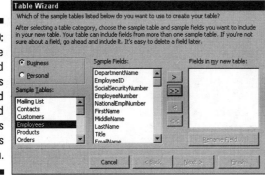

Figure 4-9:
The Table Wizard suggests tables and fields and then builds the tables for you.

3. **Click a sample table to display the available fields.**

   The Sample Tables list is a tad messy. Table names appear in no particular order, forcing you to scroll through a long list to find what's available to you. Be patient — the effort is worth it.

   The Table Wizard offers you all kinds of ready-made fields to assemble into a table.

4. **Double-click the fields you want for the table.**

   Each double-clicked field name hops into the Fields in my new table column.

Select the fields in the order you want them to appear in the new table. Don't worry if you get one or two out of order — it's easy to correct that later (Chapter 9 tells you how).

TIP

- If you like *all* the fields from a particular table, click the >> button to copy the table's entire set of fields.

- To remove a field you chose by accident, click the field name and then click the < button.

- To remove *all* the fields and start over with a clean slate, click the << button.

- If you're not happy with the current name of a field in your new table, click the field name and then click Rename Field. Type the new field name into the dialog box and click OK to make the change. Too easy, eh?

5. **Repeat Step 4 until your table is full of fields (as shown in Figure 4-10). Click <u>N</u>ext to continue building the table.**

   The field information runs off to hide as the wizard asks some more general stuff about the table.

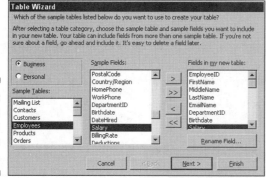

Figure 4-10: Select the fields you want in your table.

6. **Type a name for the table, and then click <u>N</u>ext.**

   Leave the primary key settings alone for now. You can mess with the settings later (see Chapter 5). Access shows you a screen listing other tables in the database and whether it thinks your new table is related to them (see Figure 4-11). Access is often spectacularly bad in its assumptions about related tables, so look at the list closely.

7. **If the Table Wizard made an incorrect assumption about table relationships and you want to help it along, do the following:**

   a. **Click the Relationships button.**

      The Relationships dialog box appears, as shown in Figure 4-12.

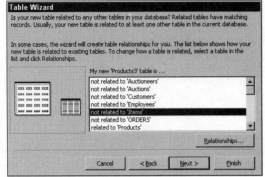

Figure 4-11:
The Table
Wizard
shows all
existing
tables and
whether
Access
thinks they
relate to
your new
table.

b. **Choose from one of the three options in the Relationships dialog box.**

In Figure 4-12, I indicate that for each record in the Products3 table, there can be many in the Items table. (Chapter 5 has more about table relationships. Look in that chapter if you're a little foggy about the hows and whys of relating tables.)

c. **Click OK.**

For more about the electronic soap opera of table relationships, see Chapter 5.

8. **Click Finish to complete the task and build the new table.**

Your table is now ready to be filled with data.

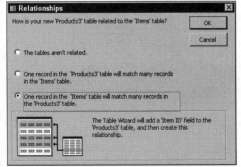

Figure 4-12:
Tell Access
how your
tables really
relate in the
Relation-
ships dialog
box.

Highlights from the sample tables

For your convenience, the following list contains some of the more useful sample tables that the wizard knows how to create. Each entry names the table and describes its purpose.

- ✔ Contacts: Full-featured customer information table; stores details about your customers

- ✔ Customers: You guessed it — a customer information list, complete with a field for e-mail address

- ✔ Employees: Solid employee information table; good example of the detail you can include in a single table

- ✔ Events: Great for meeting planners or trainers setting up their own room information

- ✔ Mailing List: General information (name, address, and so on) geared toward seminar attendees

- ✔ Orders: Tracks customer order data

- ✔ Order Details: Covers the line items for each order

- ✔ Products: General product information for a catalog and sales system

- ✔ Reservations: Handles event reservations and pre-paid fees

- ✔ Service Records: Great example of a table that manages call information for a service business

- ✔ Tasks: Tracks to-do items

Many of these tables link to form relational databases. For example, Contacts, Customers, and Tasks work together as a single system. Don't bother trying to put the individual pieces together with the Table Wizard. Use the Database Wizard instead — it's a lot easier!

Building Tables by Hand, Just like in the Old Days

Although automation is generally great, at times it plain gets in the way. For example, I appreciate the fact that with the right automatic gizmo, I can clap my hands and turn off the television. This feat becomes a problem when I start keeping time with my favorite song and accidentally drive the TV insane.

Likewise, the Table Wizard makes life easy at first, but soon you know more about what you want than the wizard does. Don't worry — when you're ready for independence, Access is there with a straightforward way to build tables by hand.

Actually, *two* easy ways exist to build a table without the Table Wizard:

✔ **Datasheet view:** Displays a blank datasheet. You just start typing data. After you've entered everything, Access looks at your entries and assigns field types based on the data it sees.

The only problem is that Access frequently misunderstands your data, leaving you to tweak the field types by hand. The bottom line: For anything more complicated than a *really* simple table, don't use datasheet view. It's a nice thought, but it drives you nuts in the end. Instead, use design view.

✔ **Design view:** The formal, almost nerd-like way to build new databases. In this mode, you have full control over the new table's fields. Don't get all weirded out because the screen looks complicated — go slowly and follow the information in the steps, and everything will turn out fine.

To create a new table by hand, cruise through these steps:

1. **Choose File⇨Open from the main menu; then double-click the database that needs a new table.**

   The database file appears.

   In the world of Access, tables live inside databases. If you don't already have a database file, start by creating one of those with the File⇨New command.

2. **On the left side of the database window, click the Tables button. Then double-click Create Table in Design View.**

   Access displays a blank table design form that looks a whole heckuva lot like Figure 4-13.

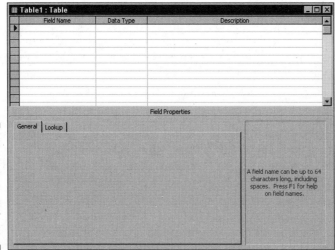

Figure 4-13: A fresh, clean table design awaiting your instruction.

3. **Type the field name and then press Tab.**

   The cursor moves to the Data Type column.

4. **Click the down arrow to list all available field types. Click the field type you want (see Figure 4-14), and then press Tab to continue.**

   Pressing the first letter of the field type scrolls you right to it. For example, if you tab into the Data Type column and press A on the keyboard, the cursor scrolls to the AutoNumber entry.

   Every time you choose a field type, the bottom portion of the window fills with new options organized below General and Lookup tabs. Just ignore all that for now. Those items help you customize and automate the way your fields work. Chapter 7 explores that area in depth.

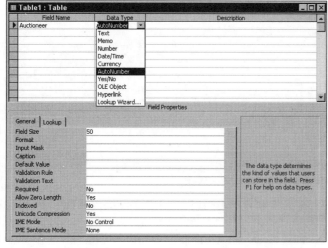

Figure 4-14:
You can select from all available field (data) types.

If you create a text field, you probably need to adjust the field size (the default size is 50, which is too much field for almost anyone). Click the Field Size box in the lower-left side of the screen *before* tabbing elsewhere; then type the correct field size.

5. **Press Tab to move the cursor to the Description field.**

6. **Type a clear, concise description of what this field contains.**

   This step is *really* important! The Description information appears in the status bar at the bottom of the screen — it's automatic help text. *Please* take the time to write a quick field description. It makes your tables much easier to use.

7. **Press Tab to move the cursor back to the Field Name column.**

8. **Repeat Steps 3 through 7 until all the fields are in place (as shown in Figure 4-15).**

   What a feeling of achievement! Your new table is almost ready.

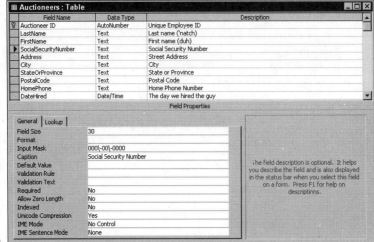

Figure 4-15:
The fields
are in
place —
time to give
your table
the stress
test!

9. **Select File➪Save or click the Save button on the toolbar to write the new table to your disk drive.**

10. **In the Save dialog box, type the name that you want to use for the table and then press Enter.**

    Access may send you a dialog box complaining "There is no primary key defined." This message means that your table won't automatically put itself into any order. Click Yes in the dialog box to create a key field and go to Chapter 5 for more about key fields.

11. **Enjoy your new table!**

    That's not bad for working without automated intervention. Congratulations on a job well done!

Chapter 5

Relationships, Keys, and Indexes (and Why You Really Do Care)

*E*very year, it's the same: Do more with less; work smarter not harder. They're not problems, they're *opportunities for achievement*. Why do I bring up such wonderful thoughts in a fun book like this? Because this chapter is at least a partial cure for these phrases that afflict you.

You need to do more in less time, right? If that's you, check out the index feature in Access 2003. This feature makes your queries fly, your sorts sing, and your hair hold firm in its current position. Are you plagued with *opportunities* because of all the duplicate data infesting your tables? Ferret out the problems with a well-placed key field. A good key field ensures that records appear once (and only once) in the table.

And what about relational databases? Can tables *really* have relationships, or do they just spend a lot of platonic time together? Thanks to the wonders of the Relationships tool in Access 2003, your tables work with each other better than ever. Of course, the matchmaking that leads to a successful relationship isn't any easier with tables than with humans, but don't let that worry you. With the tips in this chapter, you'll be a card-carrying Data Guru in no time.

The Joy (and Necessity) of a Primary Key

A table's primary key is a special field in your table. Just about every table you create should have a primary key. Here's why:

- A primary key organizes your data by *uniquely* identifying each record. For example, in a Customer table, the Customer Number would be the primary key — there's only one customer number 1, one customer number 2, and so on.

- Nerds pitch a fit if you don't have a primary key.

You need to know a few rules about the primary key before running off to create one:

- A table can have only one *primary* key. A single table can have lots of indexes, but only one primary key.

- Access automatically indexes the primary key field (that's one reason why a primary key makes your database work a little faster). For more about indexes, see the final section in this chapter, "Indexing Your Way to Fame, Fortune, and Significantly Faster Queries."

- If you create a new table without a primary key, Access automatically asks whether you want to add one. If you say yes, the program gleefully creates an AutoNumber field at the beginning of your table and sets it as the primary key. If the first field is an AutoNumber type, Access anoints it as the primary key without adding anything else to the table.

- Most of the time, the primary key is a single field, but in *very* special circumstances, two or more fields can share the job. The technical term for this type of key is a *multifield key*. The super-technical term for this type of key is *compound key*.

- You can't use the memo, OLE object, or hyperlink field types in a primary key.

- Although you *can* use the yes/no field type in a primary key, you can have only two records (Yes and No) in such a table.

- The primary key automatically sorts records in the table. This just keeps your tables neat and tidy.

- Access doesn't care where the primary key field is in the table design. The key can be the first field, the last field, or in the middle. The placement choice is all yours. For your sanity's sake, I recommend putting the key field *first* in a table. In fact, make it a habit. (You'll thank me later.)

- All primary keys must have a name, just like the field has a name. This may come as a shock, so hold on to your seat, but Access automatically names all primary keys *Primary Key*.

To nominate a field for the job of primary key, follow these steps:

1. **Open the table in design view.**

   If you're not familiar with this step, you probably shouldn't be messing with the primary key. Likewise, if you aren't comfortable with the content of Chapters 1 and 4, you aren't ready to tackle primary keys.

2. **Right-click the button next to the field you've chosen for the primary key.**

   One of those cool pop-up menus appears. For some ideas on how to choose the right field for a primary key, see the sidebar titled "Choosing the right field is a *key* issue."

3. **Choose Primary Key from the menu (as shown in Figure 5-1).**

   A little key symbol appears in the button. The primary key is set!

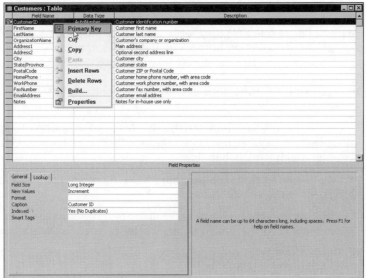

Figure 5-1: The primary key is created (and the records rejoice).

Divulging the Secrets of a Good Relationship

Relational databases split data among two or more tables. Access uses a linking field, called a *foreign key*, to tie related tables together. For example, one table may contain customer names and addresses while another table tracks the customer's payment history. The credit information is tied to the customer's address with a linking field, which, in this example, is probably a customer number. Here are a few general thoughts to keep in mind when linking tables:

✔ Usually, the linking field is one table's primary key but an average, mild-mannered field in the other table. The customer table, for example, is probably arranged by customer number, whereas the credit data is likely organized by payment number.

✔ Tables don't magically begin relating to each other just because they're cooped up inside the same database file. You explain the relationships to Access, and it handles the details. See the following section for details about explaining relationships to Access.

✔ Linking fields must be the same data type. Remember, fields of a feather flock together in the weird world of databases. Try repeating that three times quickly.

When you link two tables, they form one of four possible relationships. Although this information borders on the technical side, Access is particularly fond of these terms, so please take a minute to check them out.

✔ **One-to-one relationships** link one record in the first table to *exactly* one record in the second table.

One-to-one relationships are the simplest, but they don't happen often. Tables that have a one-to-one relationship can be combined into one table, which usually happens.

✔ **One-to-many relationships** connect one record in the first table to *many* records in the second table.

One sample customer may make many purchases at the store, so one customer record is linked to many sales records in the transaction table.

✔ **Many-to-one relationships** connect *many* records in the first table to *one* record in the second table.

Many-to-one relationships are simply the reverse of one-to-many relationships.

✔ **Many-to-many relationships** link many records in one table to many records in another. Many-to-many relationships are bad, evil, and fundamentally un-good. In fact, Access doesn't even let you to create many-to-many relationships. For a little more about the problems (and solution) to many-to-many table relationships, see the "Unraveling a many-to-many relationship" sidebar.

TIP

Choosing the right field is a key issue

What makes a good key field? How do you find the right one? Good questions — in fact, they're the two most important questions to ask about a primary key.

The top criterion for a good key field is uniqueness. The values in a key field must be unique. Access won't tolerate duplicate key values. Each and every entry in the key field(s) must be the only one of its kind. If you see a lot of table creation in your future, pin the phrase *Think unique* on your office wall.

With the word *unique* firmly imprinted in your mind, it's time to look for a natural key field in your table. Do you have any fields that always contain

unique data? Is there a Customer Number, Stock Keeping Unit, Vehicle ID, or some other field that's different in every record?

If you have a natural key, that's great. Use it! If you don't, create a unique field by adding an AutoNumber field to your table. This field type automatically inserts a new, unique number into each record of your table. AutoNumber even keeps track of numbers that you delete so that Access won't use them again. Best of all, Access takes care of the details, so you don't have to worry about programming or any special tricks to make the program work.

Linking Your Tables with the Relationship Builder Thingy

The mechanics of linking tables in Access are visual. In Access, you can look at tables, draw lines, and get on with your business. I hate to say this, but linking tables is kind of fun. Keep these three limitations in mind:

- ✔ You can link only tables that are in the same database.

- ✔ You can link queries to tables, but that's unusual.

- ✔ You need to specifically tell Access how your tables are related. And you can't tell this stuff to Access on-the-fly — linking tables is a formal process (like ballroom dancing).

When you're ready to arrange some formal relationships among your more impassioned tables, here's how to do it:

1. **From the database window, choose Tools⇨Relationships or click the Relationships button on the toolbar.**

   The Relationships window appears, probably looking quite blank at the moment.

If some tables are already listed in the window, someone (or some wizard) has defined relationships for this database. If you're in a corporate environment, *please* stop at this point and seek assistance from your Information Systems folks before mucking around with this database's relationships.

2. **Display a list of this database's tables by choosing Relationships⇨ Show Table from the main menu or by clicking the Show Table button on the toolbar.**

   The Show Table dialog box appears, listing the tables in the current database file.

3. **Click the first table involved in this would-be relationship, and then click Add.**

   A little window showing the fields in that table appears in the big Relationships workspace.

4. **Repeat the process with the other tables you want to link.**

   As you continue adding tables to the layout, more little windows appear — one for each table. You can see these windows next to the Show Table dialog box in Figure 5-2.

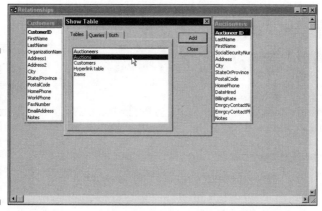

Figure 5-2:
Use the
Show Table
dialog box
to add
tables to the
Relation-
ships
diagram.

5. **Click Close after you finish adding tables.**

   With the tables present in the window, you're ready to start the relationships! (How cool — it's like a digital Valentine's Day mixer.)

6. **Decide which two tables you want to link.**

   In a one-to-many relationship, one of the tables is the *parent* and one is the *child.* In the parent, the linking field will be the primary key.

In Access, you need to see the two linking fields on the screen before you can make a relationship.

7. **Put the mouse pointer on the field you want to link in the *parent* table (which will be the primary key of that table) and hold down the left mouse button.**

   Suddenly, unexpectedly, *nothing* happens. Nothing at all. You don't see any change in the screen until the next step. I think the Access programming geeks did this to make us all wonder.

8. **While holding down the mouse button, slide the mouse from one linking field to the other.**

   The pointer becomes a rectangle. When the rectangle is on the linking field, release the mouse button. A dialog box detailing the soon-to-be relationship appears, as shown in Figure 5-3.

Figure 5-3:
The Edit Relationships dialog box details how Access connects the two tables.

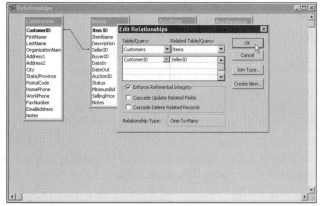

Access gets picky about your aim on this step. You must put the tip of the mouse pointer *directly* on the field you're linking to. Figure 5-3 shows the CustomerID dragged from the Customers table and dropped on the SellerID field in the Items table.

9. **Click to add a check mark to the Enforce Referential Integrity option to enforce the relationship between the two tables.**

   By turning on the Enforce Referential Integrity setting, Access makes sure that the data you put into one table's key field matches the data in the other table. In this example, Access won't let you enter a particular SellerID into the Items table unless it's a valid CustomerID in the Customers table.

10. **Click Create after you're confident that the table and field names in the dialog box are correct.**

   A line shows you that the tables are linked. Because you checked the Enforce Referential Integrity option, Access places a 1 next to the parent in the relationship and an infinity symbol next to the child, as shown in the full set of relationships in Figure 5-4. This denotes a one-to-many relationship. (Figure 5-4 also shows a one-to-many relationship between Auctioneers and Auctions, plus an as-yet-undetermined relationship between Auctions and Items.)

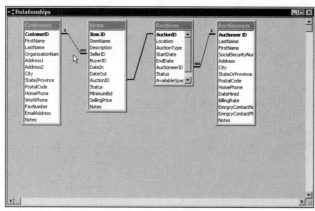

Figure 5-4:
Access displays the tables and their relationships in a neat and easy-to-see way.

   If the table names or field names listed in the dialog box are wrong, just click Cancel and try Steps 6 through 8 again.

11. **To link another pair of tables, go back to Step 3 and begin again.**

When you're finished, the Relationships window may look a little messy because relationship lines will be crossing each other. To clean it up, put the mouse pointer on the title bar of a table window and then click and drag the table window to another part of the screen. It's traditional (although not always possible) to show parents above children.

Indexing Your Way to Fame, Fortune, and Significantly Faster Queries

Psst — you with the book. Yeah, you. Want some inside information about your software? I've got a hot tip on a feature that'll blow you away. My tip speeds up your queries, makes sorting a snap, and prevents duplicate records in your tables. Pretty cool, eh? Oh, you *are* interested. Okay, then — here's the scoop.

Unraveling a many-to-many relationship

Although they sound enticing and useful, many-to-many relationships between tables just don't work. Instead of solving some weird storage problem for you, these relationships actually create lots of new problems. If your database requirements seem to demand a many-to-many relationship between a few tables, solve the problem by using what Access calls a junction table.

The *junction table* acts as a combination traffic cop and mediator between the two tables. To fulfill this role, the junction table needs a one-to-many relationship with *both* of the tables you want to connect.

For example, think about the database for a training center. The Students table lists all the center's attendees by Student ID, and the Courses table contains details about each class offered by Course ID. Each student attends many courses, and each course contains many students. Uh oh — it's a many-to-many relationship!

Now solve the problem by adding the linking table — a new third table called Schedule. The primary key for each record in the Schedule table contains both a Student ID field and the Course ID field, representing one student in one class. That gives the Schedule table a one-to-many relationship with both the Students and Courses tables. By querying the Schedule table along with the Students and Courses tables, the training center can quickly find out which students belong in each course (one Course ID, multiple Student ID records) and which courses each student attended (one Student ID, many Course ID records).

The linking table smoothly and easily solves the many-to-many relationship problem.

The cool speed secret is an *index*. An Access table index works just like the index in a book. Using the index is a whole lot faster than flipping page after page in a hopeless search for the correct passage.

An Access index works just like a book index, but instead of listing page numbers, the index tracks *record* numbers. When you sort or query a table using an indexed field, the index does most of the work. That's why indexes dramatically speed up queries and sorts — the index lets the query zero in on the information without sifting through the whole table to find it.

Here are a few random thoughts about indexes:

- ✔ Each field in a table can be indexed as long as it's not one of these field types: hyperlink, memo, or OLE object.
- ✔ Like the primary key, an index may have a unique name that's different from the field name.

✔ Although indexes make queries, searches, and sorts a whole lot faster, building too many indexes in a table slows down some tasks. Adding records to a table with several indexes takes a little longer than adding records to an unindexed table. Access spends the extra time updating all those indexes behind the scenes.

✔ Indexes either *allow* duplicate entries in your table or *prevent* them. The choice is yours. How do you choose the right one for your table? Most of the time, you want to allow duplicate records. The big exception is with primary key fields. Access always indexes primary key fields as *No duplicates* — after all, you don't want two customers with the same customer number. The No Duplicates setting tells Access to make sure that no two records have the same values in the indexed field.

✔ To list the table's indexes, open the table in design view and click the Indexes button on the toolbar.

The programmers at Microsoft made creating an index a straightforward operation. Here's how you do it:

1. **With the table open in design view, click the name of the field you want to index.**

   The blinking toothpick cursor lands in the field name.

2. **In the General tab of the Field Properties section, click the Indexed box.**

   The toothpick cursor, always eager to please, hops into the Indexed box. A down arrow appears on the right end of the box as well.

   If the Indexed display has no entry, this particular field type doesn't work with indexes. No matter how much you want to, you can't index hyperlink, memo, or OLE object fields.

3. **Click the down arrow at the end of the box to list your index options.**

   A list of index options appears.

4. **Select the index you want from the list.**

   Most of the time, click Yes (Duplicates OK). In special cases when you want every record to have a unique value in this field (such as customer numbers in your Customer table), click Yes (No Duplicates).

5. **To make the change permanent, click the Save toolbar button or choose File➪Save.**

   Depending on the size of your table, it may take a few moments of effort to create the index.

To remove an index, follow the preceding steps, but choose No in the pull-down menu in Step 4. Access wordlessly deletes the field's index.

Chapter 6

New Data, Old Data, and Data in Need of Repair

*M*aintenance adds a bundle to the cost of anything worth keeping. Whether you're talking about a house, car, stereo, television, child, pet, or significant other, maintaining your valuables in good working order usually costs a lot more than you think it will (or should).

Surprisingly, your data is one big exception to the rule. Thanks to the tools in Access, data maintenance is easy, relatively painless, and costs less than you expect. In fact, keeping your data safe, sound, and up to date is one of the program's major goals.

This chapter covers basic data upkeep: adding new records, deleting old ones, and fixing the broken ones. For table maintenance hints (such as adding new columns, renaming fields, and so on), check out Chapter 9.

Dragging Your Table into the Digital Workshop

Because records cluster together in tables, you need to open a table before worrying about records. Tables prefer company, too. They hang out inside databases. Databases don't care a whit about anything other than themselves, so you may find them lounging in a folder, sulking on a disk, or holding forth on a network drive.

That background about databases, tables, and records simply means that the first step on the road to record maintenance is opening a database. You have several ways to open a database, but ultimately they all work the same way.

When you open Access, the program displays the task pane (as shown in Figure 6-1), which offers the opportunity to create a database, reopen one you worked on recently, or wander off into another dialog box to open whichever database strikes your fancy. Each action is presented as a hyperlink.

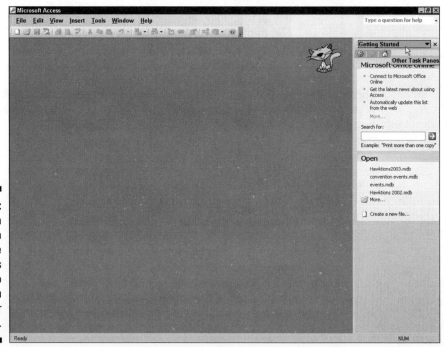

Figure 6-1:
When you open Access, the task pane is there to greet you and do your bidding.

The following list describes things you can do with the task pane:

- Click at the top of the task pane (where it says New File in Figure 6-1) to display other panes, such as Getting Started, Help, and File Search.

- To open one of the databases listed, simply click it.

- If the database you want isn't on the list, click the More Files option to display the Open dialog box. This dialog box gives you access to all the table files in a file folder.

- What? The database you want isn't there either? In that case, check out the sidebar in this chapter for some tips about the fortuitous file-finding features located in the Tools menu of the Open dialog box.

- If you're in the mood to create a table, flip to Chapter 4, where all the create-a-table stuff is.

These hints are all well and good if Access just came roaring to life, but what if it's already running and the task pane is nowhere to be found? In that case, display the task pane either by right-clicking the toolbar area and choosing Task Pane or by choosing View➪Task Pane from the main menu.

If all this stuff sounds like "task pain" to you, go through the following steps to open a database the tried-and-true way with the File menu:

1. Choose File➪Open or click the Open Database button on the toolbar.

The Open dialog box pops onto the screen, as shown in Figure 6-2.

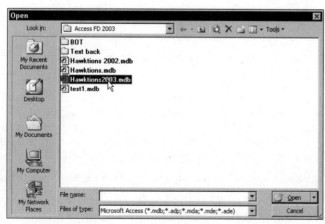

Figure 6-2:
The database list appears.

2. Scroll through the list until you find the database you're looking for.

If the database you want isn't on this list, it's probably in another folder, on another disk drive, or out on your network. To search for it, click the down arrow in the Look in box (at the top of the Open dialog box) to see a list of your local and network disk drives, and then click the drive you want to search. Access displays a list of all databases and file folders in the current folder.

To make work *really* easy, add a few shortcuts to your Favorites list. Include your most commonly used network areas, directories on your hard drive, or wherever you (or the data nerds in your company) store Access files.

3. **When you find the database, open it by double-clicking its name.**

   The database file opens with a flourish, as shown in Figure 6-3. This window shows how a normal, well-mannered database file acts in polite company. The rest of this chapter assumes that your database behaves this way.

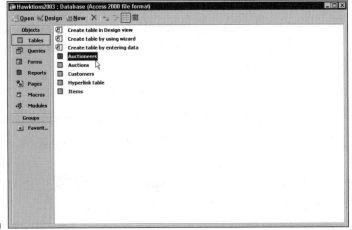

Figure 6-3:
The database file opens, and the database window displays all the tables, queries, and so on.

An introductory screen of some kind (known as a *switchboard*) may appear instead of the tabbed dialog box. Access is telling you that your database either contains some custom programming or was created by the Database Wizard. You probably have some special forms that help you interact with the information in your database.

4. **If it's not already selected, click the Tables button under the Objects bar.**

   The Tables button lists the tables in your database.

5. **Double-click the table you want to edit.**

   The screen fills with your data, displayed eloquently in datasheet view.

Adding Something to the Mix

Few tasks are more frustrating than packing your car for vacation and then suddenly discovering what you forgot to put in (and it's always something big). In the real world, this discovery is a repacking nightmare, but in the digital world of Access, adding one or a hundred extra items to your database is easy.

In fact, adding another record to a table takes only a few steps. The following instructions assume that you've opened the database file and selected the table you want to work on. (If you haven't, follow the instructions in the preceding section.) Here's how to add a new record to your table:

1. **Choose Insert⇨New Record or click the New Record button at the bottom of the datasheet window.**

   Access opens a blank record in your table and moves the toothpick cursor to the first field in that record, as shown in Figure 6-4.

   The first field in many databases is an AutoNumber type field, because this field does such a good job of assigning unique customer numbers, part numbers, or whatever kind of number you have in mind. At this point in the process, it's normal for an AutoNumber field to just sit there and stare at you. The AutoNumber field doesn't start working until the next step, when AutoNumber automagically shoves the next sequential item number into your field.

Figure 6-4:
A new record — denoted by the little pencil — sits ready for its data.

Item ID	ItemName	Description	SellerID	BuyerID	DateIn	DateOut	AuctionID
1	China setting for 8	White pattern edged in light blue	11		1/10/2004		
2	3 Cast iron toys	Lot contains three cast iron toys	15		1/11/2004		
3	Asst hardback books (1 of 4)	Box of assorted hardback books	22		1/18/2004		
4	Asst hardback books (2 of 4)	Box of assorted hardback books	22		1/18/2004		
5	Asst hardback books (3 of 4)	Box of assorted hardback books	22		1/18/2004		
6	Asst hardback books (4 of 4)	Box of assorted hardback books	22		1/18/2004		
7	Painting -- boat on lake	16x20 original oil painting	37		1/25/2004		
8	Painting -- Children	16x20 original oil painting	37		1/25/2004		
9	Painting -- Convertible	16x20 original oil painting	37		1/25/2004		
10	Painting -- Old man	16x20 original oil painting	37		1/25/2004		
11	Painting -- Round Barn	16x20 original oil painting	37		1/25/2004		
12	Mandolin	Mandolin, cherry front. Good cor	7		1/27/2004		
13	HF Radio	Ham radio transceiver. Covers 2(	24		1/29/2004		
14	2m Handi-talkie	Ham radio hand-held transceiver.	24		1/29/2004		
15	20m Yagi antenna	Single-band Yagi antenna. Incluc	24		1/30/2004		
16	SW receiver	Continuous tuning shortwave rec	24		1/30/2004		
17	Notebook computer	Pentium III notebook computer.	12		2/1/2004		
18	Portable printer	Portable ink-jet printer. Handles	12		2/1/2004		
19	Wedding dress	White silk and satin wedding dre	20		2/2/2004		
20	Asst men's clothes	Box of assorted men's casual cl	20		2/2/2004		
21	10 Jazz CDs (1 of 5)	Various jazz CDs in great condit	20		2/2/2004		
22	10 Jazz CDs (2 of 5)	Various jazz CDs in great condit	20		2/2/2004		
23	10 Jazz CDs (3 of 5)	Various jazz CDs in great condit	20		2/2/2004		
24	10 Jazz CDs (4 of 5)	Various jazz CDs in great condit	20		2/2/2004		
25	10 Jazz CDs (5 of 5)	Various jazz CDs in great condit	20		2/2/2004		
28	5 board games			0			
(AutoNumber)				0			

Record: 26 of 26

Finding those files that hide

Finding your database files isn't always such an easy thing to do. Fear not, though, because someone at Microsoft has invented a clever way to find those missing files, even if they deliberately hide from you!

In the Open dialog box, a Tools item sits at the top right. When you click it, a little drop-down menu appears, offering a helpful choice called Search. Click Search to see a variety of different ways to search for your errant databases. In the figure, I clicked the Advanced tab and told Access that I wanted to locate all databases whose file name includes the word *Northwind.* The results are displayed at the bottom. I can simply double-click to open the database or right-click for other options.

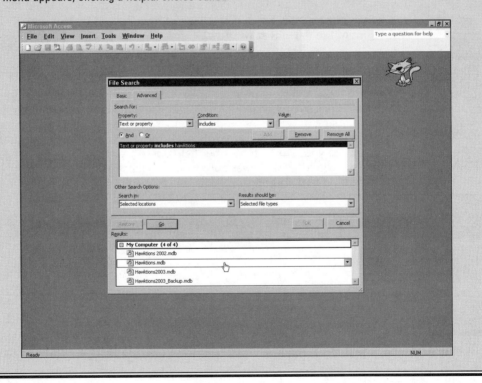

2. **Type your information.**

If the first field is an AutoNumber type, press Tab and begin typing in the second field. As soon as you start typing, the AutoNumber field generates a new number and displays it in the field (see Figure 6-5).

Don't panic if the AutoNumber field seems to skip a number when it creates an entry for your new record. When an AutoNumber field skips a number, it means that you probably entered (or at least started to enter) a record and then deleted it.

Item ID	ItemName	Description	SellerID	BuyerID	DateIn	DateOut	AuctionID
1	China setting for 8	White pattern edged in light blue	11		1/10/2004		
2	3 Cast iron toys	Lot contains three cast iron toys	15		1/11/2004		
3	Asst hardback books (1 of 4)	Box of assorted hardback books	22		1/18/2004		
4	Asst hardback books (2 of 4)	Box of assorted hardback books	22		1/18/2004		
5	Asst hardback books (3 of 4)	Box of assorted hardback books	22		1/18/2004		
6	Asst hardback books (4 of 4)	Box of assorted hardback books	22		1/18/2004		
7	Painting -- boat on lake	16x20 original oil painting	37		1/25/2004		
8	Painting -- Children	16x20 original oil painting	37		1/25/2004		
9	Painting -- Convertible	16x20 original oil painting	37		1/25/2004		
10	Painting -- Old man	16x20 original oil painting	37		1/25/2004		
11	Painting -- Round Barn	16x20 original oil painting	37		1/25/2004		
12	Mandolin	Mandolin, cherry front. Good cor	7		1/27/2004		
13	HF Radio	Ham radio transceiver. Covers 2C	24		1/29/2004		
14	2m Handi-talkie	Ham radio hand-held transceiver.	24		1/29/2004		
15	20m Yagi antenna	Single-band Yagi antenna. Incluc	24		1/30/2004		
16	SW receiver	Continuous tuning shortwave rec	24		1/30/2004		
17	Notebook computer	Pentium III notebook computer.	12		2/1/2004		
18	Portable printer	Portable ink-jet printer. Handles	12		2/1/2004		
19	Wedding dress	White silk and satin wedding dre	20		2/2/2004		
20	Asst men's clothes	Box of assorted men's casual cl	20		2/2/2004		
21	10 Jazz CDs (1 of 5)	Various jazz CDs in great condit	20		2/2/2004		
22	10 Jazz CDs (2 of 5)	Various jazz CDs in great condit	20		2/2/2004		
23	10 Jazz CDs (3 of 5)	Various jazz CDs in great condit	20		2/2/2004		
24	10 Jazz CDs (4 of 5)	Various jazz CDs in great condit	20		2/2/2004		
25	10 Jazz CDs (5 of 5)	Various jazz CDs in great condit	20		2/2/2004		
26	5 board games	Classic board games from the 19	15	0	2/27/2004		
	(AutoNumber)			0			

Record: 26 of 26

Figure 6-5:
The record
is almost
complete,
including
the
AutoNumber
entry.

3. **When you finish entering the record, you're finished!**

   Because Access automatically saves the new record while you're typing it, you have nothing more to do. Pretty cool!

   If you want to add another record, press Tab and type away.

   If you change your mind and want to kill the new addition, choose Edit⇨Undo Saved Record or press Ctrl+Z and then click Yes when Access asks about deleting the record. If the Undo Saved Record menu choice isn't available, click in the record you just added and then choose Edit⇨Delete Record. As before, click Yes when asked whether you're sure about the deletion.

Changing What's Already in a Record

Although your stuff is safely tucked away inside a table, you can reach in and make changes easily. In fact, editing your data is so easy that I'm not sure whether this is a good feature or a bad one.

Whenever you're browsing through a table, please be careful! Access doesn't warn you before saving changes to a record — even if the changes are accidental. (If I were one of those preachy authors, I'd probably make a big, guilt-laden point about how this "feature" of Access makes regular backups all the more important, but that's not my style.)

To change something inside a record, scroll through the table until you find the record that needs some adjusting. Click the field that you want to change, and the blinking toothpick cursor pops into the field.

If you have the Microsoft IntelliMouse, use the wheel button to quickly spin through the table. For such a small innovation, that wheel is a big time-saver! Chapter 8 shows you even more about browsing your data with Microsoft's little answer to the Big Wheel.

What you do next depends on what change you want to make to the field:

- To replace the entire field, press F2 to highlight the data and then type the new information. The new entry replaces the old one.

- To repair a portion of the data in a field, click the field and then use the right- and left-arrow keys to position the toothpick cursor exactly where you want to make the change. Press Backspace to remove characters to the left of the cursor; press Delete to remove them to the right. Insert new characters by typing.

- If you're in a time/date field and want to insert the current date, press Ctrl+; (semicolon). To insert the current time, press Ctrl+: (colon).

When you're finished with the record, press Enter to save your changes. If you change your mind and want to restore the original data, press Esc or Ctrl+Z to cancel your edits.

Don't press Enter until you're positively sure about the changes you typed. After you save them, the old data is gone — you can't go back.

Kicking Out Unwanted Records

There's no sense mourning unneeded records. When the time comes to bid them adieu, do it quickly and painlessly. Here's how:

1. **With the table open, right-click the button to the left of the record you want to delete.**

   A pop-up menu appears. Be sure that you click the correct record before going on to the next step! Discovering the mistake now is much less painful than finding it later.

2. **Choose Delete Record from the pop-up menu.**

   Access does a truly cool screen effect and visually swallows the old record. But it's not gone yet! Access now displays the dialog box, shown in Figure 6-6, asking you to confirm the deletion.

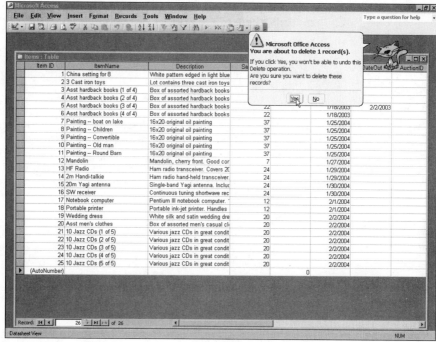

Figure 6-6:
Are you
sure you
want to
delete a
record?

3. **Click Yes to banish the record to oblivion or No if you've changed your mind.**

   If you're the slightest bit unsure, click No and do some more thinking before exercising the Delete Record command on anything in your table.

If Access tells you that it can't delete the current record, you may be trying to delete a record that contains child records in another table. If you still want to delete the record, you must first delete the child records or edit them so that they're no longer related to the record you're trying to delete. If that doesn't make sense, go to Chapter 5 and read about how to make tables relate to one another.

Recovering from a Baaaad Edit

I have only three suggestions for picking up the pieces from a bad edit. Unfortunately, none is a super-cool elixir that magically restores your lost data. I wish I had better news to close the chapter with, but I'm fresh out of headlines:

✔ **You can recover from one add or edit with the Undo command.** Unfortunately, there is no undo for deletes.

✔ **Double-check any change you make before saving it.** If the change is important, triple-check it. When you're sure that it's right, press Enter and commit the change to the table. If you're not sure about the data, don't save the changes. Instead, get your questions answered first and then feel free to edit the record.

✔ **Keep a good backup so that you can quickly recover missing data and get on with your work.** Good backups have no substitute. If you make good backups, the chance of losing data is greatly reduced, your boss promotes you, your significant other unswervingly devotes his or her life to you, and you may even win the lottery.

Chapter 7

Making Your Table Think with Formats, Masks, and Validations

• •

In This Chapter

▶ Finding where the settings live

▶ Formatting for prettier data

▶ Keeping bad data out with input masks

▶ Performing detailed testing through validations

• •

Scientists offer incredibly detailed, long-winded explanations of what it means to think, but my definition is simple. If you see dragons in the clouds, marvel at a child's playtime adventures, or wonder what makes flowers grow, you're thinking.

Whether you use my definition or one from the experts, one thing is certain: Access tables *don't* think. If you have nightmarish visions of reading this chapter and then accidentally unleashing The Table That Ate Microsoft's Competitors, have no fear; it's not going to happen. (After all, if such a scenario could happen, don't you think Microsoft would have arranged it by now?)

This chapter explains how to enlist your table's help to spot and prevent bad data from getting into your table. The chapter focuses on three tools: formats, masks, and validation rules. These tools may sound technical, but you can handle them.

Each tool has its own section, so if you're looking for specific information, feel free to jump right to the appropriate section.

Finding the Place to Make a Change

The first bit of knowledge you need is *where* to make all these cool changes to your table. Luckily, all three options are in the same place: the Table design window's General tab.

Use the following steps to put your table into design view, and then flip to the appropriate section of the chapter for the details on applying a format, input mask, or validation to a field in your table.

1. **Open the database file, and then click the table you want to adjust.**

2. **Click the Design button or right-click the table and choose Table Design (see Figure 7-1).**

   The table flips into design view, showing its nerdish underbelly to the world.

   If the table you want is already on the screen in datasheet view, just click the Design button on the far-left side of the toolbar to get into design view.

3. **Click the name of the field you want to work on.**

   The General tab in the Field Properties section (the bottom half of the window) displays the details of the current field, as shown in Figure 7-2. You're ready to do your stuff!

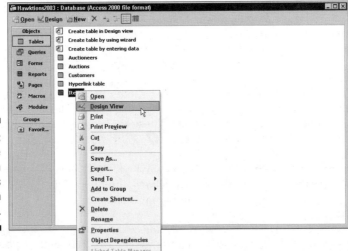

Figure 7-1:
You can see and edit a table's structure in design view.

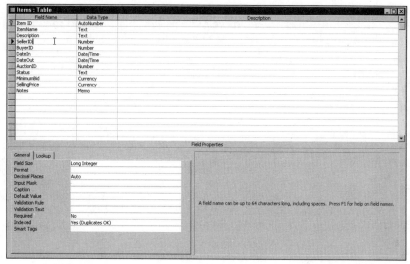

Figure 7-2:
Working
on the
SellerID
field.

4. **In the Field Properties section, click in the appropriate box and type your changes.**

   Format, Input Mask, and Validation Rule each have a box. (Validation Text has a box too, but you have to look in the "Validations: The Digital Breathalyzer Test" section, later in this chapter, to find out more about it — it's a secret for now.)

5. **If you want to work on other fields, repeat Step 2.**

6. **If you're finished, click the Design button. When Access prompts you to save your changes, click Yes.**

Granted, using formats, masks, and validations involves many more details, but the steps to get started are the same no matter which tool you apply. The following sections tackle each tool individually.

To Format, Perchance to Better See

Formats only change the way you *see* your data on the screen, not how your data is stored in the table. Although formats don't directly catch errors, they do make your information look simply marvelous.

Each field type has its own set of formats. Pay close attention to the type of field you're working with. Applying the wrong format to a field is both pointless and frustrating (and goodness knows there are enough pointless and frustrating aspects of your computer without actively courting another one) because your data can't look right, regardless of how hard you try.

To prevent that error, the following sections delve into formatting details by field type. Check the field type you're working with and then refer to the appropriate section for the available formatting options.

If your format command doesn't work the first time, double-check the field type and then review the format commands. In no time at all, you ferret out the problem.

Text and memo fields

Text and memo fields can be formatted in four ways. For some reason, the little Format box inside Access offers no ready-to-use examples of these, but that little oversight doesn't mean you can't make your own. Here's what you need to know:

- ✔ The **greater than symbol** (>) makes all the text in that field appear in uppercase, regardless of how the text was entered. To use this option, type a single greater than symbol in the Format text box. Although Access stores the data *just as it was typed,* the data appears in uppercase only.

- ✔ The **less than symbol** (<) does just the opposite of the greater than symbol. The less than symbol shows all that field's text in lowercase. Apply this format by typing a single less than symbol in the Format text box. If you entered the data in mixed case, Access displays the data as lowercase. As with the greater than symbol, only the display is changed to protect the innocent; otherwise, the data is still stored as mixed case.

- ✔ The **at sign** (@) forces Access to display either a character or a space in the field. If the field data is smaller than the format, Access adds extra spaces to fill up the format. For example, if a field uses @@@@@ as its format, but the field's data is only three characters long (such as *Tim* or *now*), Access displays three spaces and *then* the data. If the field data is four characters long, the format pads the beginning of the entry with two spaces.

- ✔ The **ampersand** (&) is the default format. It means "display a character if there's one to display; otherwise don't do anything." You can use this to create special masks. For example, a Social Security number uses the mask &&&-&&-&&&&. If someone typed 123456789 in that field, Access applies the mask and displays 123-45-6789, adding the cool dashes in the middle of the numbers by itself.

When using the @ or & characters in a mask, always include one @ or & *for each character* in the field. Masks using the greater than and less than symbols only require a single symbol for the whole field.

Number and currency fields

The friendly folks at Microsoft did all the hard work for you on the number and currency field types. They built the six most common formats into a pull-down menu right in the Format text box. To set a number or currency field format, click the Format text box and then click the down arrow that appears at the right side of the box. Figure 7-3 shows the pull-down menu, complete with your choices.

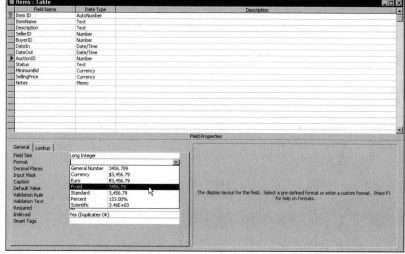

Figure 7-3: Choose a number format from the list.

Each format's given name is on the left side of the menu. The other side shows a sample of how the format works. Here's a quick rundown of the most common choices:

✔ **General Number:** This format is the Access default. It merely displays whatever you put in the field without making any editorial adjustments to it.

✔ **Currency:** This format makes a standard number field look just like a currency field. It shows the data with two decimal places, substituting zeros if decimals aren't present to begin with. Currency format also adds the appropriate currency sign and punctuation, according to the Regional Settings in the Windows Control Panel.

✔ **Euro:** Similar to Currency except uses the Euro symbol €.

✔ **Fixed:** This format locks the field's data into a specific number of decimal places. By default, this format rounds to two decimal places. To specify a different number of decimal places, use the Decimal Places setting right below the Format setting.

✔ **Standard:** This format is like Fixed but adds a thousands separator as well. Adjust the number of decimals by changing the Decimal Places setting.

✔ **Percent:** This format turns a simple decimal such as .97 into the much prettier 97%. Remember to enter the data as a decimal (.97 instead of 97); otherwise Access displays some truly awesome percentages! If your percentages are displayed only as 0.00% or 1.00%, see the next paragraph for a solution.

✔ **Scientific:** If your table lives in a world of numbers so big you can hold them captive only with scientific notation, use this format. It displays a number such as 38,000 as 3.8E+04, (which I'm sure makes perfect sense to someone).

If your entries automatically round to the nearest whole number and always display zeros in the decimal places, change the Field Size setting (right above Format) from Long Integer to Single. This setting tells Access to remember the decimal part of the number. By default, Access rounds the number to an integer as you enter it.

Date/time fields

Like the Number and Currency format options, date/time fields have a ready-to-use set of formats available in a pull-down menu. Click the Format text box and then click the down arrow that appears on the box's right side, and the menu in Figure 7-4 dutifully pops down to serve you.

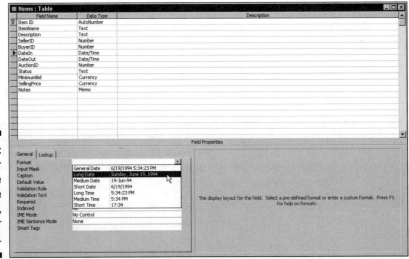

Figure 7-4: A format for every date and a date for every, uh, never mind.

Hey Access, save my place!

This tip is a certified Nerd Trick, but it's so useful that I have to tell you about it. When entering data, sometimes you need to skip a text field because you don't have that particular information at hand. Wouldn't it be great if Access automatically marked the field as blank as a reminder for you to come back and fill in the info later?

Access can create such a custom text format for you, and you don't even have to be a master magician to pull off this trick. Here's how to do it:

Type the following in the field's Format text box:

```
@;"Unknown"[Red]
```

This peculiar notation displays the word *Unknown* in red print if the field doesn't contain a value. You must type the command exactly as shown in the example (quotation marks, square brackets, and all. Feel free to substitute your own word for *Unknown*, though — the command doesn't care what you put between the quotation marks.

The choices are self-explanatory, but I want to pass along a couple of tips.

✔ When you use one of the larger formats such as General Date or Long Date, make sure that the datasheet column is wide enough to display the entire date. Otherwise, the cool-looking date doesn't make sense because a major portion of it is missing.

✔ If more than one person uses the database, choosing a format that provides *more* information rather than one that provides less is much better.

My favorite is the Medium Date format; it spells out the month and day. Dates such as 3/7/04 may cause confusion because people in different countries interpret that format differently.

Yes/No fields

You can say only so much about a field with three options. Your preset formatting choices are somewhat limited, as shown in Figure 7-5. By default, yes/no fields are set to the Yes/No formatting. Feel free to experiment with the other options, particularly if they make more sense in your table than Yes and No.

To display your *own* choices instead of a boring *Yes* and *No,* type a customized entry in the Format box. This procedure is similar to the custom text format mentioned earlier in this chapter in the "Hey Access, save my place" sidebar, except that the information goes into the Format space of the General tab. A good example format is something like this:

```
"In stock"[Green];"REORDER"[Red]
```

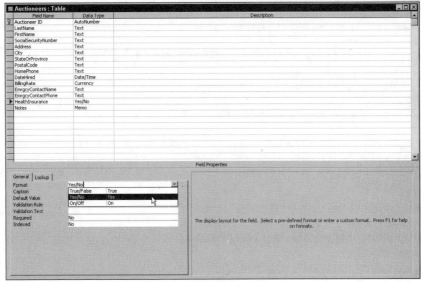

Figure 7-5:
This
format's
cupboard is
pretty bare.

If an item is in stock, the text *In stock* appears in green. Otherwise, *REORDER* screams a warning in bright red. Substitute your own words for mine if you like. Access displays whatever you put between the quotes without making any editorial decisions about the content. Make certain that Display Control in the Lookup tab (next to the General tab) is set to Text Box. Otherwise, you may have check boxes in your field.

What Is That Masked Data?

Like Western heroes riding gallantly into town, *input masks* carry a hard burden in the database world. Input masks act as frontline filters that let only certain data go into a field. When you pair them with validations (covered later in this chapter), input masks do a great job of protecting your table's fields against common data entry errors (such as transposing letters and numbers in an inventory ID number) and generally making your table safe for democracy — er, for your data.

An *input mask* is a series of characters that tells Access what data to expect in a particular field. If you want a field to contain all numbers and no letters, an input mask can do the job. It can also do the reverse (all letters and no numbers) and almost any combination in between. Input masks are stored in the Input Mask area of the field's General tab, along with everything else described in this chapter.

More than half the field types in Access can have their own input mask. Before creating the mask, you have to know exactly what the field's data looks like. Creating a mask that allows only letters into a field doesn't do any good if your goal is to store street addresses. Know your data intimately before messing around with input masks.

Input masks work best with *short, highly consistent* data. Numbers and number-and-letter combinations that all look alike are excellent candidates. Part numbers, stock-keeping units, postal codes, phone numbers, and Social Security numbers beg for input masks to ensure that the right data gets into the field.

You create an input mask in one of two ways:

  ✔ Type the mask manually
  ✔ Ask the Input Mask Wizard for help

As luck has it, the Input Mask Wizard isn't terribly bright — it only knows about text and date fields. And even then, the Input Mask Wizard offers just a few options. To accomplish anything more means cracking your knuckles and working it by hand.

Using the Input Mask Wizard

The Input Mask Wizard gleefully helps if you're making a mask for a phone number, Social Security number, United States zip code, or simple date and time field. Beyond those fields, the Input Mask Wizard is clueless, so don't look for its help with anything other than text or date/time field types.

To ask for the wizard's help, follow these steps:

1. **With the database file open, click the table you want to work with and then click Design.**

   The table flips into design view.

2. **Click the name of the field you want to adjust.**

   The General tab in the Field Properties section (the bottom half of the window) displays the details of the current field.

3. **Click the Input Mask box.**

   The cursor hops into the Input Mask box. To the right of the box, a small button with three dots appears. That's the Build button, which comes into play in the next step.

4. **Click the Build button to the right of the Input Mask text box.**

   The wizard appears, offering a choice of input masks as shown in Figure 7-6.

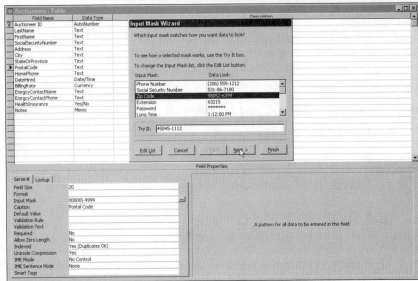

Figure 7-6:
The Input
Mask
Wizard.

You can use the wizard only with text and date/time fields.

5. **Scroll through the list of input masks to find what you want. Click your choice, and then click Finish.**

To play with the mask a bit and see how it works, click the Try It area at the bottom of the dialog box. When you're finished, click Finish to use the mask with your field.

The chosen mask appears in the Input Mask area in the table design screen, as shown in Figure 7-7.

If you click Next instead of Finish in Step 5, the wizard offers you a few screens' worth of arcane choices about changing the input mask, choosing the placeholder character, and storing the mask's extra characters (such as parentheses, dashes, and such) along with your data. Feel free to fiddle with the mask settings and avail yourself of the Try It box at the bottom of the window — it's a good way to see exactly how input masks work. Unless you really dislike the underline character, don't bother changing the placeholder setting. After clicking Next on that page, the wizard asks one final question about storing your newly masked data. The wizard wants to know whether you want the dashes, slashes, and parentheses that the input mask displays to be stored in your table along with the data you typed. The default is No, which I recommend sticking with. Click Finish to complete the process and install your completed Input Mask.

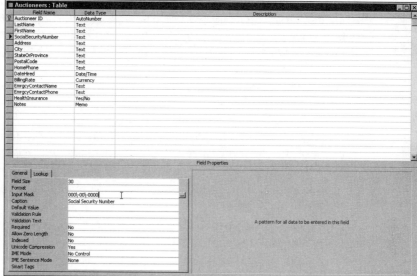

Figure 7-7:
The Input
Mask
Wizard did
all that work
for me.

Making a mask by hand

Few projects feel more gratifying than the ones where you make something yourself. Building an input mask with your bare hands, raw nerve, and these instructions *may* give you that same feeling of accomplishment. The stuff that input masks do isn't terribly complicated, but a finished mask often looks complicated. Don't worry, though. After you get the hang of it, building powerful input masks takes only a moment. The following steps, along with the information in Table 7-1, walk you through the process.

Table 7-1	Codes for the Input Mask	
Kind of Characters	*Required Code*	*Optional Code*
Digits (0 to 9) only	0 (zero)	9
Digits and + and signs	(not available)	# (U.S. pound sign)
Letters (A to Z) only	L	? (question mark)
Letters or digits only	A	a (must be lowercase)
Any character or space	& (ampersand)	C

To design and use an input mask, do this:

1. **On a piece of paper, write several examples of the data that the mask should let into the table.**

If the information you're storing has subtle variations (such as part numbers that end in either a letter/number or letter/letter combination), include examples of the various possibilities so that your input mask accepts them all. You can't build a mask if you don't know your data.

2. **Write a simple description of the data, including which elements are required and which are optional.**

If your sample is a part number that looks like 728816ABC7, write *six numbers, three letters, one number; all parts are required.* Remember to allow for the variations, if you have any. The difference between *one number* and *one letter or number* can be crucial.

Access uses different codes for required and optional data, so you need to note the difference:

- *Required* information must be entered into the field (such as a phone number).

- *Optional* elements are just that — optional (such as an area code or extension number).

3. **Enter your input mask in Access based on the codes in Table 7-1.**

Because you know what data you're storing (numbers, letters, or either one), how many characters you need, and whether each one is required or optional, working through the table and creating the mask is easy.

- To include a dash, slash, or parenthesis in your mask, put a back-slash (\) in front of it.

- To include more than one character, put quotation marks around them. For example, the mask for a phone number with an area code is !\(999"-) "000\-0000.

The phone number mask uses both the backslash and quotation mark to put parentheses around the area code plus a space between the area code and phone number. See "The exclamation point: To know it is to love it" sidebar in this chapter to find out why phone numbers include an exclamation point. (There really is a reason — it's not because they're excited.)

4. **If your field includes letters and you want them to always be upper-case, add a greater than symbol (>) to the beginning of your mask.**

To make the letters lowercase, use a less than symbol (<) instead.

You're ready to tell Access about your input mask.

5. **Click the Input Mask box.**

The blinking toothpick cursor hops into the box, ready for action.

6. **Carefully type your finished mask into the Input Mask area of Field Properties (as shown in Figure 7-8).**

   Don't worry if the mask looks like a text version of the Frankenstein monster. Beauty is optional in the world of technology.

7. **At the end of the mask, add ;;_ (two semicolons and an underscore character).**

   These three characters tell Access to display an underscore where you want each letter to appear. This step isn't required, but little things like these make input masks a little easier to use. Your mileage may vary.

8. **Click the Datasheet View button on the toolbar to check out your handiwork.**

   Try typing something into the now-masked field. The input mask should prevent you from entering an incorrect value. If it doesn't work, take the table back into design view (click the Design View button on the left side of the toolbar) and make some repairs.

   If you're adding a mask to an existing table, the mask doesn't ferret out incorrect data that's *already* in the table. You have to click each entry in the masked field (yes, that means clicking this field in *every* record of the table) to check it. If something is wrong, Access tells you, but not until you click.

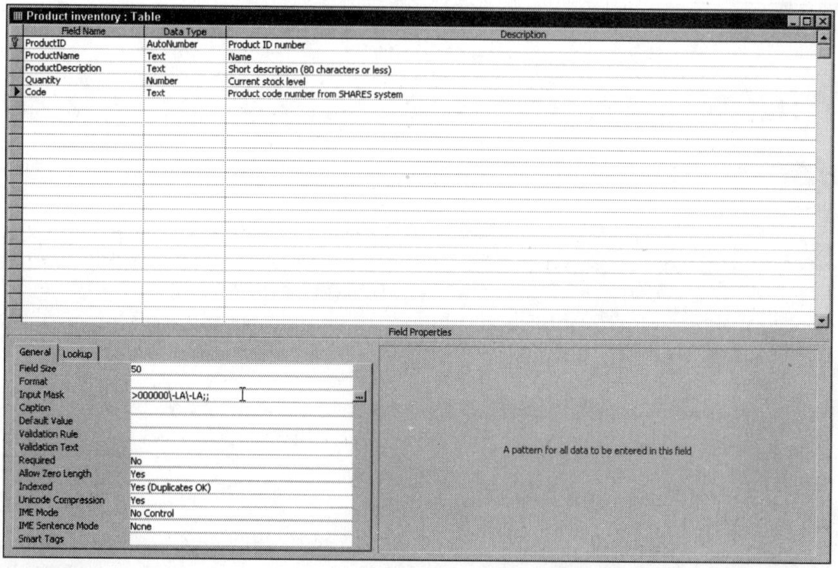

Field Name	Data Type	Description
ProductID	AutoNumber	Product ID number
ProductName	Text	Name
ProductDescription	Text	Short description (80 characters or less)
Quantity	Number	Current stock level
Code	Text	Product code number from SHARES system

Field Properties

General | Lookup

Field Size	50
Format	
Input Mask	>000000\-LA\-LA;;
Caption	
Default Value	
Validation Rule	
Validation Text	
Required	No
Allow Zero Length	Yes
Indexed	Yes (Duplicates OK)
Unicode Compression	Yes
IME Mode	No Control
IME Sentence Mode	None
Smart Tags	

A pattern for all data to be entered in this field

Figure 7-8:
Putting a mask on the Code field.

The exclamation point: To know it is to love it

Getting to know the exclamation point took me a while. After all, my input masks seemed happy without it. Even the explanation in the Access online Help file didn't change my mind. (I suppose that if the Help file's explanation had made sense, it may have had a better chance.)

While playing with the phone number example, I finally realized what the exclamation point does and why it's so useful. The exclamation point tells Access to fill up the field from the right instead of the left. Although this notion may sound like the unintelligible ramblings of an over-caffeinated nerd, it is an important point. Let me tell you why.

In the phone number example, the area code is optional, but the number itself is required. If I leave the exclamation point out of the input mask, Access lets me skip the area code and type a phone number into the phone number spaces. Everything looks fine until I press Enter. Then my seven-digit phone number displays as (555) 121-2. Eeeeewwww — not exactly what I had in mind. That's because Access filled the mask from the left, starting with the optional numbers in the area code (the numbers I didn't enter).

By adding the exclamation point to the input mask, Access takes my data and fills the mask from the right. This time, the phone number appears on the screen as ( ) 555-1212, which is what I wanted all along.

The exclamation point can go anywhere in the input mask, but try to get into the habit of putting it either at the beginning or the end. I suggest making the exclamation point the first character in the mask, simply because you won't overlook it in that position.

Validations: The Digital Breathalyzer Test

Your third (and, arguably, most powerful) tool in the War Against Bad Data is the validation. With a *validation,* Access tests the incoming data to make sure that it's what you want in the table. If the data isn't right, the validation displays an error message (you get to choose what it says) and makes you try the entry again.

Like the other options in this chapter, validations are stored in the General tab of the Field Properties area. Two options relate to validations:

- ✔ **Validation rule:** The rule is the validation itself.

- ✔ **Validation text:** The text is the error message you want Access to display when some data that violates the validation rule wanders in.

Validations work best with number, currency, and date fields. Creating a validation for a text field is possible, but the validations usually get very complicated very fast.

In the name of protecting your sanity and hairline, Table 7-2 contains some ready-to-use validations that cover the most common needs. They're organized by field type, so finding the validation rule that suits your purpose is easy.

Table 7-2	Validations for Many Occasions	
Field Type	_Validation Rule_	_What It Means_
Number	> 0	Must be greater than zero
Number	<> 0	Cannot be zero
Number	> 0 AND < 100	Must be between 0 and 100 (noninclusive)
Number	>= 0 AND <= 100	Must be between 0 and 100 (inclusive)
Number	<= 0 OR >= 100	Must be less than 0 or greater than 100 (inclusive)
Date	>= Date ()	Must be today's date or later
Date	>= Date () OR Is Null	Must be today's date, later, or blank
Date	< Date ()	Must be earlier than today's date
Date	>= #1/1/90# AND <= Date ()	Must be between January 1, 1990 and today (inclusive)

The table includes different kinds of examples to show off the power of the logical operators that validations use. Feel free to mix and match with the operators. Play around and see what you can come up with! Watch out for these gotchas:

✔ When using AND, remember that both sides of the validation rule must be true before the rule is met.

✔ With OR, only one side of the rule needs to be true for the entire rule to be true.

✔ Be careful when combining >= and <= examples. Accidentally coming up with one that can't be true (such as <= 0 AND >= 100) is too easy!

Chapter 8

Making Your Datasheets Dance

*H*aving your new datasheet look and act just like every other datasheet is pretty boring. Where's the creativity in that? Where's the individuality? Where's the life, liberty, and pursuit of ultimate coolness?

Granted, Access *is* a database program, and databases aren't generally known for being the life of the party, but that doesn't mean you're trapped in a monotonous world of look-alike datasheets. This chapter explores the tools at your disposal to turn even the most dreary datasheet into a slick-looking, easy-to-navigate presentation of your data.

The following pages focus on datasheet tricks — what to do when you're working with information in a datasheet. These tricks work with datasheets from both tables and query results, so use them to amble through and spruce up every datasheet in sight.

Wandering Here, There, and Everywhere

When a table appears in datasheet view, Access presents a window to your data. That window displays a certain number of rows and columns — not the whole enchilada (unless you have a really small table). To see more, you need to move through the table, which means moving your window around to see what else is out there.

Access offers several ways to hike through a datasheet. Which method you choose depends on how far you want to go:

✔ **To move from field to field:** Use the right- and left-arrow keys. Clicking the arrows on either end of the horizontal scroll bar does the same with the mouse.

✔ **To move between records:** Try the up- and down-arrow keys. If you're a mouse-oriented person, click the arrows at the ends of the vertical scroll bar.

✔ **To display a new page of data:** The PgUp and PgDn keys come in handy (depending on your keyboard, these may be called Page Up and Page Down, instead).

  • PgUp and PgDn scroll vertically through the datasheet.

  • Ctrl+PgUp and Ctrl+PgDn scroll horizontally.

Clicking in the horizontal or vertical scroll bars does the same.

Table 8-1 outlines the process from a keystroke-by-keystroke point of view. Between the preceding movement tips and the following table, you now know just about every possible way to move through an Access datasheet.

Table 8-1	Moving through a Table
Keystroke or Control	*What It Does*
Moving by field	
→	Moves one field to the right in the current record
←	Moves one field to the left in the current record
Home	Goes to the first field in the current record
End	Goes to the last field in the current record
Moving by record	
↓	Moves down one record in the table
↑	Moves up one record in the table
Moving by screen	
PgDn	Scrolls one screen down
PgUp	Scrolls one screen up
Ctrl+PgDn	Scrolls one screen to the right
Ctrl+PgUp	Scrolls one screen to the left

Keystroke or Control	*What It Does*
Moving in the table	
Ctrl+End	Jumps to the last field in the last record of the table
Ctrl+Home	Jumps to the first field in the first record of the table
Horizontal scroll bar	Scrolls right or left one window at a time
Vertical scroll bar	Scrolls up or down one window at a time
IntelliMouse	Turn the wheel to scroll up or down three records at a wheel time through the table (available only with IntelliPoint mouse and driver software)
IntelliMouse wheel button	Press the wheel like a button, and it becomes a super-arrow key; scroll one row or column at a time through the table (available only with IntelliPoint mouse)

Seeing More or Less of Your Data

First on the datasheet tune-up list is fiddling with the look of your datasheet. You have plenty to fiddle with, too. At first blush, your datasheet looks mundane, much like Figure 8-1. To perk it up a bit, you can change the column width, row height, and column order, and you can lock a column in place while the others scroll around it. Heck, you can even make columns disappear temporarily.

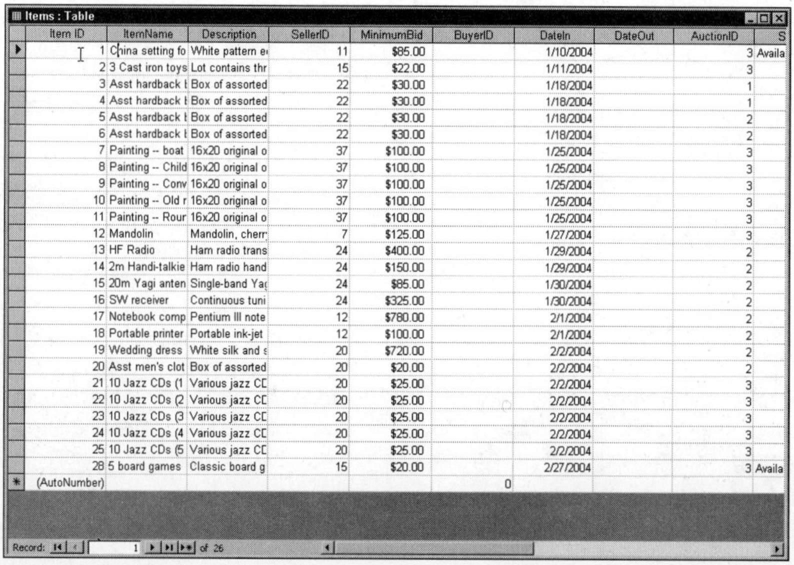

Items : Table

Item ID	ItemName	Description	SellerID	MinimumBid	BuyerID	DateIn	DateOut	AuctionID	S
1	China setting fo	White pattern e	11	$85.00		1/10/2004		3	Availa
2	3 Cast iron toys	Lot contains thr	15	$22.00		1/11/2004		3	
3	Asst hardback I	Box of assorted	22	$30.00		1/18/2004		1	
4	Asst hardback I	Box of assorted	22	$30.00		1/18/2004		1	
5	Asst hardback I	Box of assorted	22	$30.00		1/18/2004		2	
6	Asst hardback I	Box of assorted	22	$30.00		1/18/2004		2	
7	Painting -- boat	16x20 original o	37	$100.00		1/25/2004		3	
8	Painting -- Child	16x20 original o	37	$100.00		1/25/2004		3	
9	Painting -- Conv	16x20 original o	37	$100.00		1/25/2004		3	
10	Painting -- Old r	16x20 original o	37	$100.00		1/25/2004		3	
11	Painting -- Rour	16x20 original o	37	$100.00		1/25/2004		3	
12	Mandolin	Mandolin, cherr	7	$125.00		1/27/2004		3	
13	HF Radio	Ham radio trans	24	$400.00		1/29/2004		2	
14	2m Handi-talkie	Ham radio hand	24	$150.00		1/29/2004		2	
15	20m Yagi anten	Single-band Ya	24	$85.00		1/30/2004		2	
16	SW receiver	Continuous tuni	24	$325.00		1/30/2004		2	
17	Notebook comp	Pentium III note	12	$780.00		2/1/2004		2	
18	Portable printer	Portable ink-jet	12	$100.00		2/1/2004		2	
19	Wedding dress	White silk and s	20	$720.00		2/2/2004		2	
20	Asst men's clot	Box of assorted	20	$20.00		2/2/2004		2	
21	10 Jazz CDs (1	Various jazz CD	20	$25.00		2/2/2004		3	
22	10 Jazz CDs (2	Various jazz CD	20	$25.00		2/2/2004		3	
23	10 Jazz CDs (3	Various jazz CD	20	$25.00		2/2/2004		3	
24	10 Jazz CDs (4	Various jazz CD	20	$25.00		2/2/2004		3	
25	10 Jazz CDs (5	Various jazz CD	20	$25.00		2/2/2004		3	
28	5 board games	Classic board g	15	$20.00		2/27/2004		3	Availa
(AutoNumber)					0				

Record: 1 of 26

Figure 8-1: Access presents your data in rows (records) and columns (fields).

The following sections explore techniques for changing the way your data looks. You can use one option (such as changing the column width) or a number of options — you make the call. Each adjustment is independent of the others. Plus, these changes don't affect your actual data — they just present the data differently on the screen.

Most of the commands work from the mouse, but some send you back to the menu bar. If a command is in both places, it works the same either way.

After making any of these adjustments to your table, be sure to tell Access to save the table's formatting changes. (Otherwise, all your hard work is lost forever.) Choose File➪Save or simply close the window. Either way, Access automatically prompts you to save the newly made formatting changes.

Changing the column width

Although Access has become increasingly clever over the last few years, it's never quite caught the hang of column widths. In fact, it usually just gives up and sets all the column widths identically, leaving some far too wide and others way too narrow. Pretty wimpy solution for a powerful program, if you ask me.

Alternative ways of getting around

If you're blessed with a Microsoft IntelliMouse and its IntelliPoint driver software, you have an extra tool for moving through your Access datasheets. Between the two regular mouse buttons, the IntelliMouse sports a wheel that acts as a third button.

- Rolling the wheel scrolls up and down through your datasheet three lines at a time.

- Clicking and dragging with the wheel button moves the window around the datasheet in whichever direction you move the mouse. (This maneuver works just like a normal click and drag, except that you're using the wheel button instead of the left mouse button.)

If you spend a great deal of time with Access or jumping among the Office XP applications, I suggest you take the new mouse for a test drive. Each program applies the wheel button a little differently, but all the programs (and even Windows itself) use it to make your life a little easier.

But wait, there's more! In its latest incarnation, Office offers new ways of interacting with your computer. Thanks to huge advances in technology and Microsoft's continuing desire to collect more of your money by introducing you to arcane technology, Office now supports *handwriting recognition* and *voice recognition*. Although handwriting recognition looks a bit iffy to me, voice recognition sounds more useful. Voice recognition enables you to dictate to your computer, giving it commands and such. Best of all, voice recognition actually *works* these days, unlike a few years ago when YOU HAD TO TALK LIKE A MACHINE before the computer had even a fair chance of understanding what you said. Chapter 25 covers voice recognition in full detail.

Setting a new column width is a quick operation. Here's what to do:

1. **With your table in datasheet view, put the mouse pointer on the vertical bar to the right of the field name.**

   The mouse pointer changes into a bar with arrows sticking out of each side.

2. **Click and hold the left mouse button while moving the mouse appropriately (as shown in Figure 8-2).**

   Changing the field width is intuitive:

   - To make the column wider, move the mouse to the right.
   - To make it smaller, move the mouse to the left.

3. **Release the mouse button when the width is just right.**

   The column is locked into its new size, as shown in Figure 8-3.

Changing the row height

Access does a little better in the row height department than it does with column widths. It automatically leaves enough room to separate the rows while displaying plenty of information on the screen.

Even so, there's room for improvement because you can't see all the data in your table's longest fields. Changing the row height corrects this problem by showing more data in each field while displaying the same number of columns on the screen.

Figure 8-2: You can resize any column to suit your needs.

Item ID	ItemName	Description	SellerID	MinimumBid	BuyerID	DateIn	DateOut	AuctionID	S
1	China setting fo	White pattern e	11	$85.00		1/10/2004		3	Availa
2	3 Cast iron toys	Lot contains thr	15	$22.00		1/11/2004		3	
3	Asst hardback	Box of assorted	22	$30.00		1/18/2004		1	
4	Asst hardback	Box of assorted	22	$30.00		1/18/2004		1	
5	Asst hardback	Box of assorted	22	$30.00		1/18/2004		2	
6	Asst hardback	Box of assorted	22	$30.00		1/18/2004		2	
7	Painting -- boat	16x20 original o	37	$100.00		1/25/2004		3	
8	Painting -- Child	16x20 original o	37	$100.00		1/25/2004		3	
9	Painting -- Conv	16x20 original o	37	$100.00		1/25/2004		3	
10	Painting -- Old r	16x20 original o	37	$100.00		1/25/2004		3	
11	Painting -- Rour	16x20 original o	37	$100.00		1/25/2004		3	
12	Mandolin	Mandol'n, cherr	7	$125.00		1/27/2004		3	
13	HF Radio	Ham radio trans	24	$400.00		1/29/2004		2	
14	2m Handi-talkie	Ham radio hand	24	$150.00		1/29/2004		2	
15	20m Yagi anten	Single-band Ya	24	$85.00		1/30/2004		2	
16	SW receiver	Continuous tuni	24	$325.00		1/30/2004		2	
17	Notebook comp	Pentium III note	12	$780.00		2/1/2004		2	
18	Portable printer	Portable ink-jet	12	$100.00		2/1/2004		2	
19	Wedding dress	White silk and s	20	$720.00		2/2/2004		2	
20	Asst men's clot	Box of assorted	20	$20.00		2/2/2004		3	
21	10 Jazz CDs (1	Various jazz CD	20	$25.00		2/2/2004		3	
22	10 Jazz CDs (2	Various jazz CD	20	$25.00		2/2/2004		3	
23	10 Jazz CDs (3	Various jazz CD	20	$25.00		2/2/2004		3	
24	10 Jazz CDs (4	Various jazz CD	20	$25.00		2/2/2004		3	
25	10 Jazz CDs (5	Various jazz CD	20	$25.00		2/2/2004		3	
26	5 board games	Classic board g	15	$20.00		2/27/2004		3	Availa

Item ID	ItemName	Description	SellerID	MinimumBid	BuyerID	DateIn	DateOut	Auc
1	China setting for 8	White pattern edged in light	11	$85.00		1/10/2004		
2	3 Cast iron toys	Lot contains three cast iron	15	$22.00		1/11/2004		
3	Asst hardback books (1 of 4)	Box of assorted hardback bc	22	$30.00		1/18/2004		
4	Asst hardback books (2 of 4)	Box of assorted hardback bc	22	$30.00		1/18/2004		
5	Asst hardback books (3 of 4)	Box of assorted hardback bc	22	$30.00		1/18/2004		
6	Asst hardback books (4 of 4)	Box of assorted hardback bc	22	$30.00		1/18/2004		
7	Painting -- boat on lake	16x20 original oil painting	37	$100.00		1/25/2004		
8	Painting -- Children	16x20 original oil painting	37	$100.00		1/25/2004		
9	Painting -- Convertible	16x20 original oil painting	37	$100.00		1/25/2004		
10	Painting -- Old man	16x20 original oil painting	37	$100.00		1/25/2004		
11	Painting -- Round Barn	16x20 original oil painting	37	$100.00		1/25/2004		
12	Mandolin	Mandolin, cherry front. Good	7	$125.00		1/27/2004		
13	HF Radio	Ham radio transceiver. Cover	24	$400.00		1/29/2004		
14	2m Handi-talkie	Ham radio hand-held transce	24	$150.00		1/29/2004		
15	20m Yagi antenna	Single-band Yagi antenna. Ir	24	$85.00		1/30/2004		
16	SW receiver	Continuous tuning shortwave	24	$325.00		1/30/2004		
17	Notebook computer	Pentium III notebook comput	12	$780.00		2/1/2004		
18	Portable printer	Portable ink-jet printer. Hanc	12	$100.00		2/1/2004		
19	Wedding dress	White silk and satin wedding	20	$720.00		2/2/2004		
20	Asst men's clothes	Box of assorted men's casu:	20	$20.00		2/2/2004		
21	10 Jazz CDs (1 of 5)	Various jazz CDs in great cc	20	$25.00		2/2/2004		
22	10 Jazz CDs (2 of 5)	Various jazz CDs in great cc	20	$25.00		2/2/2004		
23	10 Jazz CDs (3 of 5)	Various jazz CDs in great cc	20	$25.00		2/2/2004		
24	10 Jazz CDs (4 of 5)	Various jazz CDs in great cc	20	$25.00		2/2/2004		
25	10 Jazz CDs (5 of 5)	Various jazz CDs in great cc	20	$25.00		2/2/2004		
26	5 board games	Classic board games from th	15	$20.00		2/27/2004		
	(AutoNumber)				0			

Figure 8-3:
The
ItemName
column has
been
resized to
show all of
its contents.

Like changing column width, adjusting the row height takes only a few mouse clicks:

1. **While in datasheet view, put the mouse pointer on the far-left side of the window on the line between any two rows in your spreadsheet.**

   The mouse pointer changes into a horizontal bar with arrows sticking out vertically, as shown in Figure 8-4.

2. **Click and hold the left mouse button; then move the mouse to change the row height.**

   Change the row height like this:

   • Move the mouse down to make the row higher.

   • Move the mouse up to squash the row and put the squeeze on your data.

3. **Release the mouse button when the row height is where you want it.**

   Access redisplays the table with its new row height, as shown in Figure 8-5.

Reorganizing the columns

When you laid out the table, you probably put quite a bit of thought into which field came after which other field. Most of the time, your data looks just the way you want it on the screen, but occasionally you need to stir up things a bit.

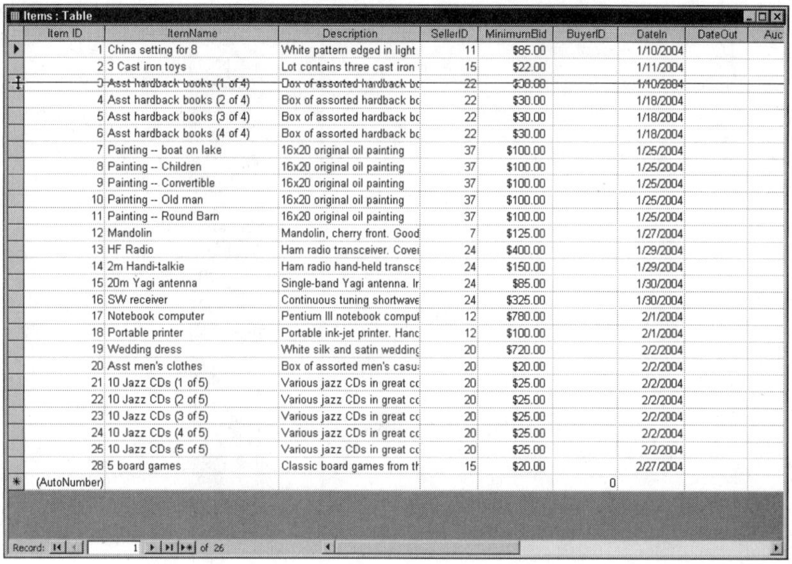

Figure 8-4:
You can modify the height of datasheet rows.

To move a field to a different place on the datasheet, use these steps:

1. **Click the field name of the column you want to move; then click and hold the left mouse button.**

   The entire column darkens, and the mouse pointer changes to an arrow with a smaller box at the base of the mouse pointer, as shown in Figure 8-6.

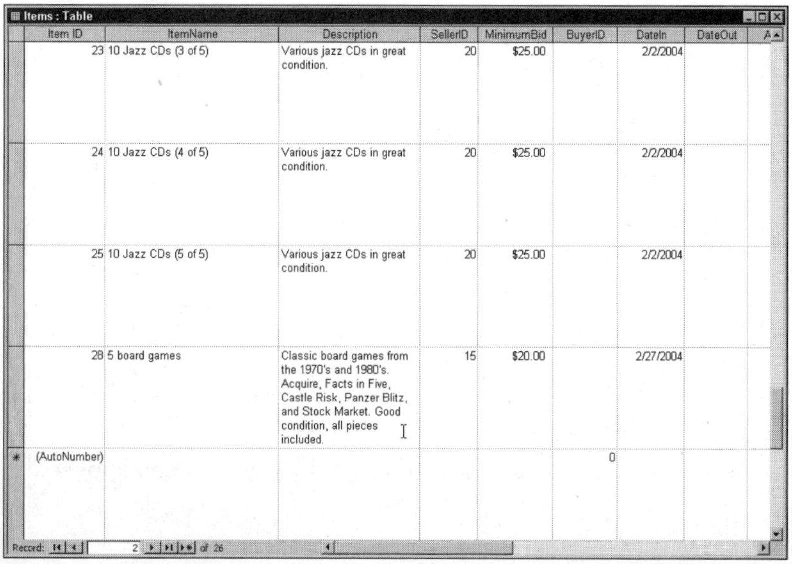

Figure 8-5:
The Description field gets enough room to wrap.

Figure 8-6:
MinimumBid
moves to
its new
location.

2. **Drag the column to its new destination.**

   As you move the mouse, a dark bar moves between the columns, show-ing you where the column will land when you release the mouse button.

   If you accidentally let go of the button before the dark bar appears, Access doesn't move the column. In that case, start again with Step 1 (and keep a tight grip on that mouse).

3. **When the column is in place, release the mouse button.**

   The column, data and all, moves to the new spot, as shown in Figure 8-7.

Hiding a column

Hiding a column is one of those features that seems totally unimportant until the moment you need it. Then it's worth its weight in gold. If you want to tem-porarily conceal a particular column, just hide the little fellow. The data is still in the table, but it doesn't appear on the screen. Too cool, eh?

To hide a column, follow these steps:

1. **With your table in datasheet view, right-click the name of the column to hide.**

   The whole column goes dark, and a pop-up menu appears.

Item ID	ItemName	Description	MinimumBid	SellerID	BuyerID	DateIn	DateOut
23	10 Jazz CDs (3 of 5)	Various jazz CDs in great condition.	$25.00	20		2/2/2004	
24	10 Jazz CDs (4 of 5)	Various jazz CDs in great condition.	$25.00	20		2/2/2004	
25	10 Jazz CDs (5 of 5)	Various jazz CDs in great condition.	$25.00	20		2/2/2004	
28	5 board games	Classic board games from the 1970's and 1980's. Acquire, Facts in Five, Castle Risk, Panzer Blitz, and Stock Market. Good condition, all pieces included.	$20.00	15		2/27/2004	
*	(AutoNumber)				0		

Figure 8-7:
The MinimumBid field now resides between Description and SellerID.

2. Choose Hide Columns from the menu, as shown in Figure 8-8.

Poof! The column vanishes.

To hide more than one column at a time, click and drag across the names of the columns you want to squirrel away, and then choose Format➪Hide Columns.

Item ID	ItemName	Description	MinimumBid	SellerID	BuyerID	DateIn	DateOut
23	10 Jazz CDs (3 of 5)	Various jazz CDs in great condition.	$25.00				
24	10 Jazz CDs (4 of 5)	Various jazz CDs in great condition.	$25.00				
25	10 Jazz CDs (5 of 5)	Various jazz CDs in great condition.	$25.00				
28	5 board games	Classic board games from the 1970's and 1980's. Acquire, Facts in Five, Castle Risk, Panzer Blitz, and Stock Market. Good condition, all pieces included.	$20.00	15		2/27/2004	
*	(AutoNumber)				0		

Menu:
- Sort Ascending
- Sort Descending
- Copy
- Paste
- Column Width...
- Hide Columns
- Freeze Columns
- Unfreeze All Columns
- Find...
- Insert Column
- Lookup Column...
- Delete Column
- Rename Column

Figure 8-8:
Hiding a field from prying eyes.

Making design changes in datasheet view — danger, Will Robinson!

Moving or hiding columns, changing column widths, adjusting row heights — these innocuous settings simply make your digital world a prettier place.

The story changes with the Rename Column, Insert Column, Lookup Column, and Delete Column options that appear on the right-click pop-up menu. These choices change the *structure* of your table, so move slowly and treat them carefully!

✔ Rename Column changes the field name.

✔ Insert Column adds a new column to the datasheet, which translates into a new field in the table.

✔ Lookup Column starts the Lookup Wizard and helps you insert a column for data pulled in from another table.

✔ Delete Column is self-explanatory (remember that Access undoes only the last action you took, so don't delete a column until you're sure that it's the right one to kill).

You alter the table's structure with these options. Have a look through Chapter 9 for more about these options and how to use them safely. (Changing the structure really *is* that important.)

When you're ready to bring back the temporarily indisposed column:

1. **Choose Format⇨Unhide Columns.**

   Up pops a small dialog box listing all the fields in the current table. The fields with a check mark in the box next to them are displayed.

2. **Click any of the unchecked check boxes next to the column that you want to see on the screen again, as shown in Figure 8-9.**

   Depending on the number of fields in the list, you may have to scroll to find all the fields.

3. **Click Close.**

Freezing a column

If you have many fields in a table, they don't all fit in the window. As you scroll from one side of the table to the other, fields are constantly appearing on one side of the window and disappearing from the other. What if you want to keep looking at a column way over on one side of the table while looking at fields from the other side?

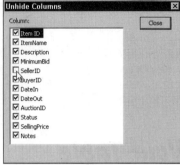

Figure 8-9:
The Unhide
Columns
dialog box
lets you
choose
which fields
to hide *and*
unhide.

The secret is to *freeze* the leftmost column in place. This action locks a column into the left side of the window so that it just sits there while you scroll merrily back and forth through the table. Of course, an unfreeze step goes along with it — you don't want your tables catching cold, do you?

Here's how to freeze a column:

1. **Right-click the name of the column you want to freeze.**

   The column turns dark, and the ever-anticipated pop-up menu appears.

2. **Choose Freeze Columns from the pop-up menu.**

   The column is now locked in place. You can scroll back and forth through your table with impunity (and you don't have any restrictions, either).

If you want to freeze more than one column, follow these steps:

1. **Figure out which columns you want to freeze.**

   Remember that the frozen columns need to all sit next to each other on the datasheet. You can't freeze a few columns, leave one free to scroll, and then freeze a couple more. (If you try to do it anyway, Access punishes you by reorganizing the columns in your datasheet so that the frozen ones all line up next to each other.)

2. **Press and hold the Shift key, then click the first column's name along the top of the datasheet.**

   Access highlights the first column.

3. **With the Shift key still held down, click the name of the column on the opposite side of the area you want to freeze.**

   All columns from the one you clicked in Step 2 to the one you just clicked are suddenly highlighted. (It's very pretty.)

4. **After the columns are highlighted, release the Shift key.**

5. **Lock the columns in place by choosing Format⇨Freeze Columns from the menu bar.**

   All highlighted columns immediately freeze.

   When you want to thaw all the frozen columns (whether you selected one or a bunch), choose Format⇨Unfreeze All Columns. Everything pops back to normal.

Fonting around with Your Table

Access displays your table in a basic, business-oriented font. You're not stuck with that font choice forever. You control the font, style, and the color of your data.

These settings apply to the *entire table,* not just a particular row or column.

To change the font, style, or color of your table, follow these steps:

1. **With the table in datasheet view, choose Format⇨Font.**

   The Font dialog box elbows its way onto the screen.

2. **Click your choice from the Font list on the left side of the dialog box.**

   Access shows the font in the Sample box on the right side of the dialog box.

   Because TrueType fonts work with almost every printer in the world and appear in any size you demand, they work best for just about everything, including datasheets. TrueType fonts display the double-T symbol at the left of the font name.

3. **Click the preferred style in the Font style list.**

   Some fonts may not have all common style options (normal, bold, italic, and bold italic).

4. **To select a different size, click a number in the Size list.**

   If you use one of the printer fonts (they have a picture of a printer next to them), you may be limited to just a few size options.

5. **If you want a new color, click the arrow next to the Color box and choose your favorite from the drop-down menu.**

6. **Click OK to apply your font selections.**

Giving Your Data the 3-D Look

This final change is purely cosmetic, but even tables like to feel good about how they look. Access gives you a couple of cool-looking, three-dimensional options for your datasheet. To turn your datasheet into a cool work of art, follow these steps:

1. **Choose Format⇨Datasheet from the menu bar.**

   The Datasheet Formatting dialog box pops onto the screen.

2. **For 3-D, click the Raised or Sunken options in the Cell Effect area.**

   The Sample box previews your selection. (I prefer Raised.)

   If you don't want the gridlines cluttering up your datasheet, leave the Cell Effect option set to Flat and uncheck the various Gridlines Shown check boxes.

3. **Click OK when you're finished.**

   The datasheet changes according to your selections.

Unless you're really good with color combinations, leave the color settings alone. Because I regularly attempt to wear stripes and plaid together, I let Access handle this option on its own.

Chapter 9

Table Remodeling Tips for the Do-It-Yourselfer

In This Chapter

▶ Hearing about the standard "worried author" disclaimer

▶ Adding a field to your table

▶ Removing a field you don't need

▶ Changing a field's name

*R*emodeling is a part of life — at least it is if you're a homeowner. A touch of paint here, a new wall there, and pretty soon your entire house is a mess because the jobs never *quite* get finished. For example, my wife gave up hope on updating the electrical outlets in our old house. I worked on the job for three years or so, and ended with eight outlets finished, eight outlets to go, and nobody left on base.

My databases, on the other hand, are a completely different story. There, I'm a digital Bob Vila, with everything organized and up-to-date. When I start changing a table, I finish the job right then and there. My wife says the difference has to do with my aversion to physical labor, but the real reason is the tools that Access provides for the job. (That and the fact that hammers simply don't like me.)

Whether you're adding a new field, removing an old one, or making some other subtle changes to your table and the data therein, this chapter guides you through the process. Be sure to read the chapter's first section before attempting any serious surgery on your tables. Some grim pitfalls await you out there, and I want you to miss them cleanly.

The steps in this chapter walk you through making changes in design view, where you're in full control of the process. Although you can do some of the tasks in this chapter in datasheet view (specifically, add and delete entire columns in your table), I don't recommend that approach. One change in datasheet view quickly turns into a full-fledged data disaster if anything goes wrong.

This Chapter Can Be Hazardous to Your Table's Design

I'm all for starting on a pleasant note, but now isn't the time. To properly set this chapter's mood, I wanted to begin with big, full-color pictures of items that have a natural *don't touch* sign on them — such as snapping alligators, high-voltage lines, and the *I dare you to audit me* box on your income tax form. My editor suggested that I use a warning icon instead. In the name of compromise (and because finding good editors is so hard these days), I agreed.

 Tread lightly in this chapter. You're tinkering with the infrastructure of your entire database system. A mistake (particularly of the *delete* kind) can cause massive hair loss, intense frustration, and large-scale data corruption. Put simply, it's bad.

Putting a New Field Next to the Piano

No matter how well you plan, sometimes you just forget to include a field in your table design. Or, after using the table for a while, you discover some unforeseen data that needs a home. Regardless of the circumstances, Access doesn't make a big deal out of adding a field.

Dropping a field into your table takes only a moment. Before starting this project, make sure that you know the following bits of information. This makes a good paper-and-pencil project, so grab your tools and figure out the following items:

- ✔ Typical examples of the data that the field holds
- ✔ The field type (text, number, yes/no, and so on)
- ✔ The size the field needs to be to hold the data, if applicable
- ✔ What you plan to call the field
- ✔ Where the field fits in the table design

With that information in hand, you're ready to make a new field. To add the field in design view, follow these steps:

1. **With the database file open, right-click the table you want to work with and choose** <u>D</u>**esign View.**

   The table structure appears in design view.

2. **Highlight the row where you want to insert your new field by clicking the row button to the left of the Field Name column.**

   Some tasks are easy when you see them, but confusing to explain — and this step is one of them. On that note, take a gander at Figure 9-1 to make sense of this maneuver.

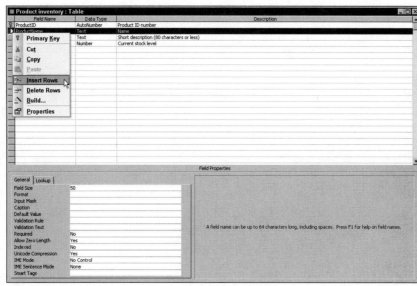

3. **Choose Insert⇨Rows from the main menu.**

   Access inserts a nice, blank row in your table design right where you clicked. Everything below that row moves down one row to make room for the new arrival.

   Don't worry about your data — Access takes good care of your work. Inserting a new row into the design doesn't hurt any data in the table itself. *Deleting* a row from the design (see the following section) is another story.

4. **Click the Field Name area of the new row, and then type the name of your new field.**

   The field name flows smoothly into the text area.

5. **Press Tab to move to the Data Type column. Click the down arrow and select the field's data type from the pull-down list (see Figure 9-2).**

   If you're uncertain which data type works best for this field, flip back to Chapter 4.

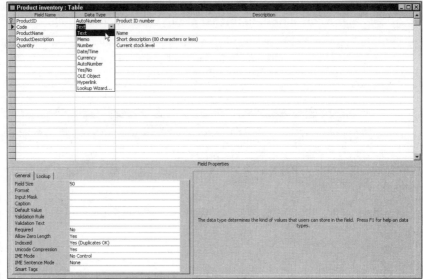

Figure 9-2:
Choose a
data type
from the list.

6. **Press Tab to hop into the Description area. Type a short description of the stuff that this field contains.**

   Although this step is optional, I *highly* recommend adding a description. Trust me on this one!

7. **Save your changes by choosing File⇨Save or by clicking the Save button on the toolbar.**

Is it a column or a field?

The answer to the lyrical question, is it a column or a field, is *yes*. In Access lingo, *columns* and *fields* are the same critters. When you insert a column into a table in datasheet view, you actually add a new field to every record. If you build a field in design view, you create a new column for the datasheet. Either way you say (or do) it, you get the same result.

So when is a field different from a column? It's different when you edit the data in a particular record. If you change one person's postal code in an address table, you aren't changing the entire column. Instead, you're changing the value of the field in that record.

Here's how to keep the two terms straight:

✔ When Access talks about columns, it means a certain field in every record of the table.

✔ When the program refers to a field, it means the data in one part of a particular record.

Saying Good-bye to a Field (and All Its Data)

Times change, and so do your data storage needs. When one of your fields is past its prime, send it to that Great Table in the Sky by deleting it from your design. Getting rid of the field *also* throws out all the data *in* the field. You probably know that already, but the point is important enough that I want to make sure you keep these suggestions in mind:

✔ Killing a field *erases all data* in the field. Proceed with caution!

✔ If the data in a table is important, make a backup copy of the database file before deleting anything. When a field is gone, the data it held is gone too, so make your backups first.

Here's how to delete a field from your table:

1. **With the database file open, right-click the table you plan to change and then choose **D**esign View from the pop-up menu.**

   The design window pops onto the screen, filled to overflowing with your table design.

2. **Click the gray button on the left side of the Field Name that you want to delete.**

   The doomed field appears highlighted.

3. **Choose **E**dit➪Delete **R**ows from the main menu.**

   A dialog box appears, asking whether you really want to do the deed (see Figure 9-3). If the Office Assistant is busily assisting you with Access, it offers a slightly friendlier version of the dialog box, but the question remains the same.

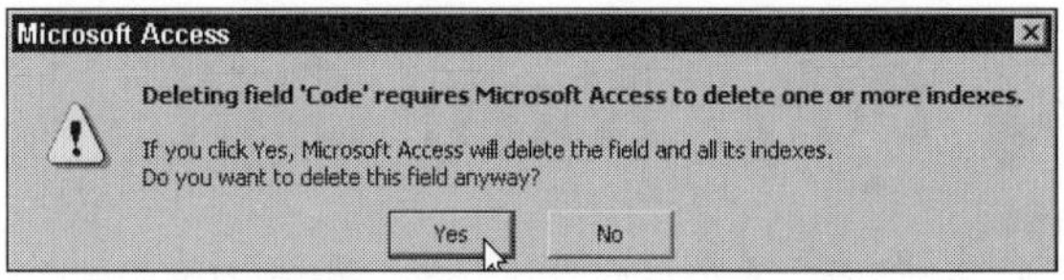

Figure 9-3:
Access warns that deleting the field means killing the data, too — permanently.

> **Microsoft Access** ✕
>
> ⚠ **Deleting field 'Code' requires Microsoft Access to delete one or more indexes.**
>
> If you click Yes, Microsoft Access will delete the field and all its indexes.
> Do you want to delete this field anyway?
>
> [Yes]   [No]

4. **Click Yes to delete the field; click No if you're having second thoughts.**

   If you delete the field and immediately wish you hadn't, press Ctrl+Z or choose Edit⇨Undo Delete (as shown in Figure 9-4). Your field instantly comes back from beyond.

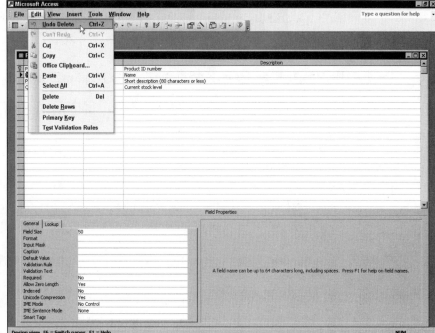

Figure 9-4:
If you get carried away deleting fields, Undo Delete can bring them back.

5. **Make the deletion permanent by choosing File⇨Save or by clicking the Save button on the toolbar.**

   The key word in this step is *permanent,* as in *never to be seen or heard from again.* You can't undo this step — when the field is gone, it's gone.

A Field by Any Other Name Still Holds the Same Stuff

Access doesn't care what you name the fields in a table. Granted, it has some technical rules for what a legal field name looks like, but editorially speaking, it leaves all the choices up to you. Field names are a human element, after all. (Silly humans, we're always running around naming stuff.)

Access offers two ways to change the name of a field:

- ✔ Retyping the name of the field in design view (the *official* way, according to Nerds Who Know)
- ✔ Right-clicking the field name in datasheet view (the intuitive way)

Which method you use is up to you — I show you both methods in the next two sections.

Changing a field name in design view

Here's how to change a field name in design view, the Access version of a digital tune-up bay for your tables:

1. **Right-click the table you want to change and choose <u>D</u>esign View from the pop-up menu.**

   The table layout appears.

2. **Click the field you plan to rename, and then press F2 to highlight it (see Figure 9-5).**

   The name of the field quivers in anticipation at the prospect of your next step.

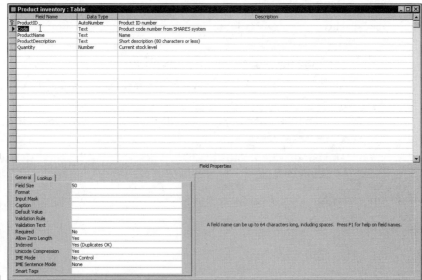

Figure 9-5:
The field name is highlighted and ready for the change.

3. **Type a new name for the field.**

   Because you highlighted the field name before typing, Access automatically overwrites the old name with the new one.

4. **To save the change, choose File⇨Save or click the Save button on the toolbar.**

   The process is complete!

Changing a field name in datasheet view

Renaming a field in datasheet view takes about the same number of steps, but some people think that this method is easier. In the name of diversity, here's how to change a field name in datasheet view:

1. **With your database file open, double-click the table you want to change.**

   Surprise — the first step here is different than all the other steps! The table appears on the screen in datasheet view.

2. **Right-click the field name that you want to change (at the top of the datasheet window).**

   The column is highlighted, and a pop-up menu appears.

3. **Select Rename Column from the pop-up menu (as shown in Figure 9-6).**

   The name of the column lights up, bracing for the impending change.

4. **Type the new name, and then press Enter.**

   Although you made the change in datasheet view, Access changes the table's design.

5. **To make the change permanent, click Save on the toolbar or choose File⇨Save.**

   And another field finds happiness and meaning in a stylish new name. Congratulations — you're finished!

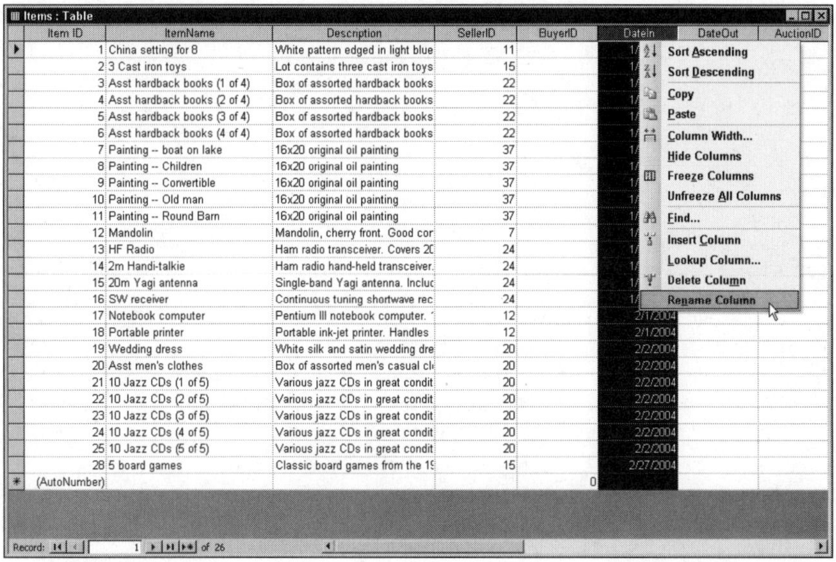

Figure 9-6:
Right-click a column heading and choose Rename Column.

Part III
Finding the Ultimate Answer to Almost Everything

The 5th Wave   By Rich Tennant

"I've been in hardware all of my life, and all of a sudden it's software that'll make me rich."

In this part . . .

Electronically collecting data together in one place is nice, but if you just moved it around on the hard disk instead of piling it around your office, what did you gain (apart from a less cluttered office)?

At the risk of sounding like a marketing brochure, the opportunity to interact with your data — to roll up your sleeves and really play with the stuff in there — is one of this program's truly cool features. With Access, you can sort, re-sort, probe, poke, average, count, add, and sub-tract (and probably fold, spin, and fluff dry) all the data in your world.

Of course, because this is a computer product (and due to the legal ramifications of the phrase), you can't describe this fun as *playing* with the data. No — that would be too easy. In proper database lingo, you're *querying* the tables.

Although saying you're going to query something sounds a lot cooler than saying you're going to ask a quick ques-tion, the basic concept is the same. This part digs into the query concept, starting out with simple questions and leading you into progressively more complex prognostica-tions. This is juicy stuff, so work up a good appetite before digging in.

Chapter 10

Quick Searches: Find, Filter, and Sort

. . . .

In This Chapter

▶ Using the Find command

▶ Sorting your database

▶ Filtering by selection

▶ Filtering by form

. . . .

*Y*ou probably don't need me to tell you what databases do: They help you store and organize the information that's important to your world. That's hardly a new concept, though — that's what 3 x 5 index cards do (and I bet you never spent $600 upgrading your index card box). To justify all the time, trauma, and accelerated hair loss associated with them, databases have to do something that a simple stack of paper products just can't match. Something like sifting through an imposing mound of data in the merest blink of an eye and immediately finding that one elusive piece of data.

Thanks to the magic of the Find, Sort, and Filter commands, Access tracks and reorganizes the stuff in your tables faster than ever. When you need a quick answer to a simple question, these three commands are ready to help. This chapter covers the commands in order, starting with the speedy Find, moving along to the organizational Sort, and ending with the flexible Filter.

Find, Sort, and Filter do a great job with *small* questions (like "Who's that customer in Tucumcari?"). Answering big, hairy questions (such as "How many people from Seattle bought wool sweaters on weekends last year?") still takes a full-fledged Access query. Don't let that threat worry you, because Chapter 11 explains queries in light and winsome detail.

Finding Stuff in Your Tables

When you want to track down a particular record *right now*, creating a query for the job is overkill. Fortunately, Access has a quick-and-dirty way to find one specific piece of data in your project's tables and forms — the Find command.

Find is available both on the toolbar and through the main menu. (Choose Edit➪Find. Keyboard-oriented folks out there can press Ctrl+F.) Access doesn't care which way you fire up the Find command — it works the same from either avenue.

Although the Find command is pretty easy to use on its own, knowing a few tricks makes it do its best work. After you know the Find basics (covered in the next section), check the tips for fine-tuning the Find command in the "Tuning a search for speed and accuracy" section, later in the chapter. That section tweaks the Find settings for more detailed search missions.

Finding first things first (and next things after that)

Using the Find command is a straightforward task. Here's how it works:

1. **Open the table or form you want to search.**

   Yes, Find works in both datasheet view and with Access forms. If you want to dive into forms right now, flip ahead to Chapter 22.

2. **Click the field that you want to search.**

   The Find command searches the *current* field in all the records of the table, so make sure that you click the right field before starting the Find process. Access doesn't care which record you click — as long as you hit the right field, Access is happy. (And it's important to keep your software happy!)

3. **Start the Find command by clicking the Find toolbar button (the one with the binoculars on it) or choosing Edit➪Find.**

   The Find and Replace dialog box pops into action.

4. **Type the text you're looking for into the Find What box, as shown in Figure 10-1.**

   Take a moment to check your spelling before starting the search. Access isn't bright enough to figure out that you actually mean *hero* when you type *zero*.

Figure 10-1:
The Find
and Replace
dialog box
gets ready
to do its
stuff.

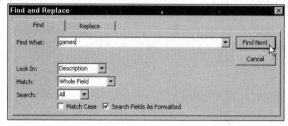

5. **Click Find Next to begin your search.**

   Before you can count to one by eighths, the Find command tracks down the record you want, moves the cursor there, and highlights the matching text. If Find doesn't locate anything, however, it laments its failure in a small dialog box.

6. **If Find didn't find what you were looking for:**

   a. **Click OK to make the dialog box go away.**

   b. **Make sure that you clicked in the correct field and spelled everything correctly in the Find What box.**

      You may also want to check the special Find options covered in the next section to see whether one of them is messing up your search.

   c. **Click Find Next again.**

What if the first record that Access finds isn't the one you're looking for? Suppose you want the second, third, or the fourteenth *John Smith* in the table? No problem — that's why the Find and Replace dialog box has a Find Next button. Keep clicking Find Next until Access works its way down to the record you want or tells you that it's giving up the search.

Tuning a search for speed and accuracy

Sometimes, just providing the information in the Find What box isn't enough. Either you find too many records or the ones that match aren't the ones that you want. The best way to reduce the number of wrong matches is to add more details to your search.

Precise adjustment makes the pursuit faster, too.

Access offers several tools for fine-tuning a Find. Open the Find and Replace dialog box by clicking the Find button on the toolbar or by choosing Edit⇔Find. The following list describes how to use the various options:

✔ **Look In:** By default, Access looks for matches only in the *current* field — whichever field you clicked in before starting the Find command. To tell Access to search the entire table instead, change the Look In setting to the Table option, as shown in Figure 10-2.

Figure 10-2:
To search
the entire
table,
change the
Look In
setting.

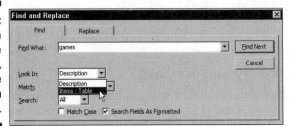

✔ **Match:** Access makes a few silly assumptions, and this setting is a good example. By default, Match is set to Whole Field, which assumes that you want to find only fields that *completely match* your search text. The Whole Field setting means that searching for *Sam* doesn't find fields containing *Samuel, Samantha,* or *Mosam.* Not too bright for such an expensive program, is it? Change this behavior by adjusting the Match setting to Any Part of Field, which allows a match anywhere in a field (finding both *Samuel* and *new sample product*), or to Start of Field, which recognizes only a match that starts from the beginning of the field. To change this setting, click the down arrow next to the field (see Figure 10-3) and then make your choice from the drop-down menu that appears.

Figure 10-3:
Look inside
all those
little fields
by using the
Match
option.

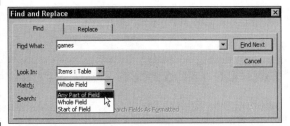

✔ **Search:** If you're finding too many matches, try limiting your search to one particular portion of the table with the Search option. Search tells the Find command to look either

- At all the records in the table (the default setting)

- Up or Down from the current record

Clicking a record halfway through the table and then telling Access to search Down from there confines your search to the bottom part of the table.

Tune your Search settings by clicking the down arrow next to the Search box and choosing the appropriate choice from the drop-down menu.

✔ **Match Case:** Match Case requires that the term you search for be exactly the same as the value stored in the database, including the case of the characters. In other words, if the database contains the oddly capitalized name `SmItH`, Match Case finds that value only if you search for the name using exactly the same odd capitalization (in this case, *SmItH*). Match Case works very well when searching your database for names.

✔ **Search Fields As Formatted:** This option instructs Access to look at the formatted version of the field instead of the actual data you typed. Limiting the search in this way is handy when searching dates, stock-keeping unit IDs, or any other field with quite a bit of specialized formatting. Turn on Search Fields As Formatted by clicking the check box next to it. This setting doesn't work with Match Case, so if Match Case is checked, Search Fields As Formatted appears dimmed. In that case, uncheck Match Case to bring back Search Fields As Formatted.

Most of the time, this option doesn't make much difference in your life. In fact, the only time you probably care about this Find option is when (or if) you search many highly formatted fields.

If your Find command isn't working the way you think it should, check the options in the preceding list. Odds are that one or more of these options aren't set quite right!

Sorting Out Life on the Planet

Very few databases are already organized into nice, convenient alphabetical lists. So what do you do when your boss wants the world neatly sorted and on her desk within the hour?

The solution is the Sort command, which is *really* easy to use! The Sort command is on the Records menu. Two buttons on the toolbar (Sort Ascending and Sort Descending) do the job as well:

✔ Sort Ascending sorts your records alphabetically from top to bottom, so records that begin with *A* are at the beginning, and records that begin with *Z* are at the end.

✔ Sort Descending does just the opposite. Records that begin with *Z* are at the top, and records that begin with *A* are at the bottom of the list.

You can sort by more than one column at a time like this:

1. **Click the heading of the first column to sort by.**

   The entire column is highlighted.

2. **Hold down the Shift key and click the heading of the last column to sort by.**

   All columns from the first one to the last one are highlighted.

3. **Choose either Sort Ascending or Sort Descending.**

   The sort is always performed from left to right. In other words, you can't sort by the contents of the fourth column and, within that, by the contents of the third column.

   The columns chosen must be contiguous (they must be all together).

Anything that's *this* useful simply must exhibit an odd behavior or two to keep life interesting. True to form, Sort has its own peculiarity when working with numbers in a text field. When sorting a field that has numbers mixed in with spaces and letters (such as street addresses), Access ranks the numbers as if they were *letters,* not numbers. Unfortunately, this behavior means that Access puts "10608 W. Vermont" before "129 Spring Mill." (Thanks to the peculiar way that your computer sorts, the 0 in the second position of 10608 comes before the 2 in the second position of 129.)

Filtering Records with Something in Common

Sometimes, you need to see a group of records that share a common value in one field — perhaps they all list a particular city, a certain job title, or the same genre of books. Ever the willing helper, Access includes a special tool for this very purpose — the Filter command.

Filter uses your criteria and displays all matching records, creating a mini-table of only the records that meet your requirements. It's like an instant query without all the extra work, hassle, and overhead (and without a *lot* of the power).

The Filter commands live on the Records menu and the toolbar. Access offers five filter commands:

- ✔ Filter For
- ✔ Filter by Selection

✔ Filter by Form

✔ Filter Excluding Selection

✔ Advanced Filter/Sort

Each command performs the same basic function, but in a different way and with different bells and whistles attached. The following sections cover the first four options. For details of the Advanced Filter/Sort option, flip to Chapter 11.

Filters work in tables, forms, and queries. Although you can apply a filter to a report, filtering reports is a different beast (and not a very friendly beast, at that). The following sections apply filters to tables, but the same concepts apply when you're working with queries and forms.

Filter For

Filter For enables you to filter your records so that you view only records meeting specific criteria. Suppose, for example, that you wanted to see all records where the minimum bid was less than $30. Here's how to do it:

1. **Right-click the first field in the column.**

   Access displays a pop-up menu like the one in Figure 10-4.

   Don't right-click the header at the top of the column (where it says *MinimumBid* in the figure). Right-clicking there displays a different pop-up menu, filled with wonderful things that you can do to that column of your table.

2. **Click the open space to the right of the Filter For item, and then type your search condition.**

   In this case, type **<30**, the symbolic equivalent of "less than 30". If you enter simply *30* without the less than symbol, Access would mistakenly assume that you meant *=30*. Whoops.

3. **Press Enter.**

   Access searches the column in which you clicked and displays only those records that meet your Filter For criterion.

 4. **To see all of the records again, click the Remove Filter button on the toolbar or right-click the field again and choose Remove Filter/Sort from the pop-up menu.**

   The entire table, full of records, pops back into view.

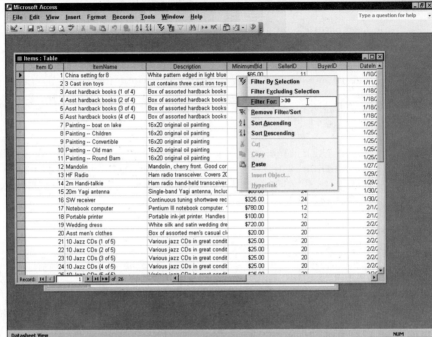

Figure 10-4:
Filter For in action.

If you right-click another column and perform another Filter For action, Access applies the new filter to only the already filtered records, giving a cumulative effect. Filtering for all items less than $30 works just fine, but then filtering *that* list for everything greater than $30 leaves you with an empty list. After all, very few things are both under 30 *and* over 30 at the same time (except, of course, the significant other in your life).

Filter by Selection

The Filter by Selection command is the easiest of the filter commands to use. It assumes that you've found one record that matches your criteria. Using Filter by Selection is much like grabbing someone in a crowd and shouting: "Okay, everybody who's like him, line up over there."

Suppose, for example, that you want to find all the items for sale at an auction with a minimum bid of exactly $30. You can use Filter by Selection in this manner:

1. **Click the field that has the information you want to match.**

   In this case, it's the MinimumBid field.

2. **Scroll through the list until you find an item whose minimum bid is $30.**

3. **Click the value you're searching for and then click the Filter by Selection button. Or you can right-click and choose Filter by Selection.**

   Access immediately displays a table containing only the items with a minimum bid of exactly $30, as shown in Figure 10-5.

Figure 10-5:
Access shows only those records matching the Filter by Selection criterion.

Item ID	ItemName	Description	MinimumBid	SellerID	BuyerID	DateIn
3	Asst hardback books (1 of 4)	Box of assorted hardback books. Printing dates rang from 1930 to 1940.	$30.00	22		1/18/2004
4	Asst hardback books (2 of 4)	Box of assorted hardback books. Printing dates rang from 1940 to 1950.	$30.00	22		1/18/2004
5	Asst hardback books (3 of 4)	Box of assorted hardback books. Printing dates rang from 1950 to 1960.	$30.00	22		1/18/2004
6	Asst hardback books (4 of 4)	Box of assorted hardback books. Printing dates rang from 1960 to 1970.	$30.00	22		1/18/2004
(AutoNumber)					0	

Items : Table — Record: 1 of 4 (Filtered)

4. **Click the Remove Filter button on the toolbar after you finish using the filter.**

   Your table or form returns to its regular display.

At this stage of the game, you may want to save a list of everything that matches your filter. Unfortunately, the Filter's simplicity and ease of use now come back to haunt you. To permanently record your filtered search, you need to create a query. See Chapter 11 for details about creating queries.

Filter by Form

You can tighten a search by using additional filters to weed out undesirable matches, but that takes a ton of extra effort. For an easier way to isolate a group of records based on the values in more than one field, turn to the Filter by Form feature (try saying that three times fast!).

Filter by Form uses more than one criterion to sift through records. (In some ways, it's like a simple query. It's so similar that you can even save your Filter by Form criteria *as* a full-fledged query!) Suppose, for example, that you need a list of all the customers at your auction who came from Illinois or Indiana. You can perform two Filter by Selection searches and write down the results of each to get your list, or you can do just *one* search with Filter by Form and see all the records in a single step.

To use Filter by Form, follow these steps:

1. **Choose Records⇨Filter⇨Filter by Form or click the Filter by Form button on the toolbar.**

   An empty replica of your table fills the screen, like the one shown in Figure 10-6.

   Normally, Access shows a down-arrow button next to the first field in the table. If you previously used a Filter command with the table, Access puts the down-arrow button in the last field you filtered, as shown in Figure 10-6. Notice that Access automatically entered the value you used in the previous Filter command. (Isn't helpful software wonderful? No, you don't have to answer that.)

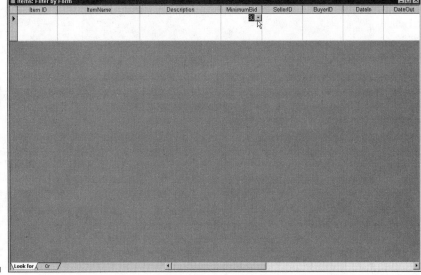

Figure 10-6:
Filter by Form remembers the last filter setting you used and assumes you want to start from there.

2. **Click the column that you want to filter with (use the scroll bars to bring the column on the screen if it's off in the ether).**

   The down arrow jumps to the column you click.

3. **Click the down arrow to see a list of values that the field contains, as shown in Figure 10-7. Click the value that you want to use in this Filter.**

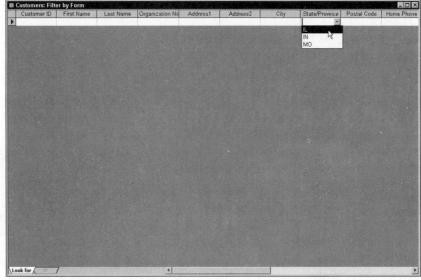

Figure 10-7:
The drop-down list shows all unique values in this field.

For instance, if you select IL from the drop-down list of a State/Province field, "IL" moves into the State/Province column. Access automatically adds the quotes on its own — one less detail that you need to remember!

4. **To add another filter option, click the Or tab in the lower-left corner of the table.**

   A new Filter by Form window appears, letting you add an alternate search condition. In addition, Access adds another Or tab to the lower-left corner of the display, as shown in Figure 10-8.

   The Filter by Form command likes to answer simple questions, such as "show me all the records containing IL in the State/Province field." Asking a more complex question (such as "show me the records with either IL or IN in the State/Province field") requires a second form. If you need to ask questions like the latter one, you probably should use a full-fledged query instead of Filter by Form. Flip ahead to Chapter 11 for more about queries.

5. **Repeat Steps 2 through 4 for each extra criterion you want to use in the filter.**

   Every trip through the steps adds another Or tab to the bottom of the window.

6. **When you finish entering all the criteria for the filter, click the Apply Filter button.**

   Figure 10-9 shows the results.

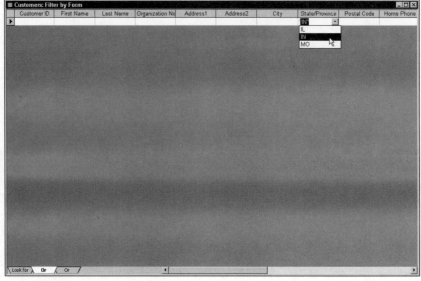

Figure 10-8:
Use as
many Or
statements
as you need
to define
the criteria.

Here are a couple of final thoughts about Filter by Form:

- ✔ Although you can get fancy by adding Or searches to your heart's content, keeping track of your creation gets tough in no time at all. Before creating *The Filter That Identified Incredibly Detailed Subsets of Manhattan*, remind yourself that queries work better than filters when the questions get complex. Flip to Chapter 11 for the lowdown on queries.

- ✔ Convert your cool Filter by Form creation into a full-fledged query by clicking the Save As Query button on the toolbar. Access dutifully remakes your work into a query and then adds it to the Query list in your database.

When you finish fiddling with your filter, click the Remove Filter by Form toolbar button. At that point, your table returns to normal (or at least as normal as data tables ever get).

Removing your mistakes (or when good criteria go bad)

What do you do when you enter criteria by mistake? Or when you decide that you really don't want to include Ohio in your filter right after you click OH? No problem — the Clear Grid button comes to the rescue!

When you click the Clear Grid button, Access dumps all the entries in the Filter by Form grid and gives you a nice, clean place to start over again.

Customer ID	First Name	Last Name	Organization Na	Address1	Address2	City	State/Province	Postal Code	Home P
1	Aan	Kermit		17757 S. Lyons		Fairland	IN	44879-2271	(317) 924
2	Rex	Morris		3627 Glenarm D	Apt. A	Beech Grove	IN	47827-	(317) 827
3	Ginny	Stevenson	Stevenson Antic	28 W. Washing	Suite 203	Indianapolis	IN	46204-4827	
4	Gary	Holko		2557 Fisher Dri		Anderson	IN	49877-2211	(317) 298
6	Oslo	Bergenman		4278 Eden Ct.		Indianapolis	IN	46205-	(317) 464
7	Anistasia	Kimmerly		6774 Wildemes	Apt. 11A	Greenwood	IN	46733-8927	(317) 687
8	Todd	Yosemite	Yosemite Conci	8379 RR 1	Box 38	Hope	IN	40288-7367	
9	Patricia	Philips	BHMS, Inc.	1010 Skyeway		Fishers	IN	46038-8915	
10	Kathryn	Grant	Universal Transp	3872 Port of Wa		Chicago	IL	49022-8279	
11	Travis	Cooksey		5807 Layman A		Noblesville	IN	46039-3726	(317) 864
12	Kevin	Davis		5646 Candelite		Greenfield	IN	44763-	(317) 363
13	Jack	Laux		25 Lower Bay L		Highland	IN	48572-8229	(317) 589
14	Vincent	Steffers	Cardinal Antique	6917 N. Meridia		Indianapolis	IN	46206-4271	
15	Edward	Anderson		431 Brentwood		Oakland	IN	45884-	(317) 783
16	King	Daniels	Baystorm, Inc.	9 Graceland Pl.		Muncie	IN	48443-2879	(317) 499
17	Lindsay	Travers		102 Windsor Dr	Apt. F	Brownsburg	IN	45777-	(317) 939
18	Clyde & Carmer	White		P.O. Box 3387		Carmel	IN	44893-3387	(317) 484
19	Paula	Ritter		229 Waterbury		Carmel	IN	44795-	(317) 449
20	Erika	Whitechurch		3872 E. Sedlak		Brownsburg	IN	44873-9287	(317) 298
21	Bruce	Yatsak	BY Collectibles	1 Captain's Squ	Suite 3100	Indianapolis	IN	46206-8376	
22	Sam	Gregory	Whimseco	1620 Edmondsc		Plainfield	IN	48667-3382	
23	Amanda	Tillery		6 E. Market	Suite 201	Indianapolis	IN	46206-	(317) 454
24	Gretchen	Hankla	Daisyfield Shop	227 Daisyfield D		Noblesville	IN	44879-8373	
25	Byron	Jiles		1122 Belden Dr.		Greenwood	IN	41988-7113	(317) 284
26	Clarence	Micy		385 Carlton Arm		Newton	IN	44879-2822	(317) 891
27	Mario	Schussler		1625 Euclid Ave		Fortville	IN	47334-1912	(317) 389
28	Harry	Nelson		19474 Vermeer		Carmel	IN	47934-3762	(317) 478
29	Callie	Logan	Eye 4 Antiques	227 Polk		Zionsville	IN	44023-9372	
30	Judith	Reginald		338 Kealing Ave		Indianapolis	IN	46206-	(317) 587
31	Charles	Polliet		430 Rimwood Li		Indianapolis	IN	46207-3287	(317) 875
32	Jean	Quillican	The Sharper Qu	1235 Washingto		Woodfield	IN	48339-	

Record: 1 of 42 (Filtered)

Figure 10-9: Access finds all customers from either Illinois (IL) or Indiana (IN).

If you want to get rid of just a single Or tab instead of clearing the whole grid, click that tab and then choose Edit⇨Delete Tab.

Filter by excluding selection

Filter Excluding Selection is the inverse of Filter by Selection: It selects everything *except* a certain value. It works great for times when you want to briefly hide a bunch of records that all share a unique attribute (a particular zip code, a certain state, a given phone exchange, and so on).

Here's how to make Filter Excluding Selection work for you:

1. **Scroll through the table until you find the value you want to exclude.**

2. **Right-click the value and choose Filter Excluding Selection, as shown in Figure 10-10.**

   You right-click the field containing the value, just like you do when using Filter by Selection.

3. **Press Enter.**

   Access shows everything *except* the records containing the value you chose. And you did it all with a single click, too!

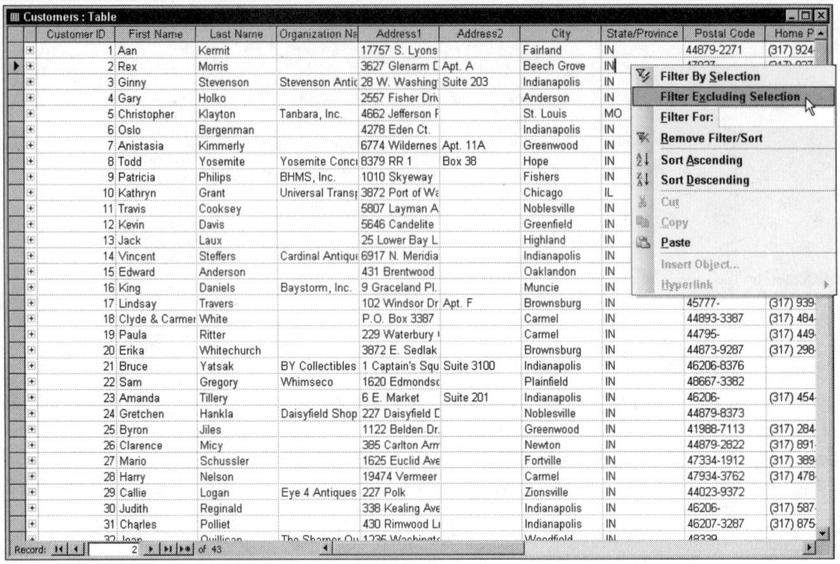

Figure 10-10:
In just a
moment,
Access will
hide all
records for
customers
living in
Indiana.

Chapter 11

Pose a Simple Query, Get 10,000 Answers

Someone infinitely smarter than me once observed that the most interesting insights in life spring not from the answers that life gives us, but instead from the questions that we pose along the way. One way or another, *everything* that we know — every shred of information in our minds — springs from questions that we asked aloud, pondered silently, or whispered furtively to the student at the next desk in hopes that he or she would take the risk of broaching the subject in class for us.

Databases follow this rule of life pretty well. Gathering your information into a database isn't easy, nor does the simple act of *gathering* really make the data easier to use. (After all, when you're finished, all you have is an electronic pile of the same stuff that previously lived in file cabinets.) The real power of a database flows from the questions you ask of it and the answers that it provides.

Access uses its own terminology for questions posed to your database — as do all databases in general. Access calls these questions *queries,* and they're the wily technological animals that this chapter covers.

The chapter starts with an introduction to the gentle (and frequently arcane) art of asking questions about the information in your database. Next, the chapter explores the basics of the simplest query in Access, which is *so* simple that the programmers gave this query the confusing name advanced filter/sort just to keep it murky. From there, the chapter guides you deeper into the data jungle where you find the true power of Access, the select query.

Don't worry if your first few queries produce odd results. That's how queries start for everybody (myself included). Queries aren't easy to master, but the payoff at the end is huge. Go slowly, be patient with yourself, and take comfort in the fact that others before you trod the same path you now walk — the path called "Hmm, that's not the answer to the question I thought I asked."

Database Interrogation for Fun and Profit

Of all the cool features in Access, the query takes the medal as the true hero in the ongoing Battle to Enhance Your On-the-Job Performance. Queries help you make sense of all the data that you, your co-workers, and a cast of a thousand others have slavishly typed over the course of too many hours, days, months, years, biannual bird migrations, and deep space satellite voyages.

Just as tables prepare your data for work by lining up all the information in neat rows and columns, queries make the data work for you by culling out the irrelevant details and shining light on murky mysteries. When you use queries, your data starts paying a return on all your labor.

All this querying sounds great, but it leaves open a simple question: *What the heck is a query?* Simply put, a *query* is a question about the data in one or more of the tables in your database. Queries make lists, count records, and even do calculations based on the data lurking in your database.

Queries discover useful information such as how many spools of purple silk thread sit in your warehouse, which customers bought the organic cactus face cream (in both non-prickly and extra-prickly varieties), and how weather affects carry-out pizza sales. In short, queries put the power behind your Access data.

Query magic doesn't stop with just answering questions. More advanced queries can add or delete records in your tables, calculate summary figures, perform statistical analyses, and with the right add-ons from Microsoft, probably even wash your dog.

On Your Way with a Simple Query — Advanced Filter/Sort

At first glance, you may wonder why I just spent all this time talking about queries if the first technical issue in the chapter is a *filter*. Trust me — there's a method to my madness. (Nice for a change, isn't it?)

The folks who created Access know that different searches require different techniques. For different searches, they include two search tools in the software: filters and queries.

Filters, the simpler tool of the two, quickly scan a single table for whatever data you seek. Filters are fast but not terribly smart or flexible. For example, if you want to quickly see a list of all records for people living in Nevada, a filter works wonderfully. If you want to do more than merely *see* the list, the filter falls short. Chapter 10 covers filters in their limited but useful glory.

Queries go far beyond filters. But to get there, queries add more complexity. After all, a bicycle may be easy to ride, but a bike won't go as far or as fast as a motorcycle. For all its power, the motorcycle is a tad more complex to operate than your average two-wheeler. And so it goes with queries. Queries work with one or more tables, let you search one or more fields, and even offer the option to save your results for further analysis.

For all the differences between filters and queries, the most advanced filter is, in reality, a simple query, which makes some perverse sense. Your first step into the world of queries is also your last step from the domain of filters. Welcome to advanced filter/sort, the super filter of Access, masquerading as a mild-mannered query.

As its name implies, advanced filter/sort is more powerful than a run-of-the-mill filter. The filter is so powerful that it's really a simple query. You use the same steps to build an advanced filter/sort that you use to create a query — and the results look quite a bit alike, too.

Even though it looks, acts, and behaves like a query, advanced filter/sort is still a filter at heart and constrained by a filter's limits. The limitations of advanced filter/sort include the following:

- ✔ Advanced filter/sort works with only one table or form in your database at a time, so you can't use it on a bunch of linked tables.

- ✔ You can ask only simple questions with the filter. Real, honest-to-goodness queries do a lot more than that (which is why an entire part in this book is about queries).

- ✔ The filter displays all the columns for every matching record in your table. With a query, *you* choose the columns that you want to appear in the results. If you don't want a particular column, leave it out of the query. Filters aren't bright enough to do that.

Even with those limitations, advanced filter/sort makes a great training ground to practice your query-building skills.

Although this section talks about applying filters to only tables, you can also filter a query. You might wonder why anyone would want to apply a filter to a query. Actually, there's a good reason: As you will see in your new career as Query Master, some queries take a long time to run. Suppose, for example, that you run a complicated Sales Report query, look at the results, and notice that it includes data from every state, but you only wanted to see sales from Wisconsin. Rather than modify the query and run it again, you can simply apply a filter to your query's results. Poof! You get the same results in a fraction of the time.

Peering into the filter window

The filter window is split into two distinct sections:

- ✔ The upper half of the window holds the *field list,* which displays all the fields in the current table or form.

    For now, don't worry about this portion of the window — the upper half comes more into play when you start working with full queries.

- ✔ The lower half of the screen contains a blank *query grid* where the details of your filter go. Even though you're building a filter, Access calls the area at the bottom of the screen a query grid. You see almost the same grid later in the chapter in the section about building real queries.

To build the filter, you simply fill in the spaces of the query grid at the bottom of the window, as shown in Figure 11-1. Access even helps you along the way, with pull-down menus and rows that do specific tasks. The following sections cover each portion of the query grid in more detail.

Figure 11-1:
The
advanced
filter/sort
window
looks a lot
like a
regular
query
window.

CustomersFilter1 : Filter

Customers
*
CustomerID
FirstName
LastName
OrganizationN

Field:
Sort:
Criteria:
or:

Building a simple query — er, filter

Start your filter adventure by firing up the basic query tool of Access, the advanced filter/sort. Here's what to do:

1. **Open the table that you want to interrogate.**

   With good luck and wind from the east, your table hops into view.

   The advanced filter/sort tool also works on forms. If you feel particularly adventuresome (or if you mainly work with your data through some ready-made forms), give the filter a try. Filtering a form works just like filtering a table, so just follow the rest of these steps.

2. **Decide what question you need to ask and which fields the question involves.**

   You may want a list of products that have been in inventory more than 60 days, customers who live in Munich or Amsterdam, books by your favorite author, or recipes that take less than an hour to cook and contain spinach. Whatever you want, nail down your question first and then locate the fields in your table that contain the answer.

   Don't worry if your question includes more than one field (such as the recipe problem) or multiple options (such as the customer city example). Filters — and queries — can handle multiple-field and multiple-option questions.

3. **Choose Records➪Filter➪Advanced Filter/Sort.**

   The filter window appears, ready to accept your command (see Figure 11-1). If you previously used a filter of any kind with this table, Access shoves that same filter information into the new window. Otherwise, the Filter/Sort window looks pretty blank.

   The filter window is nothing but a simplified query window. The filter looks, acts, and behaves a lot like a real query. More about full queries comes later in the chapter, so flip ahead to the next section if that's what you need.

4. **Click the first box in the Field row and then click the down arrow that appears to the right of the box.**

   The drop-down menu lists all the fields in your table.

5. **Click the first field you identified in Step 2.**

   Access helpfully puts the field name in the Field box on the query grid. So far, so good.

6. **To sort your filter results by this particular field, click the Sort box, and then click the down arrow that appears. Select Ascending or Descending from the drop-down menu.**

   If you want to see the results in the same order that your data always appears in, just skip this step.

Ascending order means lowest to highest (for example, *A, B, C . . .*);
descending is highest to lowest (for example, *Z, Y, X . . .*).

**7. Click the Criteria box under your field, and then type the question
for your filter to answer.**

Setting the criteria is the most complex part of building a query — it's
the make-or-break item in the entire process. The criteria is your actual
question, formatted in a way that Access understands. Building a query
with the right criteria can involve a lot, but Table 11-1 gives you a quick
introduction to the process.

Flip to Chapter 13 for a deeper look into the world of Boolean logic, the
language of Access criteria.

Table 11-1		Basic Comparison Operators	
Name	*Symbol*	*What It Means*	*Example*
Equals	(none)	Displays all records that exactly match whatever you type.	To find all items from customer 37, put 37 into the Criteria row.
Less Than	<	Lists all values that are less than your criterion.	<30 in the MinimumBid field finds all bids from $29.99 on down.
Greater Than	>	Lists all values in the field that are greater than the criterion.	30 in the MinimumBid field finds all bids that are more than $30 (starting with $30.01).
Greater Than or Equal To	>=	Works just like Greater Than, except it also includes all entries that exactly match the criterion.	>=30 finds all values from 30 to infinity.
Less Than or Equal To	<=	If you add = to Less Than, your query includes all records that have values below or equal to the criterion value.	<=30 includes not only those records with values less than 30, but also those with a value of 30.
Not Equal To	<>	Finds all entries that don't match the criteria.	If you want a list of all records except those with a value of 30, enter <>30.

8. **If your question includes more than one possible value for this field, click the Or box and type your next criterion.**

   Feel free to include as many Or options as you need. Just keep scrolling down to open up a new row for your criterion.

   If you type a bunch of Or lines, your first entries seem to disappear. Don't worry — you didn't mess up anything. Access just scrolled the table up a bit to make room for the new criterion. Click the up arrow on the scroll bar to see your original entries again.

9. **Repeat Steps 4 through 8 if your question involves more than one field.**

   With all the criterion in place, it's time to take your filter for a test drive.

10. **To turn on the filter, choose Filter➪Apply Filter/Sort or click the Apply Filter button on the toolbar.**

    After a moment of thinking (or whatever Access does when it's figuring out something), your table view changes, and only the records that match your filter are left on display, as shown in Figure 11-2. Pretty cool, eh?

    To see all the data again, click the Apply Filter button one more time. The filtered records join their unfiltered brethren in a touching moment of digital homecoming.

Figure 11-2:
Ta-dah! Your
filtered data
appears as
if by magic!

	Customer ID	First Name	Last Name	Organization Na	Address1	Address2	City	State/Province	Postal Code	Home F
	2	Christopher	Klayton	Tanbara, Inc.	4662 Jefferson F		St. Louis	MO	58837-7911	(314) 826
	10	Kathryn	Grant	Universal Trans;	3872 Port of Wa		Chicago	IL	49022-8279	
*	(AutoNumber)									

Record: 1 of 2 (Filtered)

If you *really* love this particular filter, save it like this:

1. **Click the Save As Query button on the toolbar (the picture of a disk with a funnel over it).**

   Access displays a dialog box asking what you want to call the query.

2. **Type a name and then click OK.**

   Access carefully saves your filter as a query, including this query with the others of its kind on the Queries page in your database window.

Plagued by Tough Questions? Try an Industrial Strength Query!

Sometimes, quick and easy information is all that you need — ask the question, get the answer, and then go on with life. At other moments though, you need introspection, analysis, and concerted thought — in other words, your information calls for work. Thanks to the Access query tools, that work just got easier.

The basic query tool, created to make your life easier, is the select query. Because developers use all their creativity writing programs, they tend to name their creations according to what the software actually does — hence, a select query *selects* matching records from your database and displays the results according to your instructions.

Unlike its simplified predecessor in this chapter, a select query offers all kinds of helpful and powerful options. These options include:

- ✔ **More than one table in a query.** Because a select query understands the relational side of Access, this query can pull together data from more than one table.

- ✔ **Show only the fields that you want in your results.** Select queries include the ever-popular Show setting, which tells Access which fields you really care about seeing.

- ✔ **Put the fields into any order you want in the results.** Organize your answers with fields where *you* want them, without changing anything in your original table.

- ✔ **List only as many matching entries as you need.** If you need only the top 5, 25, or 100 records, or even a percentage such as 5% or 25%, Access meets your need through the Top Value's setting.

The following section covers the basics of building a single-table select query. The other chapters in this part dig into detail on the goodies mentioned in the preceding list.

Build a Better Query and the Answers Beat a Path to Your Monitor

Creating a select query is a lot like putting together one of those advanced filter/sort thingies, but the select query includes a few extra interesting buttons and levers. The following steps run through the process and toss out some tips about advanced stuff that you don't want to miss:

1. **Open the database that you want to interrogate, and then click the Queries button on the left side of the screen.**

   Access lists all your existing queries (assuming that you have some in there), plus a few options for query creation.

2. **Decide what question you're asking with the query, which fields you need to answer the question, and which fields you want in your results.**

   Because select queries let you pick and choose with more detail, you need to think through more options than you did with the advanced filter/sort. The basic step remains the same, though. Which fields contain the data you want to know about? Which fields do you need in the solution? Think it through carefully, because these decisions form the major groundwork of your query.

TIP

Putting everything in *your* order

Access has a nice tool for sorting the results from a query. After all, queries don't get much easier than clicking a little box labeled *Sort,* and then telling the program whether Ascending or Descending is your choice for sort-flavor-of-the-moment.

The only problem with this little arrangement is that Access automatically sorts the results from *left* to *right.* If you only request one sort, this order is no big deal. But if you request *two* sorts (for example, organize the results by both Customer ID *and* Item ID), the column that's closest to the *left* side of the query automatically becomes the primary sort, with any other field playing second (or third) fiddle.

Taking control of the sort order isn't hard, but it also isn't obvious. Because Access looks at the query grid and performs the sorts from left to right, the trick is to move the column for the main sorting instruction to the left side of the grid. (Only a computer jockey can come up with a solution like this.)

To move a column in the grid, put the tip of the mouse pointer in the thin gray box just above the field name on the query grid. When the mouse turns into a down-pointing arrow, click once. All of a sudden, the chosen field is highlighted. (Fear not — highlighting the field is the hard part of the process.)

With the mouse pointer aimed at the same little gray area right above the field name, hold down the mouse button and drag the field to its new position on the grid. As you move the mouse, a black bar moves through the grid, showing you where the field lands when you let up on the mouse button. When the black bar is in the right place, release the mouse button. The field information pops into view again, safe and happy in its new home.

In addition to changing the sort order of your query, this moving trick also changes the order in which the fields appears in your query results. Feel free to move fields here, there, or anywhere, depending on your needs. Is this some great flexibility or what?

3. Double-click Create query in design view.

The screen does a quick change, and you get two new windows:

- Blank select query screen
- Show Table dialog box

4. In the Show Table dialog box, click the table you want to use and then click <u>A</u>dd. Click <u>C</u>lose to get rid of the Show Table dialog box.

Access puts a little window listing the table's fields into the top of the select query window.

5. Select the first field for your query by clicking the down arrow in the Field box. Then click the name of the field in the drop-down menu.

Access automatically puts the name of the table in the Table box and assumes that you want to include the field in your results by putting a check mark in the Show box.

You can also scroll through the field list in the small table window (the one that's in the upper part of the query window) and double-click each field that you want in the query. As you double-click, Access fills the field names in the query grid. I prefer this way, particularly when you start using multiple-table queries (which I cover in the next chapter).

6. Repeat Step 5 until all of the fields you want are in the query grid.

Now you're ready to adjust the sorting options.

7. To sort the query results by a particular field, click in that field's Sort box, click the down arrow, and select Ascending or Descending from the drop-down menu.

Just like advanced filter/sort, Access gives you the little-to-big and big-to-little options you know and love.

If you tell Access to sort with more than one field, Access starts with the field closest to the left of the query grid, and then sorts the other fields when it runs into identical records in the first field. See the "Putting everything in *your* order" sidebar, later in this chapter, for more information about sorting your data.

8. If you don't want a field to appear in the results, uncheck the Show box for that field.

9. Enter the criteria for each field that's part of the question.

Select queries use the same rules as the advanced filter/sort, including all the operators in Table 11-1. If you need some Or criteria (such as customers in Indiana or Illinois), use the Or lines in the query grid (see Figure 11-3).

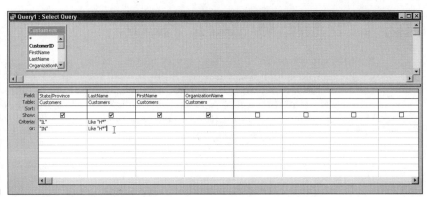

Figure 11-3:
This query
finds
Customers
whose last
names begin
with *H* and
who live in
IL or IN.

Thanks to their extra power, select queries support some special operators in the Criteria section in addition to the ones in the table. Flip ahead
to Chapter 13 to see the super-duper cool operators from Mr. Boole's
bag of tricks.

10. **Take one last look at everything, take a deep breath, and click the
    Run button.**

    After a few (or perhaps *many*) moments of chunking and thunking,
    your query results pop onto the screen, looking like Figure 11-4.

    If what you see *isn't* exactly what you thought you asked for (isn't that
    just like a computer?), double-check your query instructions. Common
    problems include mixing up the greater than (>) and less than (<) signs,
    leaving out an equals sign (=) in your greater-than-or-equal-to state-
    ments, or simply misspelling a region name, state, or postal code.

If you love this select query (in a friendly and useful way), be sure to save it!
If you forget to save the query manually, Access pointedly reminds you about
saving the moment that you try to close the query window.

Figure 11-4:
Here's the
result of
the select
query in
Figure 11-3.
Only Indiana
and Illinois
customers
need apply!

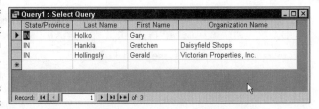

Toto, Can the Wizard Help?

Besides the advanced filter/sort query and the select query, you can rely on the Simple Query Wizard. If you know how to build queries by hand with the New Query function, the Simple Query Wizard is a breeze. Like all of the other wizards in the land of Access, the Simple Query Wizard takes care of the behind-the-scenes work for you, but you have to enter the sorting and criteria information on your own.

If you want to use the Simple Query Wizard instead of New Query, follow these steps:

1. **In the Database window, click the Query category, and then click the New command and select the Simple Query Wizard.**

   The Simple Query Wizard appears, asking which fields you want in your query, as shown in Figure 11-5.

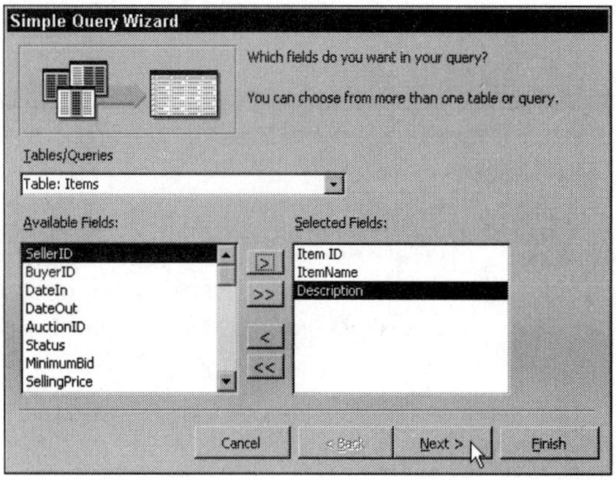

Figure 11-5:
The Simple Query Wizard holds your hand while you ask questions of the database.

2. **Click the down arrow in the Tables/Queries box. In the list that appears, click the name of the tables that you want to use in your query.**

   The wizard lets you choose fields from any of the related tables in your database, as well as from other queries that you previously built.

3. **Tell the wizard which fields to use in the query:**

   - To move a field from the Available Fields list to the Selected Fields list, highlight the field and then click the > button.

   - To transfer all the fields in the table to the Selected Fields list, highlight them and then click the >> button.

- If you decide that you don't want a field that you've transferred, highlight that field in the Selected Fields list and click the < button.

- If you want to remove all the fields in the Selected Fields list, highlight them and click the << button.

- To see the fields from a different table or query, click the down-arrow button in the Tables/Queries box, and then choose the new table or query from the drop-down list. The Available Field list automatically shows you the fields contained therein.

4. **Click <u>N</u>ext.**

   The wizard thinks for a moment, and then does one of two things, depending on whether you chose fields from a single table or from multiple ones. If the query includes fields from two or more tables or queries, the wizard *usually* offers you a dialog box of summary and detail options. If your query uses fields from only one table (or if the wizard arbitrarily decides that it doesn't feel like offering any summary options), you go straight to naming the query.

   How does the wizard choose whether or not it feels like summarizing things? That's a good question. (Hang on tight — this gets a little rough.) The wizard's decision has a lot to do with the first field you add to your query, as well as the relationships between the tables. Remember the one-to-many table relationship thing in Chapter 5? Here's where it comes into play. If the *first* field in the query is the key field of a one-to-many relationship with another table in your query, the wizard offers to do some summaries for you. If the first field in the query *isn't* that special key used in the one-to-many link, the wizard won't do a summary. (I guess he just feels cranky about it.) For more about the emotional world of table relationships, flip back to Chapter 5.

5. **If the wizard offers you the Summary and Detail options, make your choice and then click <u>N</u>ext.**

   If you want to see every field of every record, choose Detail. To show an overview, including automatic totals of any appropriate numeric fields laying around your query, select the Summary option.

6. **Type a name for your query, as shown in Figure 11-6.**

   The check box at the bottom of the screen opens a Help file that explains how you can customize your query.

7. **If you want to dress up the query by adding some cool extras, click the Modify the Query Design option.**

   This option tells the wizard to send your newly created query directly into the shop for more work, such as sorting and totals.

8. **If you're satisfied with your options at this point, click the Open the Query to View Information option to see the datasheet view.**

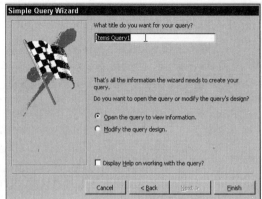

Figure 11-6:
Every good
query
deserves
a name.

This option runs the query and presents your query results in a typical Access datasheet. The other option, Modify the Query Design, sends you back to the Query Design screen to do some manual touch-ups on the query itself.

9. **Click Finish to see your handiwork.**

   Lo and behold, your results appear. Congratulations on a job well done (or at least a query well asked).

Chapter 12

Searching a Slew of Tables

In This Chapter
- ▶ Setting up queries with more than one table
- ▶ Enlisting the Query Wizard's help
- ▶ Building multiple-table queries in design view

*Q*uestioning just one table at a time kind of defeats the purpose of a relational database program. After all, relational database programs, which Access proudly claims to be, spend all their time and energy encouraging you to organize your data into *multiple* tables. Why would they do that without including some way to link the various tables and ask intelligent questions? (Well, they may do it just to be annoying, but assume that's not a possibility here.)

In keeping with its membership in the Relational Database Application Club of America, Access does indeed include tools for querying multiple tables. Because the process is on the arcane side, this chapter focuses on enlisting the Query Wizard to help you through the process. For the more technically inclined out there, this chapter explains how to build a multiple-table query by hand, too.

There's no shame in using the wizard's help when building a multiple-table query. The process isn't easy — remember, some people spend their college careers *studying* databases — but the Query Wizard covers the hard parts for you.

Some General Thoughts about Multiple-Table Queries

To make the most of your data, you often need to connect and compare stuff from a variety of tables — especially if you live in the corporate world. Fortunately, Access knows all about linking tables. That's why the computer folks call Access a *relational database program*. Like the high-tech equivalent of the village matchmaker, Access lets you define relationships between the various tables you work with. The relational thing works in queries too, meaning that Access can dig up information from two or more tables at the same time and (with your help and guidance) recognize stuff that goes together.

In most cases, a multiple-table query works the same as a single-table query. You merely need to let Access know that you are drawing on information from different tables, and the software does the rest.

Access maintains links between the tables in your database. Usually you (or your Information Systems department) create this link when you first design the database. When you build the tables and organize them with special key fields, you actually prepare the tables to work with a query.

Key fields link your Access tables. Queries use key fields to match records in one table with their mates in another. Figure 12-1 shows a key field in action. In the figure, you see two linked tables for an auction company: Customers and Items.

Figure 12-1:
In a multiple-table query, the tables are linked to share their data.

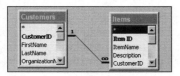

The Customers table stores contact information for everyone who sells goods through the auction. To prevent mixing up customers who have similar names, the company assigns each customer a unique number (the CustomerID). No two customers can have the same CustomerID; it's the key field in the Customer table.

The second table, Items, lists all the things that those customers offer for sale. To keep the items straight, each one gets a unique ItemID. Because every item comes from someone listed in the Customers table, the company puts the seller's number (the number stored in the CustomerID field of the Customer table) in the SellerID field of the Items table. That links the two tables. Through that link, every SellerID in the Items table matches a CustomerID in the Customers table. To find out who offered a particular item in an auction, the company just finds the item's SellerID number and looks that up in the Customer table's CustomerID field. Voila — instant information!

Before building a bunch of multiple-table queries, you *must* understand how the tables in your database work. More specifically, you need to know which fields the tables use to link the data. If you don't know, you're begging for trouble (which arrives in the form of queries that don't tell you anything useful). To find out more about relationships in general and how to use the relationship-building tools of Access, flip back to Chapter 5.

Calling on the Query Wizard

The Query Wizard isn't much of a wizard if all it does is create single-table queries. Luckily, it's one *heckuva* wizard because it comprehends the multiple-table query details as well.

To create a multiple-table query, follow these steps:

1. **In the database window, click the Queries button (in the Objects bar on the left side of the window).**

   The window lists all the queries currently living in the database.

2. **Double-click Create Query by Using Wizard.**

   The Simple Query Wizard window appears. Don't be surprised if the window looks familiar — it's the same one you use to make single-table queries. With a twist of the wrist (and a click of the mouse), it also builds multiple-table queries!

3. **Click the down arrow next to the Tables/Queries box (as shown in Figure 12-2), and then click the name of the first table to include in this query.**

   The Available Fields list changes and displays the fields available in the table (but you probably guessed that).

Figure 12-2:
Use the
Simple
Query
Wizard to
select from
more than
one table.

4. **In the Available Fields list, double-click each field that you want to include in the query.**

   If you add the wrong field, just double-click it in the Selected Fields list. The field promptly jumps back to the Available Fields side of the window.

5. **When you finish adding fields from this table, repeat Steps 3 and 4 for the next table you want to use in the query.**

   After you list all the fields you want in the Selected Fields area, go to Step 6.

6. **Click Next to continue building the query.**

   A screen amazingly similar to Figure 12-3 *may* hop into action if the first field in your query list is the key field that ties your tables together. If you don't see the screen, don't panic. Access wants you to name the query instead. (For a more detailed explanation, flip to the "Toto, Can the Wizard Help?" section in Chapter 11. Specifically, take a look at Step 4 over there.)

   If you include fields from two tables that aren't related, the Access Office Assistant leaps into action when you click Next. Office Assistant reminds you that the tables must be related and suggests that you correct the problem before continuing. Actually, *suggests* isn't quite correct — it politely *demands* that you correct the relationship before trying to create the query. If this error appears, click the OK button in the Office Assistant's message to go directly to the Relationships window. Repair the relationship and then restart the Query Wizard to try again. I tell you about table relationships in Chapters 4 and 5.

7. **If the wizard asks you to choose between a Detail and a Summary query, click the radio button next to your choice, and then click Next:**

   • **Detail** creates a datasheet that lists all the records that match the query. As the name implies, you get all the details.

   • **Summary** tells the wizard that you aren't interested in seeing every single record; you want to see a summary of the information instead.

   If you want to make any special adjustments to the summary, click Summary Options to display the Summary Options dialog box shown in Figure 12-4. Select your summary options from the list and then click OK.

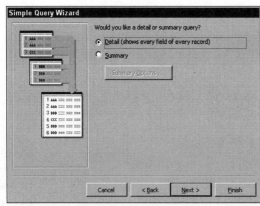

Figure 12-3: Depending on the types of information in your query, the Query Wizard may offer to summarize the data for you.

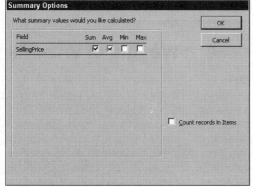

Figure 12-4:
Access
offers
different
ways of
summarizing
the data.

8. **Type a title for your query in the text box and then click Finish.**

   The query does its thing, and Access displays the results, as shown in Figure 12-5. Congratulations!

Figure 12-5:
The
datasheet
view of the
multiple-
table
summarized
query.

First Name	Last Name	Work Phone	Sum Of SellingPrice	Avg Of SellingP
Anastasia	Kimmerly	(317) 687-0819	$44.60	$44.60
Edward	Anderson	(317) 388-1842	$5.00	$5.00
Erika	Whitechurch	(317) 388-2727	$58.86	$8.41
Gerald	Hollingsly	(317) 237-7965	$265.36	$53.07
Gretchen	Hankla	(317) 779-4773	$147.94	$36.99
Kevin	Davis	(317) 367-2827	$12.10	$6.05
Sam	Gregory	(317) 292-8367	$47.00	$11.75
Travis	Cooksey		$14.12	$14.12

Record: ◄◄ ◄ 1 ► ►► ►✱ of 8

Rolling Up Your Sleeves and Building the Query by Hand

Using a wizard to build your multiple-table queries isn't always the best solution. Maybe the query is too complex or requires some special summaries (or perhaps you just don't feel up to tangling with the Query Wizard at the moment). For those times when creating a query by hand is the best choice, use design view instead.

Although it sometimes looks a bit complicated, design view is nothing to be afraid of. After you get the hang of it, you may discover that you *prefer* building queries this way. (What a scary thought!)

A gaggle of geese, a waggle of wizards

Is there a collective noun for a group of wizards? If not, there should be, because Access is loaded down with a plethora of wizardly assistants. Chapter 11 introduces the Simple Query Wizard, the most useful wizard for your general Access query needs. But the wizard corps doesn't stop there. Access includes three other query wizards that await your call: the Crosstab Query Wizard, the Find Duplicates Query Wizard, and the Find Unmatched Query Wizard.

Unfortunately, not all wizards are as straightforward as the Simple Query Wizard. Of the remaining three, the Crosstab Query Wizard is the only one that normal humans are likely to use. To find out about the Crosstab Query Wizard, check out Chapter 14. The remaining two wizards (Find Duplicates Query Wizard and Find Unmatched Query Wizard) are so weird that you don't need to worry about them.

Before starting a new multiple-table query, make sure that the tables are related! If you aren't sure about the table relationships, get back to the database window and click the Relationships button on the toolbar. (See Chapter 5 for more about table relationships.)

To build a multiple-table query by hand in design view, follow these steps:

1. **On the left side of the database window, click the Queries button.**

   The database window lists all your queries, ready for action.

2. **Double-click Create a Query in Design View.**

   After a moment, the Show Table dialog box appears. Behind it, you see the blank query window where your query takes shape.

3. **Double-click the name of the first table you want to include in the query.**

   A small window for the table appears in the query window (see Figure 12-6).

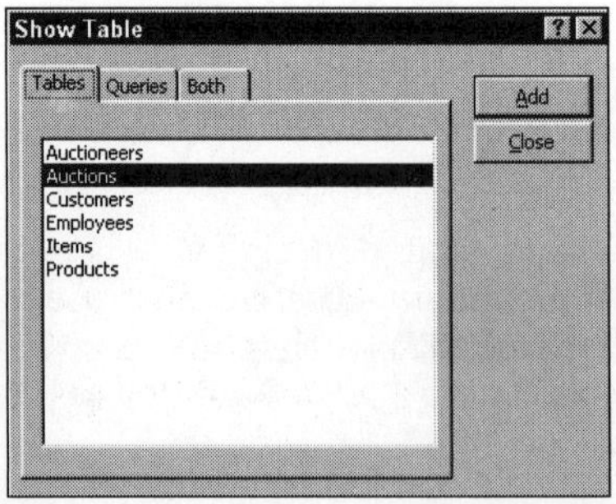

Figure 12-6:
The first table takes its place in the query.

Show Table

Tables | Queries | Both

Auctioneers
Auctions
Customers
Employees
Items
Products

Add
Close

4. **Repeat Step 3 for each table you want to add to the query. When you're finished, click Close to make the Show Table dialog box go away.**

   Don't worry if lines appear between your tables in the query window (as shown in Figure 12-7). That's good — it shows that Access knows how to link the two tables.

   What happens if you create a query but no line appears between the tables? Access is telling you that it doesn't have a clue how to link the tables. You can easily correct this. One solution is to cancel the query by closing the query window, and then use the Relationships button to build some relationships. Another solution is to create the relationship right in the Query window by dragging a field from the first table and dropping it onto the related field in the second table.

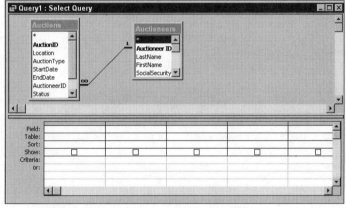

Figure 12-7:
Access knows how to link the Auctions and Auctioneers tables.

5. **Add a field to the query grid by double-clicking its entry in the field list boxes at the top of the Query window (shown in Figure 12-8). Repeat this step for each field you want to include in the query.**

   Choose your fields in the order you want them to appear in the query results. Feel free to include fields from any or all of the tables at the top of the query window. After all, that's why you included the tables in the query to begin with.

   If you accidentally choose the wrong field, you can easily correct your mistake. Click the field name's entry in the query grid and then select the oddly named Edit➪Delete Columns option from the menu bar. The incorrect field's entry (its column) is gone.

6. **If you want to sort by a particular field, click the Sort box under the field name and then click the down arrow that appears at the edge of the Sort box. Click either Ascending or Descending (as shown in Figure 12-9).**

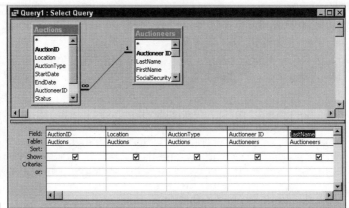

Figure 12-8:
You can mix
and match
the fields
from
different
tables in a
single
query.

If you want to sort by more than one field, repeat this step. Remember, though, that sorts are performed from left to right. If you want to sort by the second field and then by the first, you should first rearrange your columns.

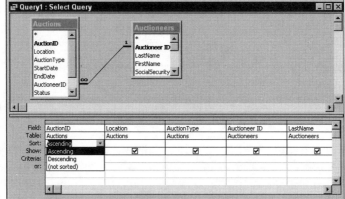

Figure 12-9:
A sorting we
will go . . .
ascending,
that is.

7. In the Criteria box for each field, set up the selection information for the query.

Even though this is a multiple-table query, you build criteria in the same way you do for single-table queries. Refer to Chapter 11 for help.

8. **If you want to include a field in the query but you don't want that field to appear in the final results, click the check box in the Show row for that field.**

   The Show setting really stands out in your query grid. There's only one check box in there, and that's the Show option.

9. **Review your work one more time. When you're sure it looks good, save the query by choosing File⇨Save.**

10. **In the Save As dialog box, type a name for the query and then click OK.**

    You don't want to lose all that hard work by not saving your query!

11. **Cross your fingers and then choose Query⇨Run (or click the Run button) to run your query.**

How did it work? Did you get the answer you hoped for? If not, take your query back into design view for some more work. To do so, choose View⇨Design View (or click the Design button).

Chapter 13

Lions AND Tigers OR Bears? Oh My!

● ●

● ●

*I*t's a fact of life: The longer you work with Access, the more complex are the questions that you ask of your data. Sorting your stuff up, down, right, and left, and filtering it through and through is not enough — now you want it to march in formation while doing animal impressions. (Well, you always did set high goals.)

Access queries may make your data do tricks, but even queries need some help to complete the most advanced prestidigitation. That's where Dr. Boole and his magic operators enter the picture. By enlisting the unique capabilities of Boolean operators, your queries can scale new heights, perform amazing acrobatics, and generally amuse and astound both you and your coworkers. They may even surprise your boss!

This chapter looks at AND and OR, the two main operators in the world of Access. It explains what the operators do, how they do it, and (most importantly) why you care. Get ready for a wild ride through the world of logic — strap your data in tight!

Comparing AND to OR

AND and OR are the stars of the Boolean sky. In spoken and written language, AND sticks phrases together into a complex whole, whereas OR describes a bunch of options from which to choose. In the world of databases, they perform much the same duties.

For example, if the woods are full of *lions AND tigers,* you can expect to find both types of animals anticipating your arrival. On the other hand, if the woods are full of *lions OR tigers,* you know that *one or the other* is out there, but you don't expect to see both. In database terminology, AND means *both,* whereas OR means *either* (egad — this sounds like a grammar class).

Here's an easy rule to keep the two operators straight:

- ✔ **AND** narrows your query, making it more restrictive.
- ✔ **OR** opens up your query, so more records match.

If you start looking for an individual with blue eyes AND red hair AND more than six feet tall AND male, you have a relatively small group of candidates (and I'm not among them). On the other hand, if you look for people with blue eyes OR red hair OR more than six feet tall OR male, the matching group is much, much bigger. In fact, half the folks who worked on the book — including both of the family gerbils — meet the criteria.

Finding Things between Kansas AND Oz

One of the most common queries involves listing items that fall between two particular values. For example, you may want to find all the records that were entered on or after January 1, 2003 but before January 1, 2004. To ask this type of question, you use an AND criteria.

Using an AND criteria is pretty easy:

- ✔ Put the two conditions together on the same line.
- ✔ Separate the conditions with an AND.

Figure 13-1 shows the query screen restricting DateIn in the Items table of the Auction database to sometime during the year 2003.

Don't worry about the pound signs — Access puts those in automatically so it can feel like it contributes to your query. Wait a minute! Since when do we put pound signs around a date? Call it a condition of the drinking water in Redmond, Washington, that caused the engineers there to come up with this one, but for some reason, dates are surrounded by pound signs . . . if you forget, Access inserts them for you.

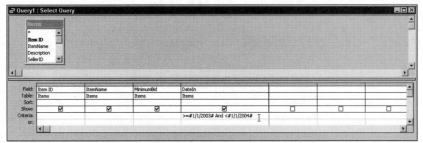

Figure 13-1:
The AND
operator
finds all
dates from
Jan. 1, 2003
to the day
before
Jan. 1, 2004.

Take a close look at the formula in the query. Access begins processing the query by sifting through the records in the table and asking the first question in the criteria, "Was the record entered *on or after* January 1, 2003?" If the record was entered before this date, Access ignores it and goes on to the next one. If the record was entered on or after January 1, 2003, Access asks the second question, "Was the record entered before January 1, 2004?" If yes, Access includes the record in the results. If not, the record gets rejected, and Access moves on to the next one.

The comparison uses greater than or equal for the first date (January 1, 2003) to include records written on the first day of the year as well.

This type of "between" instruction works for any type of data. You can list numeric values that fall between two other numbers, names that fall in a range of letters, or dates that fall in a given area of the calendar. Access doesn't care *what* data you test.

You could also search for dates in 2003 with the BETWEEN operator (see Figure 13-2 for an example of BETWEEN in action). The criteria BETWEEN #1/1/03# AND #12/31/03# selects records if the dates land on or between January 1, 2003 and December 31, 2003.

Figure 13-2:
An even
better
BETWEEN!

Multiple ANDs: AND Then What Happened?

One of the best features of Access is its flexibility. Overall, Access lets you do whatever you want in a query. For example, Access doesn't limit you to just *one* criterion in each line of a query. You can include as many criteria as you want. Access treats the criteria as if you typed an AND between each one.

Multiple criteria queries are tricky, though. Each AND criterion that you add must sit together on the same row. When you run the query, Access checks each record to make sure that it matches all the expressions in the given criteria row of the query before putting that record into the result table. Figure 13-3 shows a query that uses three criteria. Because all the criteria sit together on a single row, Access treats the three criteria as if they were part of a big AND statement. This query returns only records for auctions held at The Ranch that included items from customer Donati that had a minimum bid of less than $25.

Figure 13-3:
Show me
only records
that meet
all my
require-
ments,
please.

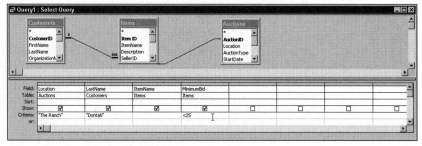

When you have a very large database and want to restrict your results to a minimum of records, combining a few criteria is the most useful way to go.

Need to narrow your results even more? (Wow, your boss *is* demanding!) Because Access displays the query results in datasheet view, all cool datasheet view tools work with the query — tools such as your old friend, the filter! Just use any of the filter commands (on the Records⇨Filter menu) to limit and massage your query results. If you need a quick refresher about filters, flip back to Chapter 10.

Are You a Good Witch OR a Bad Witch?

Often, you want to find a group of records that match one of several different possibilities (such as people who live in France or Belgium or the United States). This search calls for the OR criteria, the master of multiple options.

Access makes using an OR criteria almost too easy for words. There's nothing special to type, nothing to buy, and no salesperson will call. In fact, the OR option is built right into the Access query dialog box, ready and waiting for your call.

To make a group of criteria work together as a big OR statement, list each criterion on its own line at the bottom of the query. Each line can include criterion for whichever fields you want, even if another line in the query *already* has a criterion in that field. (Trust me, this is easier than it sounds.) Figure 13-4 shows a query asking to see all records where the last name is Anderson or Smith or Rivendell.

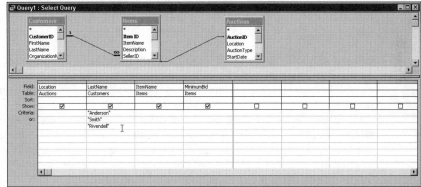

Figure 13-4:
Looking for auctions by these three families.

Of course, you can list the criteria in different columns, too. For example, Figure 13-5 shows the Items table of the auction database with a request for items that were entered by the Anderson, Smith, or Rivendell families OR that have a MinimumBid less than $30. So, all items entered by Anderson, Smith, or Rivendell will appear in my report as will any item with a minimum bid of less than $30 regardless of who sent it to the auction.

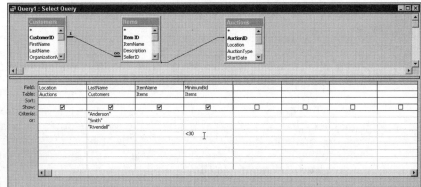

Figure 13-5:
Create OR criteria from different fields.

Each criterion is on a separate line. If the criteria are on the same line, you are performing an AND operation — only records that match both rules appear.

AND and OR? AND or OR?

Sometimes, using the AND and OR operators by themselves isn't enough. You need to ask a question about several different groups. Part of the question involves restricting the groups (with an AND), and other parts require including records based on a different criteria (with an OR).

Be careful with these logically complex queries. They get really fancy *really* fast. If a query grows to the point that you're losing track of which AND the last OR affected, you're in over your head, and it's time to start over again.

Instead of adding layer upon layer of conditions into a single query, break down your immense question into a series of smaller queries that build on each other. Begin with a simple query with one or two criteria. From there, build another query that starts with the first query's results. If you need more refining, create a third query that chews on the second query's answers. Each successive query whittles down your results until the final set of records appear. As a bonus, doing things this way lets you double-check every step of your logic, so it minimizes the chance of any errors accidentally slipping into your results.

The most important point to remember is that each OR line (each line within the criteria) is evaluated separately. If you want to combine several different criteria, you need to make sure that each OR line represents one aspect of what you're searching.

For example, in the Auctions database, knowing which items sell for less than $30 or more than $100 at a single auction site may be useful. Finding the items in those price ranges requires the use of an OR condition. (To find items with a MinimumBid *between* $30 and $100, use an AND criteria instead.) Using an OR condition means that the criteria go on separate lines.

However, that restriction isn't enough. You only want the items that are for sale at one site (in this example, it's The Ranch). For this query to work, you need to repeat the site information on each OR line. Congratulations — you have a bouncing baby AND/OR combination query.

To set up this query, you need a two-criteria line. One line asks for items that are less than $30 AND are for sale at site one; the other criteria calls out items that are more than $100 AND are for sale at site one. Because the criteria are on two lines, Access treats them as a big OR statement. Figure 13-6 shows the two ANDs with an OR.

Figure 13-6:
Any criteria
on the same
line are AND
operators
and restrict
the search.
Any criteria
on separate
lines are OR
operators
and expand
the search.

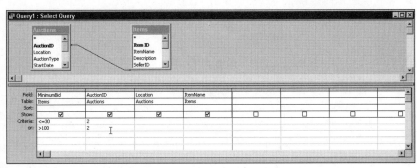

When reviewing your criteria, look at each line separately to make sure that line represents a group that you want included in the final answer. Then check to see that the individual lines work together to distill the answer you're seeking:

- ✔ AND criteria all go on the same line and are evaluated together.

- ✔ OR criteria go on separate lines, and each line is evaluated separately.

- ✔ Criteria that you want to use in each OR statement must be repeated on each of the separate lines.

Chapter 14

Teaching Queries to Think and Count

Getting quick answers to simple questions about the stuff in your database is nice, but there's more to life than finding out precisely how many folks from Montreal or Bombay bought pastel-colored back-scratchers between January and May of last year. Sometimes you need a big picture rather than a detailed, item-by-item analysis. What if you want to know the total amount of money the Montreal folks spent on back-scratchers? Or the number of orders people in Bombay placed during each month of the year? Or which 25 cities in your worldwide marketing effort purchased the most products?

That's precisely where the super-secret Access summary tool, the Total row, comes into play. Thanks to its many special capabilities, your queries can accumulate totals, count matching entries, organize your results in all kinds of helpful ways, and perform a number of other clever tricks.

How do you make this amazing stuff happen? Ah, that's always the question. The answer involves coaxing the Total row into your query and then choosing the right options to do what you need. This chapter walks you through the process, explaining the inner workings of the Total row and its helpful functions. Read on to make your queries do more for you!

Super-Powering Queries with the Total Row

You already know what a basic query does: You ask Access a question, and it shuffles and scurries through one or more of your tables, hunting up the answer. It might send back just a few matching records, or it might ship in a metric ton of data. Either way, it dumps all this stuff in your lap, leaving you to do the hard work of sifting everything into a useful form.

There's more to an Access query than meets the eye, though. In addition to answering basic questions and burping up huge lists of matching records, queries can also perform simple calculations on the data in your tables. You know that a query can list the customers from Germany. But why just ask for a raw list when Access can count at the same time? And while you're at it, why not have Access tell you how many items those customers purchased last year from your different product lines? Ah, now you're catching the vision!

Best of all, asking a big question like that with an Access query is a lot easier than it sounds. Why? Because all the computational complexity in there — the totals, the counts, and all the organization — comes from one place: the Total row of your query grid (shown in Figure 14-1). Whether you want to count, sum, sort, or find the highest or the lowest, the Total line does it all with just a click of your mouse.

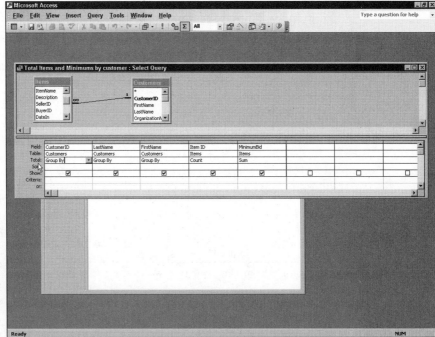

Figure 14-1:
The Total row appears between the Table and the Sort rows.

The Total row might look pretty small and insignificant, but it packs a lot of punch. Take a look at Table 14-1, which lists all the options available in the Total row's vocabulary. The table also gives you a quick description of the service each entry performs in your queries.

The most universally helpful tools among the Total row's offerings are Group By, Sum, Count, and the odd-sounding option Where. Later sections in this chapter go into more depth about these items, explaining what they do, how to use them, and why you really *do* care about all this stuff.

After you feel comfortable working with these options, try a few queries using the Total row's more esoteric choices. Although they do more special-ized tasks such as calculating standard deviations or finding the largest and smallest items in your table, all Total row functions work basically the same way. After you know how to make one option do its thing, the other options make perfect sense, too.

Table 14-1	Total Row Functions
Function	**What It Does**
Group By	Groups the query results by the field's values
Sum	Totals all the values from this field in the query results
Avg	Averages the values in this field in your query results
Min	Tells you the lowest value found in the field
Max	Reports the highest value found in the field)
Count	Counts the number of records that match the query criteria
StDev	Figures the statistical standard deviation of the values in the field
Var	Calculates the statistical variance of the values in the field
First	Displays the first record that meets the query criteria
Last	Displays the last matching record that Access finds
Expression	Tells Access that you want a calculated field (see Chapter 15 for the different calculations Access can perform)
Where	Uses this field for selecting records but doesn't summarize anything with it

Adding the Magical Total Row to Your Queries

In a confusing twist, the Total line usually *doesn't* appear on the query grid — you must coax the Total line out of hiding with the right command, explained in the upcoming steps. After doing that, Access adds the Total row to your query grid.

Why doesn't the Total row appear in your query grid all the time? Frankly, because Microsoft wants to make queries *look* a little simpler. With all those various rows, columns, buttons, and things, queries appear pretty complicated — particularly at first glance. In the name of reducing the clutter even a little bit, thus making queries more accessible to everybody, Access hides the Total row by default.

So what's the secret password that puts a Total row in your query grid and lets you choose a ready-to-go calculation to use? Follow these steps and find out:

1. **Set up an average, normal query, just as you usually do.**

   By now, you probably know the drill for opening a new query and choosing the tables and fields that you want to see in your results. If you need a quick refresher, flip to Chapter 11.

Σ

2. **Turn on the Total row by either clicking the Totals button on the toolbar or selecting <u>V</u>iew⇨Tota<u>l</u>s from the main menu.**

   The Total row appears. For every field already in your query, Access automatically fills the Total row with its default entry, Group By.

   In case you wondered, the Totals button displays the Greek letter sigma. Mathematicians, engineers, and others with deep interpersonal communication difficulties use this symbol when they mean "give me a total."

3. **To change a field's Total entry from Group By to something else, click that field's Total row.**

   The blinking line cursor appears in the Total row, right next to a down-arrow button.

4. **Click the down-arrow button in the field's Total row, and then select the new Total entry you want from drop-down list.**

   The new entry appears in the Total row.

5. **Make any other changes you want, and then run the query.**

   With the Total line in action, the query results automatically include the summary (or summaries) you selected. Too cool, eh?

The following section goes into detail about using the most popular and useful Total row options.

Putting the Total Row to Work

After coaxing the Total row into making an appearance on your query form (the preceding section explains that part of the trick), you can start using its myriad capabilities to save you time, effort, and frustration. This section focuses on the four most commonly used options in the Total row's toolbox: Group By, Sum, Count, and Where. Each section explains what the option does and gives some examples of how to make it work for you.

When you get the hang of the basic options on the Total row, experiment with the others. You set all of them up basically the same way — they just differ in their ultimate results. For details about how the advanced options work, check the Access help system (Help➪Microsoft Access Help).

Most of the Total row options perform well by themselves, but they also work and play well with others. When running multiple queries, try mixing differ- ent options together to save yourself time. It takes some practice to ensure that everything works the way you want, but the benefits (namely, more information with less effort) make up for the investment.

Organizing things with Group By

The Group By instruction organizes your query results into groups based on the values in one or more fields. Group By also eliminates duplicate entries in your results. When you turn on the Total row in your query grid, Access automati- cally puts in a Group By for every field on the grid. Group By pools the records that the other Total row instructions such as Sum and Count summarize for you.

Putting a single Group By instruction in a query tells Access to total your results by each unique value in that field (by each customer number or product name, for instance). Each unique item appears only once in the results, on a single line with its summary info. If you include more than one Group By instruction in a single query (like the one shown in Figure 14-2), Access builds a summary line for every unique combination of the fields with the Group By instruction.

Put the Group By instruction into the field you want to summarize — the one that answers the question, "What do you want to count *by?*" For example, if you want to count the number of products purchased *by each customer,* the Group By instruction goes into a field containing a customer number or other unique, customer-identifying information. For a count of your customers *by the state* where they live, the Group By instruction lands in the field contain- ing their state.

Figure 14-2:
This query
tallies a
summary
line for
every
combination
of data in
the State/
Province
and
PostalCode
fields.

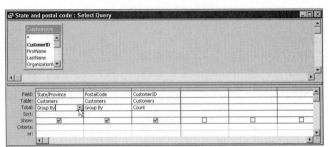

When you use Group By, Access automatically sorts the results in order based on the field with the Group By instruction. If you put Group By in the State/Province field, for example, Access sorts your results alphabetically by the contents of that field. To override this behavior and choose a different sorting order, use the Sort row in your query grid, as shown in Figure 14-3. Choose the field that you want to sort everything by, and then put the appropriate sorting command (ascending or descending, depending on your needs) in that field's Sort row. Access does the rest by itself, and automatically organizes the query results in the right order.

Figure 14-3:
Make
Access sort
your results
the way
you want
with a quick
click in the
query grid's
Sort row.

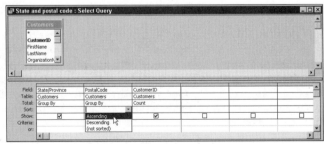

Adding a total with Sum

Sum works only with numeric fields. When you put the Sum instruction in a field, Access totals the values in that field. If you use the Sum instruction all by itself in a query grid, Access calculates a grand total of the values in that field for the entire table. By pairing a Sum instruction with a Group By instruction (as shown in Figure 14-4), your results display a sum for each unique entry in the Group By field.

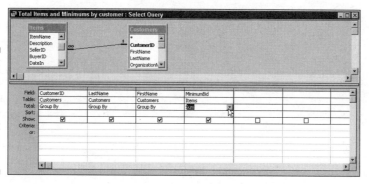

Figure 14-4: Put the Sum instruction in a numeric field so it can do its thing.

Pair the Sum instruction with any other Total row option to get more than one summary for each line of your results. Count and Sum naturally go together, as do Sum and Average, Minimum, and Maximum. To limit the range of the records totaled in Sum, use the Where instruction (described shortly).

Counting the good count

Use the Count instruction in the query when you want to know how many rather than how much. Because Count doesn't attempt any math on a field's data, it works with any field in your tables.

When used by itself in a query (as shown in Figure 14-5), Count tallies the number of entries in a particular field across every record in the entire table, and then displays the answer. By using Count with one or more Group By instructions in other fields, Access counts the number of items relating to each unique entry in the Group By field.

For a quick and accurate count of the number of records in a group, point the Group By and Count instructions at the same field in your query grid, as shown in Figure 14-6. To be part of the group, the records need matching data in a certain field. Because you *know* that the field for your Group By instruction contains something (namely, the data that defines groups for the query results), that field is a perfect candidate for the Count instruction as well. Add the field to your query grid a second time by choosing the same field name again in a new column, and then selecting Count in the Total row.

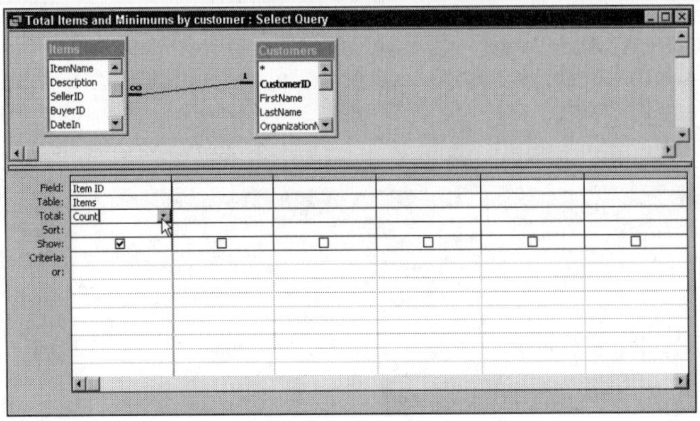

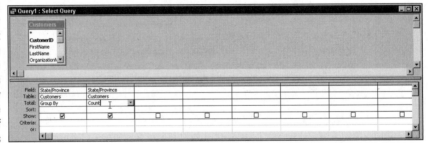

Figure 14-5:
Use Count
on a single
field to
easily count
the number
of records
in a table.

Figure 14-6:
By putting
both a
Group By
and Count
instruction
in the same
field, this
query easily
counts the
number of
customers
in each
state.

Narrowing the results with Where

The Where instruction works a bit differently than the other options in the Total row. Instead of calculating, counting, tallying, or figuring, the Where instruction lets you add more criteria to the query (showing customers from certain states, only including orders after a certain date, and so on) without cluttering your results with a bunch of extraneous fields.

The query in Figure 14-7 uses a Where instruction to limit which records appear in the query results. Normally, that query would count customers by State/Province and PostalCode, listing every record in the table. Adding a Where instruction in the second State/Province field tells the query that it needs to test the data before including it in the results. In this case, the Where instruction's criteria admit records for people living in only Indiana or Georgia (the data in State/Province matches either IN or GA).

Figure 14-7:
The Where
instruction
in the
right-hand
State/
Province
field
prevents
nonmatching
records
from getting
into the
results.

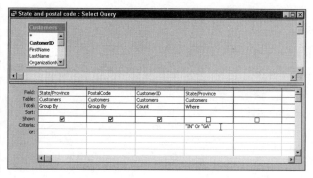

Choose the Right Field for the Summary Instruction

Deciding which field gets a Sum, Count, or other Total row instruction *greatly* affects your query results. If you accidentally choose the wrong field, Access suddenly (and rather spectacularly) fails to tally things correctly.

Why would an advanced program like Access suddenly lapse into a digital coma while doing simple things like counting or adding? Access doesn't summarize *every* matching record that it finds in your table. Instead, it notices only fields that contain something. If the field containing the Total row instruction doesn't contain any data, Access ignores the record, leaving it out of the count. Figure 14-8 sheds more light on this weird behavior. The first three fields of every record in that table (CustomerID, Last Name, and Address1) contain information, making them great candidates for a Count instruction. Because every single record in the table has a value of some kind in the Customer ID, Last Name, and Address1 fields, Access could make a perfect count of the records in the table.

Now, compare those three completely filled-in fields with all the blank spaces in the Address2, Home Phone, and Work Phone fields. If you used a Count instruction in any of those fields, Access would count only the records that had data in those fields. That's a great thing if you want to know how many customers in your database provided their phone number at work, but it hurts if your question pertains to the number of customers in various states.

Correcting query results

If your multi-table queries display too many or too few results, you likely face a problem with the way Access thinks about the two connected tables. Luckily, that's an easy problem to correct — after you know how to find the Join Properties dialog box, that is.

When you connect two tables in a query, Access displays the tables above your query grid and draws a line between them, showing how the relationship works. But that little line does more than it seems. The line also leads to the Join Properties dialog box, a secret haven of information about how Access deals with the information it finds in those related tables.

To display the Join Properties dialog box, double-click precisely on the line that connects your two tables. The little dialog box shown in the figure appears. (If a bigger dialog box called Query Properties pops up instead, just close it and try again; Access thinks you missed the line.)

Look at the three options filling the bottom half of the dialog box. Those options govern how Access chooses which rows to include in the results of the query. By default, Access chooses the first option, which displays only matching records from both related tables. Most of the time, that's how you want Access to behave. In this option, if a record in one table doesn't have a matching record in the other, Access doesn't display that record in its results. If no query results display a zero in the summary, this option probably caused the problem.

On those rare occasions when you want to see all the records from one table or the other in your results, choose option two or three in the Join Properties dialog box. These options display more records in your results because you get all the records that match *plus* all the ones that don't.

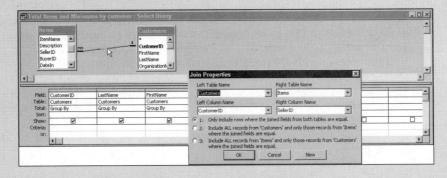

The moral of the story: Avoid embarrassing errors in your results by putting your Count instruction in a field that contains data. As long as Access peers into the field and finds something, it's happy. (And keeping Access happy is, after all, the goal.)

Figure 14-8:
Putting
Count or
other
summary
instructions
in fields with
a lot of blank
entries will
mess up the
calculations!

	Customer ID	Last Name	Address1	Address2	Home Phone	Work Phone	First Name	C
+	1	Kermit	17757 S. Lyons Ave		(576) 924-119	(317) 447-362	Aan	Fairland
+	2	Morris	3627 Glenarm Dr.	Apt. A	(576) 827-228		Rex	Beech
+	3	Stevenson	28 W. Washington	Suite 203		(317) 727-909	Ginny	Indiana
+	4	Holko	2557 Fisher Drive		(576) 298-277		Gary	Anders
+	5	Klayton	4662 Jefferson Pkwy		(314) 826-772	(314) 826-090	Christopher	St. Lou
+	6	Bergenman	4278 Eden Ct.		(317) 464-294	(317) 466-278	Oslo	Indiana
+	7	Kimmerly	6774 Wilderness Trail Dr.	Apt. 11A	(317) 687-499	(317) 687-081	Anistasia	Greenw
+	8	Yosemite	8379 RR 1	Box 38		(812) 488-227	Todd	Hope
+	9	Philips	1010 Skyeway			(317) 554-790	Patricia	Fishers
+	10	Grant	3872 Port of Washington			(312) 399-827	Kathryn	Chicag
+	11	Cooksey	5807 Layman Ave		(317) 864-773		Travis	Nobles
+	12	Davis	5646 Candelite Dr.		(317) 363-009	(317) 367-282	Kevin	Greenfi
+	13	Laux	25 Lower Bay Ln		(317) 589-333	(317) 448-844	Jack	Highlar
+	14	Steffers	6917 N. Meridian St.			(317) 576-338	Vincent	Indiana
+	15	Anderson	431 Brentwood Pl.		(317) 783-919	(317) 388-184	Edward	Oaklan
+	16	Daniels	9 Graceland Pl.		(317) 499-382	(317) 837-289	King	Muncie

Record: 14 ◀ 4 ▶ ▶I ▶* of 43

Chapter 15

Calculating Your Way to Fame and Fortune

*O*ne of the big rules in database creation is that a table should contain as few fields as possible. Smaller tables load faster, are easier to document and maintain, and take up less disk space. One extra field isn't much by itself, but it adds up when your table contains several hundred thousand records!

So how do the pros keep their tables small? By storing only what they really need and using calculations to figure out whatever else they require. For example, if your table contains the wholesale cost and the retail price of an item, why bother storing the markup percentage? When you need that information, use a calculated field to create it on the fly!

A *calculated field* takes information from another field in the database and performs some arithmetic to come up with new information. In fact, a calculated field can take data from more than one field and combine information to create an entirely new field, if that's what you want.

In this chapter, you build all kinds of calculations into your queries. From simple sums to complex equations, the information you need is right here.

Although the examples in this chapter deal with calculated fields in queries, the same concept applies to calculated fields in reports. For a few tips about calculating fields and reports, flip ahead to Chapter 20.

A Simple Calculation

When you want to create a calculated field in a query, first list the fields needed for the calculation, and then write down which tables contain those fields. The query must include all of the tables in your list. If the fields live together in one table, include only that table in the query. If the fields are split among several tables, make sure to include every one of those tables at the top of the query screen. If you miss a table or two, Access can't do the calculations. (Even with its sometimes-amazing antics, Access is *still* merely software — it's not terribly bright, and it gets confused easily.)

Start building the calculated field by clicking the empty field name box of any column. Access puts the results of the calculation in the same grid position as the calculation itself, so if the calculation sits in the third column of your query grid, the calculation's results will be in the third column, too. Just choose the spot where you want the results to appear, and put the calculation there. Then, instead of selecting an existing field for that column, type the calculation that you want Access to perform.

As you may suspect, Access uses a special syntax for building calculated fields. Although you can't just type *add these together and display the result* (that's *way* too simple and understandable) calculating isn't much tougher than that.

Basically, you type the calculation just like you'd enter it in a pocket calculator, except you substitute field names for at least some of the numbers. The key to the process is the square bracket symbols ([ ]). To make Access understand which parts of the calculation are fields, you put square brackets around the field names. Access miraculously recognizes that those entries refer to fields in your table. Access treats anything else it finds in the calculation as constants (which is the math nerd term for *it means whatever it says*).

Using the auction example, suppose that research says that most items sell for 47 percent more than the minimum bid price (or 147% of the minimum bid). To calculate the expected price, you need to multiply MinimumBid by 147%. Because Access isn't smart enough to recognize the percent sign, you need to convert percentages to decimals (thus 147% turns into 1.47). Translated into an Access calculation, it looks like this:

```
[MinimumBid] * 1.47
```

The square brackets around MinimumBid tell Access that MinimumBid is a field in the table, not just a bunch of text that accidentally wandered into the calculation. Because the 1.47 isn't surrounded by brackets, Access assumes that you mean the numeric value 1.47. Figure 15-1 shows the finished formula, all ready to go.

Why Access names all your calculations *Expr*

Despite its massive computational capabilities, Access just isn't very creative. When you make your first calculation in a query, Access cleverly calls it Expr1, which is math shorthand for *expression one,* the first calculation (or expression) in the query. If you add a second calculation to the query grid, Access automatically calls it Expr2 (for *expression two).* It does that to keep the expressions organized in its own mind, and so it has something to put above the calculated results in the results window.

Luckily, Access knows that these monikers look pretty stupid, so it lets you name calculated fields yourself. To replace Expr1 with a more descriptive name of your choice, click the Design View button. This switches the screen from the results display back to the query grid. Find your calculation in the grid, and then carefully replace the *Expr1* text with the name you want. Make sure you leave the colon between your field name and the calculation! The finished product, complete with its new field name and nifty calculation, should look something like the figure.

By the way, Access calls this text (the name above your calculated field) a *label.* That's a long-standing computer geek term for "text that describes something."

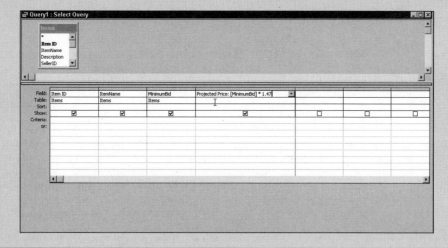

Figure 15-1:
The cal-
culation
takes shape
next to the
regular
fields in
the query,
complete
with Expr1
in front of it.

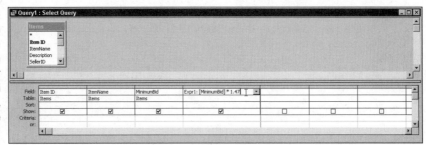

Access doesn't mind if you use the same field name twice in a single calculation. For instance, you could solve the preceding example also with this formula, which does a little better job of showing how the calculation works:

```
[MinimumBid] + ([MinimumBid] * .47)
```

The moment you click outside your finished calculation, Access shoves the
Expr1: text in front of whatever you typed. Why did it do that? Well, that's a
good question. For a good answer (and, more importantly, an explanation of
how to change it), look in this chapter's sidebar.

When creating formulas, keep these general guidelines in mind:

- ✔ You must manually type the field names and such into your
  formula — you can't just drag and drop stuff from the table list.

- ✔ Dragging the field name adds it as a new field in your query,
  which isn't *quite* what you had in mind.

- ✔ Don't worry if your calculation grows past the edge of the Field box.
  Access still remembers everything, even if it doesn't appear on the screen.
  To make the query column wider, aim the mouse pointer at the line on right
  side of the thin bar above the calculation entry. When you get it right over
  the line, the pointer changes into a line with a horizontal arrow through it.
  When that happens, click and drag the mouse to the right and left. As you
  do, the column expands and contracts according to your movements. This
  trick changes the size of any column in your query grid in one easy step!

- ✔ If you want fields from more than one table in a single calculation, you
  must tell Access both the table name and field name instead of just the
  field name alone. To do that, type the table name in square brackets,
  type an exclamation point, and then type the field name in square brackets. The format of the finished entry looks like this:

```
[TableName]![FieldName]
```

When you run a query containing a calculation, Access produces a datasheet showing the fields you specified, plus it adds a new column for the calculated field. In Figure 15-2, the datasheet shows the item name, the minimum bid, and the calculated field containing the expected price for each item.

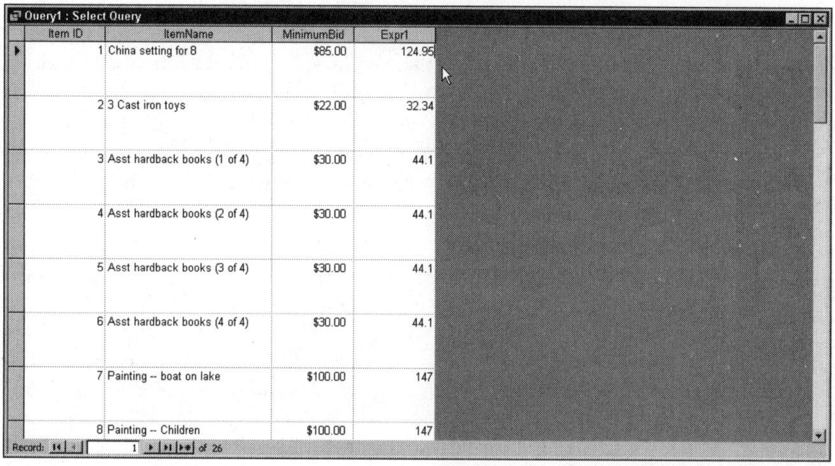

Figure 15-2:
The calculation worked, but Access gave the results an odd name.

Item ID	ItemName	MinimumBid	Expr1
1	China setting for 8	$85.00	124.95
2	3 Cast iron toys	$22.00	32.34
3	Asst hardback books (1 of 4)	$30.00	44.1
4	Asst hardback books (2 of 4)	$30.00	44.1
5	Asst hardback books (3 of 4)	$30.00	44.1
6	Asst hardback books (4 of 4)	$30.00	44.1
7	Painting -- boat on lake	$100.00	147
8	Painting -- Children	$100.00	147

Record: 1 of 26

Bigger, Better (and More Complicated) Calculations

After getting the hang of simple calculations, you can easily expand your repertoire into more powerful operations, such as using multiple calculations and building expressions that use values from other calculations in the same query. This stuff really adds to the flexibility and power of queries.

Add another calculation — go ahead, add two!

Access makes it easy to put multiple calculations into a single query. After building the first calculation, just repeat the process in the next empty Field box. Keep inserting calculations across the query grid until you just don't care anymore — Access gleefully lets you keep right on going.

You can use the same field in several calculations. Access doesn't mind at all.

Using one expression to solve a different question

One of the most powerful calculated field tricks involves using the solution from one calculated field as part of another calculation in the same query. The calculation not only creates a field in the query results, but also supplies data to other calculations in the same query, just like a real field in the table.

Although the details are simple, the technique borders on the realm of true techno-magic. Tread carefully because a small error in one calculation quickly compounds into a huge mistake when other calculations rely on an accuracy-challenged number.

Access identifies each calculation with a unique label — the name that sits in front of the calculation in the query grid and above the answer in the results. The default labels always start with Expr. You can change the label to something more colorful (such as DaysInStock) by using the technique explained in the "Why Access names all your calculations *Expr*" sidebar in this chapter.

To use the results from one calculation as part of another, just include the name of the first calculation in square brackets. In short, treat the first calculation like a field in your table.

The query in Figure 15-3 shows this technique in action. The answer to the first calculation (Projected Price) feeds into the second calculation (Projected Profit). In the second calculation, Expected Price looks just a normal field, complete with the square brackets around it. Access treats it that way, despite the fact that it's a different calculation in the same query.

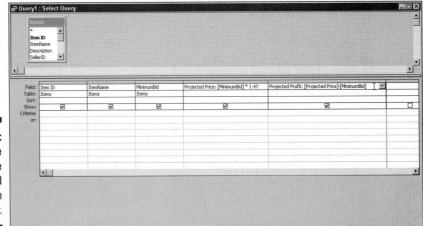

Figure 15-3:
Use the result of one calculated field in another.

Figure 15-4 shows the results from running the query. Access displays the results from the two calculations under the same custom label names that appear in the calculations: Projected Price and Projected Profit.

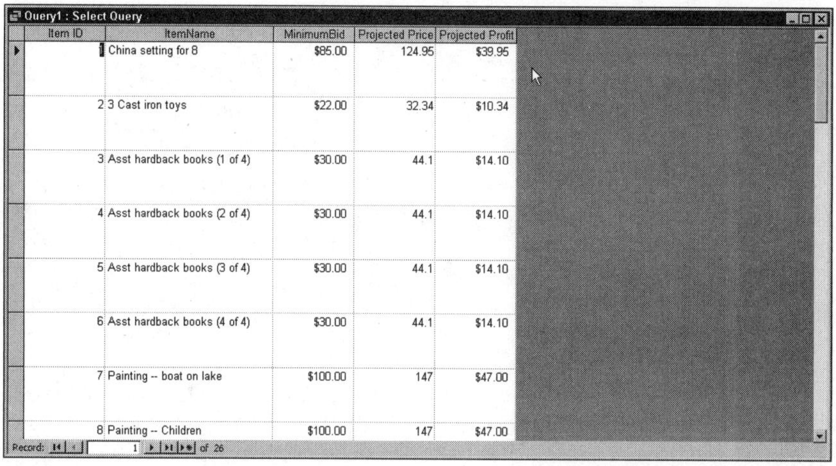

Figure 15-4:
Access displays results that it calculated for projected price and projected profit.

Making Access ask nicely for help

At times, you may want to include a value in a formula that doesn't exist anywhere in your database (for example, the number 1.47 for 147 percent in the calculation example earlier in this chapter). If you know the value, you can type it directly into the formula.

But what if the number changes all the time? You don't want to constantly rebuild a query — that's a mistake just waiting to happen. Instead of building the ever-changing number into your formula, why not make Access *ask* you for the number when you run the query?

You won't believe how easy this trick is — really. To coax Access into asking for a number, just think of an appropriate name for the value (such as Current Rate, Last Price, or Percent Increase), and then use the name in your formula as if it were a regular field. Put square brackets around it and shove it into your calculation, just like you did with the other fields.

When you run the query, Access displays a dialog box like the one shown in Figure 15-5. Just enter the value of your expected increase (as a decimal value), and Access does the rest. This option means that you can use the same query with different values to see how changing that value affects your results.

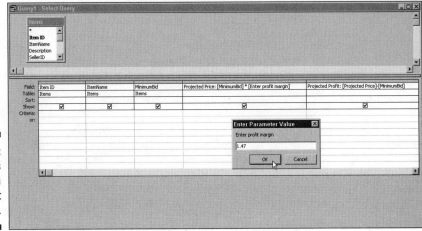

Figure 15-5:
Access
asks for a
profit
margin.

When choosing a name for this value, don't use the name of an existing field in your table. (Otherwise, you confuse the daylights out of Access.) Instead, go with something that describes the number or value itself. As you can see in the query grid shown in Figure 15-5, I lean toward things like [Enter profit margin] because that name explains itself. When you look at this query months (or even years) from now, you easily recognize that something called [Enter profit margin] probably isn't a normal field, but rather a value that Access asks for when the query runs. Besides, names like that look really nice in the little pop-up window Access displays to collect the value, too.

Working with words

Number fields aren't the only things you can use in calculations. In fact, performing calculations with a text field often comes in a lot handier than just fiddling with numbers.

Access treats text fields in calculations much like it handles number fields — you still surround the field name with square brackets and carefully type the field name by hand. There *is* one important difference, though: Instead of connecting several text fields with a plus sign (+) like you would when doing simple math, you use the ampersand character (&). Granted, the ampersand does almost the same thing as the plus sign, but the technical gurus at Microsoft really, *really* prefer that you use the ampersand. They call the ampersand the *concatenation operation,* which is a fancy way to say that it connects things.

Figure 15-6 shows a calculated text field in action. This example solves a common database issue: making one name out of the pieces in two separate fields. The formula shown in the figure combines the FirstName and LastName fields into a single full name, ready to appear on a mailing label, yacht club membership report, or some whatever useful purpose you devise.

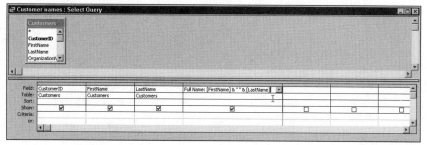

Figure 15-6:
Turning two names into a single calculated field.

This formula consists of the FirstName field, an ampersand (instead of a plus sign, because the gurus want it that way), a single space inside quotation marks, followed by another ampersand, and then the LastName field:

```
[FirstName]&" "&[LastName]
```

When you run this query, Access takes the information from the two fields and puts them together, inserting the space between them so they don't run straight into each other. Figure 15-7 shows the results of this query.

Figure 15-7:
First and last names combine for the more aesthetically pleasing, single field, Full Name.

Expression Builder (Somewhat) to the Rescue

Creating calculated fields presents you with two basic challenges:

✔ Figuring out what the formula should say

✔ Entering the formula so Access recognizes it

Although Access can't help you with the first problem, it tries hard to offer some assistance with the second. When all else fails and you just can't assemble a calculated field exactly the way Access wants it, click the Build button on the toolbar to bring out the Expression Builder.

In theory, Expression Builder walks you through the frustrating syntax of building a calculation (what Access calls an *expression*) that meets all the weird requirements Access puts in place. Theory is a wonderful thing, but it doesn't always bear up to the harsh realities of experience. Although Expression Builder might help some nerdy programmer develop the ultimate formula to unlock time travel, it usually gets in the way of a normal person who simply wants to make a formula that works.

Before resorting to Expression Builder, try a little troubleshooting on your own. If your formulas don't work the way you think they should, double-check the spelling of every field. Most problems come from those simple errors. Also, try including table names with your field names with the [TableName]![FieldName] construction mentioned previously in the chapter. If none of that works, take a deep breath and dive into Expression Builder. Who knows — it might actually help.

The Expression Builder has several parts, as shown in Figure 15-8. You create the expression in the big window at the top. Immediately below that, you find a bunch of buttons for the mathematical and comparison operators available to your formula.

Figure 15-8: The Expression Builder in action.

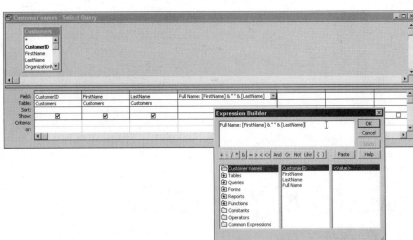

The first of these operators does simple mathematical things: addition, subtraction, division, and multiplication. Next comes the ampersand (&), which combines two text fields, just like a plus sign does for numbers. Continuing to the right, the next two groups of operators (=, >, <, <> and And, Or, Not, and Like) do logical comparisons. Use them to develop expressions for the Criteria section of your queries, when you need a response of *True* or *False*. The final two buttons in this collection shove parentheses into your formulas. Don't bother with them — it's a lot easier to simply press the parenthesis keys on the keyboard.

The lower half of the dialog box contains three windows that work as a team. When you click something in the first window, its contents spill into the second and third windows, depending on how much stuff Access needs to display. The first window on the left lists folders for all the tables, queries, forms, and other stuff in the current database.

Near the bottom of the list in the first window, Access also includes a few items for the Truly Technical Person. These folders contain constants (things such as *true* and *false),* another list of operators available for comparisons and formulas, plus a folder called Common Expressions, which contains stuff that makes sense only when building a report.

Expression Builder works like a big calculator crossed with a word processor. Double-click things in the triple-window display at the bottom to include them in your expression at the top. Click once on the buttons just below the top window to include different operators in the expression. And the entire time you do that, you can always click anywhere in the big pane on top and type whatever you feel like typing.

Does Expression Builder help or hinder? That's a darned good question. It depends on how you learn things and what kind of assistance makes the most sense to you. If you think that Expression Builder might help you, I highly recommend clicking the Help button in the Expression Builder window and letting the Office Assistant walk you through the window personally. As the Office Assistant offers thoughts, explanations, and samples of most everything that Expression Builder knows how to do, you might just hit an epiphany.

Chapter 16

Automated Editing for Big Changes

In This Chapter

▶ Anguishing over the process

▶ Replacing data

▶ Deleting data

▶ Updating data

Correcting an incorrect entry in an Access table is pretty easy. A few clicks, some typing, and {poof!} the problem is gone. But what if you need to correct 26,281 records? Now you're talking about a whole bunch of clicking and typing and clicking and typing. Editing an entire table by hand doesn't sound like a *poof!* experience to me. It sounds more like a clean-the-elephant-herd-with-a-toothbrush kind of thing.

Fortunately, Access has a variety of large-scale housekeeping and editing tools. These tools enable you to make widespread changes to your database without wearing down your fingers in the process. This chapter explores the tools available within Access and gives you examples of how to use them to make quick work of the elephant herd in your life.

First, This Word from Our Paranoid Sponsor

Please, oh *please* read this chapter carefully. The queries explained in here are wonderful tools, but they're also double-edged swords. Used correctly, these automated editing queries save incredible amounts of time. But if something goes wrong, they can inflict incredible amounts of damage to your table with a single click. Any time you plan to remove, change, or add to the data in your tables with one of these queries, take a moment and make a backup copy of at least the table, if not the entire database.

To back up a table, follow these steps:

1. **Open the database file, and click the Tables button on the left side of the Database window.**

   Access displays a list of all the tables in the database.

2. **Right-click the table you plan to edit and choose Copy.**

   Access places a copy of the table onto the Windows clipboard.

3. **Right-click anywhere in the open space of the database window and choose Paste from the pop-up menu.**

   The Paste Table As dialog box appears.

4. **Type a name for the new table (such as Customer table backup), and then click OK.**

   Don't worry about the other options in the dialog box. The default settings work just fine. The dialog box closes, and you now have a copy of the original table.

Quick and Easy Fixes: Replacing Your Mistakes

Automated editing queries have a lot of power. But before hauling out the *really* big guns, here's a technique for small-scale editing. The technique may seem simplistic, but don't be fooled; it's quite handy.

You can practice small-scale editing by using the Replace command as follows:

1. **Open a table in datasheet view.**

2. **Click the column in which you want to change data and choose Edit⇨Replace.**

   The Find and Replace dialog box appears, as shown in Figure 16-1.

3. **In the Find What box, type the value you want to change. In the Replace With box, type a new value.**

   With this information in place, you're ready to start making changes.

4. **Depending on how you want to apply the changes to your table, click one of the buttons on the right side of the window.**

Figure 16-1:
The Find
and Replace
dialog box
enables you
to change
information
throughout
your table.

The moment you click either the Replace or Replace All button, Access *permanently* changes the data in your table. Remember that Access lets you undo only the last change you made, so if you clicked Replace All and updated 12,528 records, Access lets you undo only the very last record that you changed — the other 12,527 records stay in their new form.

- **To find the next thing to change, click Find Next.** The cursor jumps to the next record in the table that contains the text you entered in the Find What box. No changes get made at this point — Access only finds a matching candidate. To make a change, click the Replace button, explained next.

- **To apply your change to the current record, click Replace.** This makes the change *and* moves the cursor to the next matching record in the database. Click Replace again to continue the process. To skip a record without changing it, click Find Next.

- **To make the change *everywhere* in your table, click the Replace All button.** Access won't ask about each individual change. The program assumes that it has your permission to correct everything it finds. Don't choose this option unless you are *absolutely certain* that you want the change made everywhere.

5. **When you finish, click Cancel or the X button at the top-right of the dialog box.**

   The Find and Replace dialog box closes.

If you misspell *munchkin* throughout your data (I *hate* it when that happens) and need to change all its occurrences to the proper spelling, you can simply put the incorrect spelling in Find What, the proper spelling in Replace With, and click the Replace All button. Your computer goes off and does your bidding, changing each and every instance of the word in the Find What box to the word in the Replace With box.

Access gives you a lot of control over the process. In addition to the options you know and love from the Find command (discussed in Chapter 10), Replace offers additional options:

- ✓ **Match Whole Field:** Activates when you click the drop-down arrow. It tells Access to look only for cases where the information in the Find What box *completely matches* an entry in the table. (If the data in your table includes any additional characters in the field — even a single letter — Match Whole Field tells Access to skip it.)

- ✓ **Match Any Part of Field:** Performs the replace action whenever it finds the text in *any portion* of the matching text in the field. For instance, this setting picks the area code out of a phone number. Unfortunately, it also replaces those same three numbers if they appear anywhere else in the phone number, too.

- ✓ **Start of Field:** Replaces the matching text only if it appears at the beginning of the field. This one would replace only the area code in a series of phone numbers without touching the rest of the numbers.

If your editing goes awry, remember that the wonderful Undo option corrects only the *very last record* that Access changed. Just choose Edit⇨Undo from the main menu or press Ctrl+Z.

Different Queries for Different Jobs

Although Select queries do most of the work in Access, they're only one of several query types available to you. You can change the type of query you use by selecting a new query type from the Query menu (found in query design view) or by clicking the Query Type button. Whether you click the down arrow at the right side of the Query Type button or click the Query menu item, a list of query types appears, as shown in Figure 16-2.

Figure 16-2:
Choose a
different
query type
from the list.

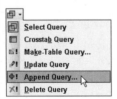

The last four types of queries (Make-Table, Update, Append, and Delete) contain exclamation points to remind you that these types of queries change the way your information is organized. When you work with these four types of queries, you can click the Query View button to preview which records the query affects. I strongly recommend that you do a preview before running any of these queries, because previewing is the only way to make sure that the changes you're making are the ones you intend.

With most types of queries, the difference between using the Run button and the Query View button is minor. But when you use the delete query or the update query, whether you use the Run or the Query View button makes a big difference. When you use the Query View button with these two functions, you see the results without changing your database. If you use the Run button instead, your information changes for all time and eternity (well, unless you have a backup — which you *made,* right?).

You're Outta Here: The Delete Query

The easiest of the editing queries is the delete query. Unfortunately, the Delete query is also one of the most dangerous. (Why do *easy* and *dangerous* always go together in computer programs?)

Creating a delete query works just like creating a select query. In fact, they're identical, except for the query type setting. Before you create a delete query, create a select query to test your criteria and make sure that the query finds the records you want. After you know that the criteria work correctly, change the select query to a delete query with the Query Type setting mentioned in the preceding section.

Here's how to build a delete query:

1. **Create a normal select query.**

2. **Set up criteria to identify the records you want to delete.**

3. **Run the select query to make sure that it finds *only* the records that you want to work with.**

   If the select query finds *other* records as well, adjust the criteria so that the extras don't match.

4. **Return to design view.**

5. **Click the Query Type button, and then choose Delete Query from the drop-down list that appears (or choose Query⇨Delete Query).**

   To show that Access heard your command, it changes the name of the query in the title bar to *Delete Query.* The query form itself also changes. Instead of a Sort line, the query now shows a Delete line, just like the one in Figure 16-3.

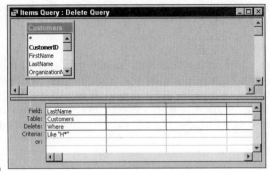

6. **Start the query by clicking the Run Query button.**

   Access somberly displays a message saying that it's about to delete a bunch of rows from your table, and asking whether you really, *really* want to go ahead with the process. It also reminds you that after it deletes records, it can't get the data back.

7. **If you want to delete the records, click Yes.**

   The query runs; Access finds the records that match the criteria, and removes those records from the table.

That's all you need to do.

You can't undo changes you make by using the delete query. After you delete these records, they're gone for good, never to be seen again.

You can create delete queries that use more than one table to locate information. However, be careful when you use multiple tables because the number of changes you make can increase dramatically if your queries don't work quite right. Again, I suggest backing up your database and running a select query first to list the records that you want to delete.

Making changes gets a bit more complicated when deleting records from more than one table. Access can do this only if the records are linked one-to-one — if each record in one table is linked to one record in the other table. When you look at the relationship grid at the top of the query screen, one-to-one links appear with the number 1 above both ends of the connection.

One-to-many links, on the other hand, show a number 1 on one side and an infinity sign (∞) on the other. You can't delete records in a one-to-many relationship with only one query. Instead, it takes two separate delete queries — one removes records from the first table, and another yanks them from the other end of the relationship.

Depending on the database settings, Access may not even *let* you delete the records. One-to-many deletions involve the touchy technical issue of *referential integrity*. Loosely translated, this means that records *must* exist in one table because *matching* records depend on them in some other table. Life gets weird with referential integrity, but many corporate databases use referential integrity because it ensures that huge mistakes don't happen by accident. If you work in a big company and think that you need to delete data but keep running into a referential integrity error, contact your Information Systems folks. After they stop hyperventilating, they can help you.

Making Big Changes

There comes a time in every database's life when it needs to change. Fortunately, you can make radical changes to a database automatically by using the update query. The update query enables you to select certain records and then change specific data in the records as you want.

As with other types of queries that modify your data (particularly the delete query discussed earlier in the chapter), make sure that your query works with only the records that you want to change. Setting up and testing your criteria with a select query before running the query for real is always a good idea.

When you select the update query by choosing Update Query from the Query menu or the Query Type list, your query grid changes to resemble the one shown in Figure 16-4.

Although the query looks normal overall, this grid includes a new line labeled Update To. You can use any criteria to select your records, just as in a normal select query. For example, you may want to select all the records where the customer's last name is Harrison. To do so, set up your criterion with the LastName field and the entry Harrison on the Criteria line.

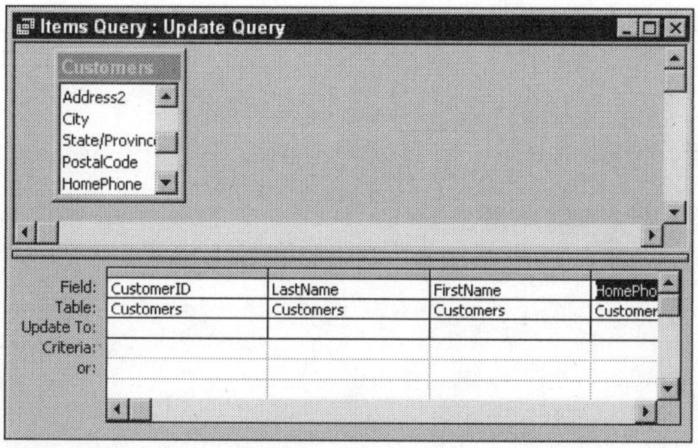

Figure 16-4:
An update query has a new row called Update To.

For some reason, the Harrison family has decided to reduce complexity and increase ambiguity by adopting the same first name: Ralph. You can go through and change each record by hand, but using an update query is easier: Simply type Ralph on the Update To line below FirstName. Your update query screen looks like the one shown in Figure 16-5.

Figure 16-5:
The update
query
finds all
customers
whose last
name is
Harrison and
changes the
first name
to Ralph.

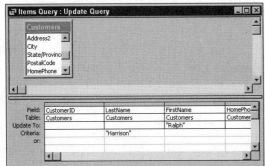

When you run the query, you get a warning message that you're about to update records. Click Yes to go ahead and make your changes.

An update query can involve more than one table. Suppose that you want to add a notation for each customer who has an auction item with a minimum bid of more than $100. Here's how to involve multiple tables:

1. **In the query design window, select the tables you need to find the records that you want to update.**

   In this case, you need the Customers and Items tables.

2. **Select the fields that you need to create the select query.**

   For the sample query, I needed the Notes column from the Customers table (because it gets updated) and the MinimumBid column from the Items table. For your query, choose the fields that help you find the records to change, plus the fields that get changed during the process.

3. **Click the Query Type button to change, um, the query type.**

   Access shifts a few rows in the query form, leaving you with a new row marked Update To, along with the Criteria rows you know and love.

4. **Enter the search (select) criteria to locate the records that you want to update.**

   In this example, I want to change records with a minimum bid that's greater than 100. To find those, I put > **100** in the Criteria row under MinimumBid.

5. **Enter the new value(s) for the field(s) to be updated.**

This item tells Access what to do in the rows that match your specification in the previous step. For this example, I want Access to add the phrase *Big Bucks* to the Notes field for every auction item with a minimum bid over 100. In Figure 16-6, I entered "Big Bucks!" in the Update To row in the Notes column.

Figure 16-6:
This query finds all records of items bought for more than $100 and enters the helpful notation "Big Bucks!" in the record's Note field.

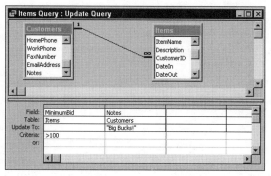

6. **Run the query by clicking the Run button or by choosing Query⇨Run from the main menu.**

Access dutifully tells you how many rows will be updated and offers you a chance to change your mind (click Cancel). Too cool!

You can also make changes based upon the existing value in a field. To do that, you use a calculation like the ones I describe in Chapter 15. Suppose, for example, that you want to add 10 percent to the MinimumBid of all items from customers in Ohio. To make changes based on an existing value in a field, follow these steps:

1. **In the update query window, select the field that you want to search with and enter an appropriate search condition.**

In this example, I chose the State/Province field and entered a criterion of OH.

2. **Select the field that you want to update, and then enter the new value in the Update To row.**

In the example, I entered the formula **[Items]![MinimumBid] * 1.1** under MinimumBid, as shown in Figure 16-7.

The square brackets tell Access that you're talking about a table or a field. The first set of square brackets contains the table name, and the second set contains the field name. An exclamation point separates them.

3. Run the update query to make the changes to your data.

Figure 16-7:
This query
finds all
Ohio cus-
tomers and
increases
their
minimum
bids by 10
percent.

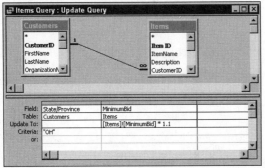

I know I said it already, but I'll say it again: *Be careful.* The update and delete queries can affect a lot of data and cannot be undone. If you run a query without entering any criteria, the update (or delete) is performed on *every* record in the table! At a minimum, run the query as a select query first to make sure that you're selecting the right records; then change the query to an update or delete query. Better still, have a good backup in place.

Part IV
Turning Your Table into a Book

Now maybe these folks got a decent disaster recovery plan and maybe they don't...

DANGER
WILD RHINOCEROS

In this part . . .

Someone said that the computer revolution would do away with paper. Needless to say, that person was wrong. (Last I heard, that person is now compiling the annual psychic predictions page for one of the national tabloids.)

In other chapters, you put data into tables and then mix it up a little. Now it's time to pull the data out, clean it up a bit, and record it for posterity on the printed page.

Access has some strong reporting tools to make your multi-thousand-page reports look truly cool. Better still, it offers some great summary tools to make those multi-thousand-page reports a thing of the past. Stick your head into this part and see what you can see!

Chapter 17

AutoReport: Like the Model-T, It's Clunky but It Runs

*W*hat do you do if someone (for example, your boss) wants to see all the revelations you made using your datasheets, tables, and queries? And then, what if your boss wants to share the aforementioned revelations with the rest of the company? The odds are good that the entire management team doesn't want to crowd around your monitor and study thousands of records and dozens of queries (besides, your cubicle isn't *that* big).

Lucky for you, Access includes tools for creating and printing reports. In fact, Access sees report-making as just another part of the database experience. Reports take information from your database (specifically, reports can draw from tables or queries) and organize that information according to your instructions. Access even includes report wizards to walk you through the steps of designing a report to meet your needs.

You probably found this chapter because the boss wants a report *right now,* so the following pages take you to the AutoReport factory, where a cadre of digital elves are anxious to create a quick report for you. If your boss gives you the time, the last section in this chapter (plus the other chapters in this part) helps you spruce up the finished report a bit, making it a thing of beauty in addition to an object of truth.

AutoReport Basics for High-Speed Information

Think of AutoReport as your very own information assembly line. The AutoReport tools excel at one task: building a single-table report according to your specifications. Fire up the software, tell it what you want, and your report is as good as finished.

Although AutoReport works with only one table or query at a time, it still offers some choices. AutoReport builds two kinds of reports: tabular and columnar. Both reports organize the same data, but in different ways:

- **Tabular AutoReport:** Places all information for each record on one row, with a separate column for each field. The tabular format puts the field names above each column (often trimming the names until you can't make heads or tails of what they are) and squashes the columns themselves together in the name of fitting everything horizontally on a single page.

- **Columnar AutoReport:** Organizes each record vertically on the page, in two columns — one for the names of the fields and one for the contents of the fields. If the table has more than 15 or so fields, each record generally starts on a new page.

I don't have a profound answer for when to use one AutoReport layout or the other. The choice is more a matter of taste and aesthetics than anything else. The only advice I can offer is that the tabular format is generally more useful if your report has lots of records with small fields, and the columnar format is often better for reports with large fields but fewer records.

The query advantage

The fact that Access lets you base a report on a query is wonderful. When you build a report on a table, you get a report containing each and every record in the table. But what if you want only a few of the records?

Access makes it easy. Create a query and then base the report upon that query.

The advantages don't stop there. If you create a query based on multiple tables, Access neatly organizes your results into a single datasheet. If your query produces the information that you want in its datasheet, a report based on that query's results organizes and presents the information in the way you want. (In Chapter 12, I show you how to create queries using more than one table.)

Whether you choose the tabular or columnar format, feel free to change AutoReport's creation however you want. Use the report as a starting point, and add titles, headers, footers, cool formatting, and more. Because AutoReport builds a normal Access report, a quick trip to design mode puts all report development and formatting tools at your command. Check out Chapters 19 and 20 for more information about formatting, headers, and the other cool tricks available in the report system.

Putting the Wheels of Informational Progress in Motion

Although AutoReport includes separate tools for building columnar and tabular reports, the good news is that both systems work the same way. The only difference between these two styles is in how they organize the data in the finished report. From a *how this works* standpoint, they're the same.

Follow these steps to create either a columnar or tabular AutoReport:

1. **In your database window, click the Reports button in the Objects bar, and then click <u>N</u>ew.**

   The New Report dialog box appears, showing all the report types from which you can choose.

2. **Click AutoReport: Columnar or AutoReport: Tabular depending on your informational needs.**

   After you click the AutoReport entry in the list, the graphic in the New Report window changes to a tiny image of the report layout.

3. **Click the drop-down list at the bottom of the dialog box to select which table or query you want to use.**

   Scroll through the options until you find the table or query on which you want to base your report (like Figure 17-1). Remember that each AutoReport covers only one query or table.

Figure 17-1: The wizard creates a columnar report based on the Auctions table.

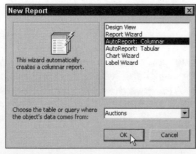

4. **Click OK.**

   After a bit of clunking and thunking, Access displays your finished report in print preview mode (as shown in Figure 17-2), which is programmerese for "This is what the report looks like if you print it." I show you some neat print preview tools in the next section, "Previewing Your Informational Masterpiece."

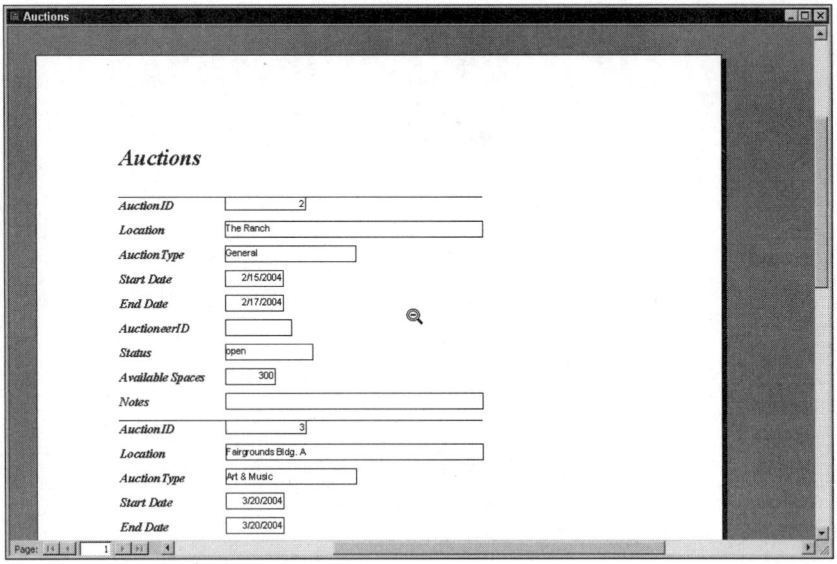

Figure 17-2:
Use the print preview window to, well, preview what your report will look like when it's printed.

![Screenshot of the Auctions print preview window showing report fields including Auction ID, Location, Auction Type, Start Date, End Date, AuctioneerID, Status, Available Spaces, and Notes.]

Although Access thinks quite a lot of the report (it's having one of those proud parent moments), usually the report has a look that only a digital parent can love. Before sending the report out into the cold, cruel world, you probably should take it into design view and dress it up a bit. See the "Truth Is Beauty, So Make Your Reports Look Great" section, later in this chapter, for the basics of spiffing up a dull AutoReport.

Previewing Your Informational Masterpiece

When you're in print preview mode, you can't do a whole lot with your report except print it. But print preview does enable you to check out exactly what your document looks like. Table 17-1 shows the tools print preview provides to help with your inspection.

Table 17-1	Print Preview Tools	
Tool	*What It Is*	*What It Does*
	View button	Allows you to flip back and forth from design view to print preview
	Print button	Sends your report to the you know-what
	Zoom button	Alternates zooming levels (between fit to screen and 100%)
	One Page button	Displays one page at a time
	Two Pages button	Displays two pages at a time
	Multiple Pages button	Displays up to six pages at a time
100%	Zoom control	Unlike the other Zoom button, selects one of ten zoom levels
Close	Close button	Closes the print preview window
Setup	Setup button	Sets up the page and the printer
W	Office Links button	Sends the report to Microsoft Word or Excel (assuming that Word or Excel are installed on your computer)

Zooming around your report

In Figure 17-2, the entire page is not visible. The parts that show look pretty good, but you can't see the whole record, let alone the whole page. In Figure 17-3, Access displays the report full-size, just like it looks on the printed page.

Thankfully, Access knows a lot more display tricks than simply shrinking the page until it fits onto your monitor. Here's a quick romp through the visual toolbox awaiting you in the report system:

✔ Need to see what the whole page looks like? Click the Zoom button and change the setting to Fit. This displays the full-page view shown in Figure 17-3. Access calls the full-page view the Fit view because it *fits* the whole page on your screen.

✔ Alternatively, you can use the Zoom control (the one with the text in it, not the one that looks like a magnifying glass) and choose other zooming levels from 10% all the way to 1000%. If, for some reason, you wanted 82%, you can also type a value directly into the box and press Enter to see the results.

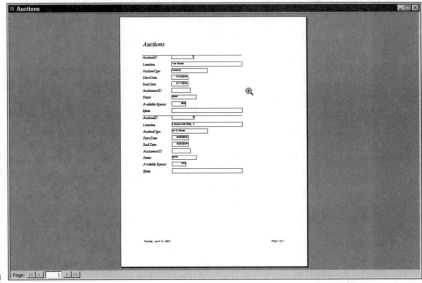

When you move your mouse pointer over the preview of your report, your pointer changes to look like a magnifying glass. Use this to zoom in to the report and check individual sections. Just click what you want to see, and Access swoops down, enlarging that portion of the report so you can see it clearly. Click again, and your view changes back to the previous setting.

Note that clicking any of the page-number buttons (one page, two page, multiple pages) sets the zoom view to the Fit view setting. When you have two pages showing, the odd-numbered page is always on the left, unlike book publishing, which puts the odd-numbered page on the right — unless the typesetting department is having a very bad day.

If you choose View➪Pages from the main menu, Access offers quite the selection of page view options, as you see in Figure 17-4. Set your system to show one page, two pages, or a mind-numbing (and eye-squinting) twelve pages on a single screen.

Calling on the pop-up menu

You can right-click anywhere on the print preview screen to see a pop-up menu that gives you the choice of switching the zoom or viewing a specific number of pages. When you select the Zoom command, a submenu appears with the same choices that appear on the Zoom control. Two other commands are available when you right-click the print preview screen:

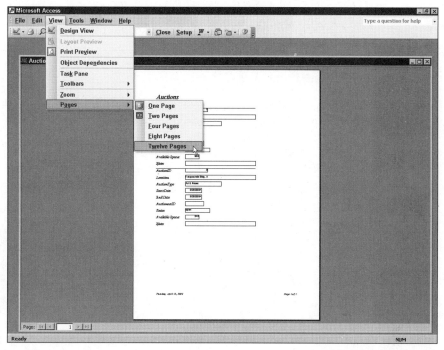

Figure 17-4:
Preview up to 12 pages of your report at a time.

✔ **Save As/Export:** Choose this command to save your Access report in a format used by another program.

A very cool feature of Access is its capability of exporting to HTML. That's right — you can create a report and then save it as a Web page by exporting to HTML.

✔ **Send:** Choose this command to take a copy of your Access report and send it as an e-mail message.

Truth Is Beauty, So Make Your Reports Look Great

After looking at your report in the print preview window, you have a decision to make. If you're happy with how your report looks, great! Go ahead and print the document. However, a few minutes of extra work does wonders for even the simplest reports.

Start with the basics in the Page Setup dialog box. To get there, choose File➪ Page Setup from any Report view in Access or simply click the Setup button on the toolbar. This dialog box provides three tabs of options to ensure that your report is as effective and attractive as it can be.

The Margins tab

The Margins tab of the Page Setup dialog box controls the width of the margins in your report — no surprises here. Figure 17-5 displays your options. The page has four margins, so the dialog box includes a setting for each one (Top, Bottom, Left, and Right).

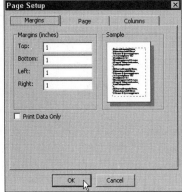

Figure 17-5:
Set the margins of your report on the, uh, Margins tab.

Here is how you set or change margins:

1. **Double-click in the appropriate box (Top, Bottom, Left, or Right) and type a new setting.**

   Access automatically uses whatever Windows thinks is your local unit of measurement (inches, centimeters, or whatever else you measure with). On the right side of the dialog box, Access displays a sample image, which shows you how your current margin settings work on a page.

2. **Make all the changes you want to your report's layout, and then click OK.**

3. **Look at your report in print preview to check your adjustments.**

   If you need to tweak the report, simply go back to Page Setup and play with the options until everything looks just right.

The last item on the Margins tab is the Print Data Only check box. I guess the programmers can't think of anywhere else to put this box, because it has nothing to do with margin settings. If you select this option by checking its box, Access prints only the data in your records; field headings won't appear on the printed document. Use Print Data Only if you plan to use preprinted forms. Otherwise, leave it alone, because your report looks pretty odd without any field labels.

The Page tab

The Page tab tells Access about the sheet of paper you print your report on, including its size and layout, as well as what printer you keep the paper in. You make some of the most fundamental decisions about how your report looks from the Page tab of the Page Setup dialog box (see Figure 17-6).

Figure 17-6:
The Page tab enables you to choose a printer, page size, and more.

The Orientation box sets the direction that your report prints on paper:

✔ Portrait (the way that this book and most magazines appear) is the default choice.

✔ Landscape pages lie on their side, giving you more horizontal room but less vertical space.

Deciding whether to use Portrait or Landscape is more important than you may think. For tabular reports, landscape orientation displays more information for each field, thanks to the wider columns. Unfortunately, the columns get shorter in the process. (After all, that piece of paper is only so big.) Columnar reports don't do very well in a landscape orientation because they usually need more vertical space than horizontal space.

Your other choices for the Page tab are determined by your printing capabilities. The Size drop-down list in the Paper section of the tab enables you to choose the size of the paper you want to use (refer to Figure 17-6). The Source drop-down list gives you the option to use your regular paper feed (the Automatically Select choice), use another automatic source, or manually feed your paper into the printer.

The last part of the Page tab lets you choose a specific printer for this report. You can choose the Default Printer option (Access uses whatever printer Windows says to use) or the Use Specific Printer option (where you choose the printer yourself). Most of the time, you can leave this setting alone; it's useful only if you want to force this report to always come from one specific printer at your location. If you click the Use Specific Printer option, the Printer button comes to life. Click this button to choose from among your available printers.

The Columns tab

You get to make more decisions about your report's size and layout on the Columns tab, as shown in Figure 17-7.

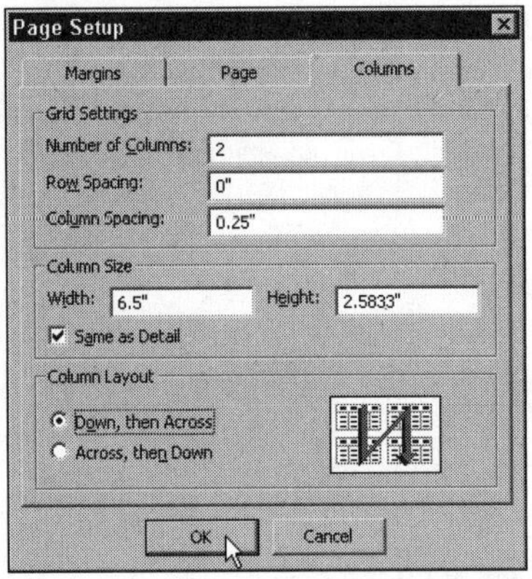

Figure 17-7: The Column Layout area of the Columns tab enables you to format a report with snaking columns, like a telephone directory.

The Columns tab of the Page Setup dialog box is divided into three sections:

✓ **Grid Settings:** Controls how many columns your report uses and how far apart the different elements are from each other

✓ **Column Size:** Adjusts the height and width of your columns

✔ **Column Layout:** Defines the way that Access places your data in columns (and uses an easy-to-understand graphic to show you as well)

The default number of columns is one column to a page, but you can easily change the setting to suit your particular report. Just keep in mind that with more columns, your report may show less information for each record. If you use so many columns that some of the information won't fit, Access conveniently displays a warning.

If the number of columns you select fit (or if you're willing to lose your view of the information in some of your fields), click OK to see a view of how your document looks with multiple columns.

The Grid Settings section of the Columns tab also adjusts row and column spacing:

✔ **Row Spacing:** Adjusts the space (measured in your local unit of distance) between the horizontal rows. Simply click the Row Spacing box and enter the amount of space that you want to appear between each row. Again, this setting is a matter of personal preference.

✔ **Column Spacing:** Adjusts the width of your columns. If you narrow this width, you make more room, but your entries are more difficult to read.

The bottom section of the Columns tab, called Column Layout, lets you control how your columns are organized on the page. You have two options here:

✔ **Down, then Across:** Access starts a new record in the same column (if the preceding record has not filled up the page). For example, Record 13 starts below Record 12 on the page (provided there's enough room), and then Records 14 and 15 appear in the second column.

✔ **Across, then Down:** Access starts Record 13 across from Record 12, and then puts Record 14 below Record 12, and Record 15 below Record 13, and so on.

If your columns don't look exactly right the first time, keep trying. Small adjustments to the row and column spacing produce big changes across a long report. The on-screen preview gives you an easy check on how the report looks — and prevents you from killing multiple trees in the quest for perfection.

Chapter 18

Wizardly Help with Labels, Charts, and Multilevel Reports

*A*utoReports (covered in Chapter 17) are just the tip of the Access report iceberg. If you're so inclined, you can use Access to generate more complex reports. You can even create useful printouts that you probably never thought of as reports — mailing labels and charts. Don't be daunted — Access provides kind, gentle wizards to help you along your report-creating journey.

Creating Labels

When the bulk-mailing urge strikes, there's nothing like a good stack of mailing labels to really make your day. At moments like this, Access rides to the rescue with the Label Wizard, one of the many report wizards in Access.

The Label Wizard formats your data for use with any size or type of label on the planet. Mailing labels, file labels, shipping labels, name tags — the list goes on forever. Best of all, the Label Wizard does all the hard stuff with the wave of a wand.

In the past, one of the hardest aspects of making labels was explaining the label layout to the software. At some point, Microsoft engineers obviously endured this hardship themselves because they built the specifications for hundreds of labels from popular manufacturers right into the Label Wizard.

If you happen to use labels from Avery, Herma, Zweckform, or any other maker listed in the wizard's manufacturer list, just tell the wizard the manufacturer's product number. The wizard sets up the report dimensions for you according to the maker's specifications. Life just doesn't get much easier than that.

Before firing up the Label Wizard, figure out what information you want on the labels. Unless you want a label for everything in the table, you need to create a query that chooses the right pieces from your table, sorts them into order, and generally gets them ready for their trip to the sticky-backed paper. Refer to Part III to review the procedures for creating queries.

With your table or query in hand, you can make the labels. Follow these steps to create your label report:

1. **In the database window, click the Reports button in the Objects bar.**

   Access lists the reports in your database.

2. **Click New to create a new report.**

   The New Report dialog box appears, showing you all the available report types, including the all-important Label Wizard.

3. **Click Label Wizard.**

   The little picture to the left of the list changes into a page of labels to confirm that Access heard you correctly, as shown in Figure 18-1.

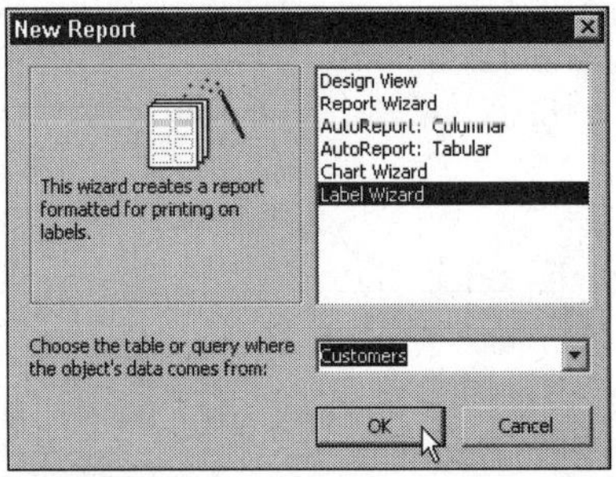

Figure 18-1:
Access prepares to prepare your labels.

4. **Click the down arrow near the bottom of the dialog box.**

   A drop-down list appears, asking you to choose the table or query that you want the object's data to come from.

5. **Click the query or table that you want to use with the labels.**

   The wizard is ready, and the data awaits!

6. Click OK to start the Label Wizard.

In a flurry of disk activity, the Label Wizard dialog box appears, as shown in Figure 18-2.

7. Click the down arrow next to the Filter by Manufacturer box and select your label's manufacturer from the drop-down list that appears.

Access makes creating labels as painless as possible — provided that you use labels from a company that the Microsoft developers know about:

a. If your label manufacturer is on the Label Wizard's list, click the company name. In the top of the Label Wizard window, Access displays that company's labels by product number. Scroll through the list until you find the number that matches the one on your label box. When you find it, skip merrily along to Step 9. (Lucky you!) If the number isn't on the list, proceed to the next step.

b. If your label manufacturer isn't in the Label Wizard's list, take another look at your box of labels. Because Avery controls so much of the label market, other manufacturers often put the equivalent Avery code on their product, usually with the notation like Avery *xxxx* labels, with the *xxxx* part replaced by an Avery code. If you see that on your label box, select Avery as the label maker, and then look for the right label number in the list. If you find it, skip ahead to Step 9. If you still don't find the number, go to Step 8.

If all else fails and you simply cannot find in the list a label like yours, you can easily define one. Simply click the Customize button and follow the prompts. The biggest trick is telling Access the size of your labels (use a ruler for that) and how many labels across there are on a sheet (use your fingers to count those).

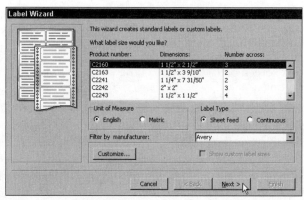

Figure 18-2: The Label Wizard knows almost every label type ever made.

8. **If the Label Wizard doesn't know the details of your labels, click Customize to add them to the Wizard's repertoire.**

Building a customized label entry isn't hard, but it *does* take a few steps. Thankfully, Access walks you through them pretty painlessly. True, the software asks for a rather obnoxious number of measurements that describe your labels, but at least it uses them all. Refer to the information sheet or configuration details that came with your labels for help finding the required measurements. When you finish entering the information, click OK to continue with Step 10, the font selection.

9. **Click Next.**

The dialog shown in Figure 18-3 appears, offering you a slew of font choices.

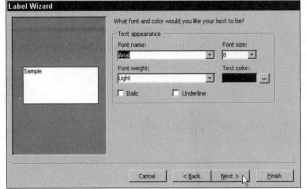

Figure 18-3:
Choose your font wisely; the entire label will use it.

10. **Choose the font, size, weight, and color for the text on your label and then click Next.**

You can choose any font available in Windows. Change the text size, change how bold it looks (what the technogeeks call *font weight*), and even add italics, underline, and a new text color (you need a color printer for that). As you make changes, the sample text screen on the left side of the window shows your current settings.

Keep in mind that the formatting you choose applies to *all* the text on *every* label. If you add italics, the *entire label* — and every label — comes out that way. Add special formatting sparingly because a little goes a long way.

11. **Select the data you want to appear on the label and type any other text that you want to print.**

12. **Select the fields from the Available Fields list and click the > button to transfer the field to the Prototype Label box, as shown in Figure 18-4.**

    If you want fields on separate rows, press Enter or use an arrow key to move to the next row. When you double-click a field (or click the > button), that field always transfers to the highlighted line in the Prototype Label box. Access figures out how many lines can print on your label, based on the label's size and the font size you're using.

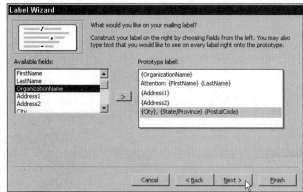

Figure 18-4: Choose the fields that you want Access to print on your labels.

If you want to print a particular character, word, or other text message on every label, just click wherever you want it to appear and then type your text. For example, to insert a comma between the city, state, or province on your mailing labels, select the City field, type a comma, press the spacebar, and then select the State/Province field. When Access prints each label, it puts the city name, adds a comma, and then fills in the rest of the information.

13. **Click Next when the fields look simply marvelous (or at least passably cute).**

    Now Access wants to know how to sort the labels.

14. **Choose the field for Access to use to sort your labels, as shown in Figure 18-5, and then click Next.**

If you plan a bulk mailing with discounted postage, check with your local postal authority for details about how it wants your mail organized. They're picky about such things, but you and Access can handle it.

15. **Type a name for the label report, and then click Finish to see your creation in action.**

    If the labels are *almost* right but still need a few tweaks, click the Design button on the toolbar (the one that looks like a triangle and pencil) and modify the design as needed.

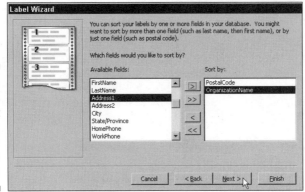

Figure 18-5:
Tell Access
in what
order you
want the
labels to
print.

Using the Chart Wizard in Your Report

Generally, reports are just a collection of words and numbers, organized to allow you to make sense of the information. But sometimes words and numbers don't paint enough of the story. At times like these, a graph makes the perfect antidote, filling in the heads, tails, and other sundry parts of your report's informational picture. As the saying goes, a picture is worth a thousand words (so add a few graphs and save a bunch of trees).

Access includes an artsy wizard for just such occasions. Say hello to the Chart Wizard, creator of preeminent pies, beautiful bars, and luscious lines with just a few mouse clicks.

To build a chart (or graph, because Access uses the terms interchangeably), you need at least two fields (but no more than six). One field contains the numbers making up the bars, lines, pie slices, or other graphical representations in your graph. The other field should hold labels identifying the various numbers (otherwise, your graph looks swell but says nothing). All the fields must come from a single table or query.

Because the wizard is fluent in several types of charts, finding a layout that works perfectly for your data is easy. The wizard offers five major types of charts:

- **Line charts:** The classic chart from geometry class is reborn into the digital world. The line chart is great for showing trends over time.

- **Bar, cone, and column charts:** Variations of the line chart, these charts use vertical or horizontal bars to display your data. Good for comparing groups of data against each other (such as sales by quarter over a period of years).

✔ **Pie and donut charts:** These charts take a series of numbers and display them as percentages of a total. Perfect for showing how much each division contributed to total corporate profit, how many people from various countries buy a product, and anything else that requires a slice-of-the-pie approach. (They also add a nice touch to breakfast meetings, particularly when accompanied by a steaming cappuccino or nice cup of hot chocolate.)

✔ **Area charts:** A cross between a line chart and pie chart, these graphs show how the total of a *group* of figures changed over time. Perfect for showing how costs and profits add up to total revenue over several quarters.

✔ **XY and bubble charts:** These charts are the odd uncles and peculiar third cousins of the Access chart family. They chart two data points as they relate to a third data point (such as the number of women who visited the club each month, displayed by income group). In the vernacular, this translates to *unless you have a darn good reason, don't even bother with these charts.* These charts are wonderful for engineers, economists, scientists, statisticians, and anyone else who probably needs more to do with their free time.

Building the chart-of-your-heart takes only a few minutes, thanks to the wizard's helpful and competent assistance. Follow these steps to build a chart:

1. **In the database window, click the Reports button and then click <u>N</u>ew.**

   The New Report dialog box appears, proudly displaying your report options.

2. **Choose Chart Wizard.**

3. **Click the down arrow next to the Choose the Table or Query box, and then select a table or query for your chart.**

4. **Click OK.**

   Access opens the table or query you selected, takes a look inside, and then displays the fields available for the chart.

5. **Select the numeric and text fields for your chart, and then click <u>N</u>ext.**

6. **Use the > and < buttons to add or remove fields in the list.**

   The >> and << buttons move *all* the available fields.

7. **Click <u>N</u>ext.**

   Access displays samples of every graph it knows how to make.

8. **Click the picture of your chart type and then click <u>N</u>ext.**

As you click a chart (see Figure 18-6), the wizard briefly describes the chart and offers a few technical thoughts on how it works. The wizard explains how to display the data in your chart, but ultimately lets you make whatever changes you want.

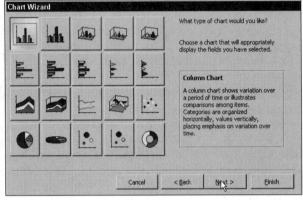

Figure 18-6:
Access displays and describes its available graphs.

9. **Click Next when the chart meets your expectations (or when you simply tire of messing with the whole affair).**

10. **Drag and drop fields from the column on the left into the various positions in the graph. Double-click the graph items to change their summary options, and make whatever adjustments you want.**

11. **Click the Preview Chart button (as shown in Figure 18-7) to see how the chart looks as you make changes.**

12. **Click Next when you're satisfied with your chart.**

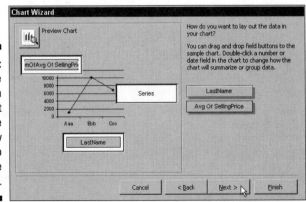

Figure 18-7:
Make changes in your chart and use the Preview button to see the result.

13. **Type a name for your new chart in the window that appears.**

14. **Click Finish to see the product of your labor.**

Creating More Advanced Reports

The AutoReport Wizard (refer to Chapter 17 for details) quickly creates simple reports from a single query or table. When you (or, more likely, your boss) need something *right now,* the AutoReport Wizard is a great tool.

Sometimes, however, your reporting needs call for more detail, more organization, or simply more data. For these more complex reports, seek help from the Report Wizard. This master of informational presentation lets you add fields from as many tables as you want and organize those fields into as many levels as you choose. Each new level gets its own personalized section of the report, complete with a custom header and footer. After a spin with the Report Wizard, your data won't want to go anywhere else.

Creating complex reports involves more steps than creating the simple ones, but the results are *definitely* worth the extra effort. Because complex reports include a lot more options, I split the steps to build the report into several sections according to topic. Each section includes some explanations of what the settings do and how to use them.

Starting the wizard and choosing some fields

In the end, a multilevel report looks a lot different than a basic report, but they both start out the same way. Begin your report creation safari by following these steps:

1. **In the database window, click the Objects bar's Reports button.**

   As usual, Access displays the reports currently in your database.

2. **Click New to create a new report.**

   The New Report dialog box appears, showing you all the report types you can choose from. (Bored? Don't worry — the cool stuff comes soon!)

3. **Click Report Wizard, and then click OK.**

   Don't choose a table or query for the Report Wizard to use — just leave that space blank and click OK. The dialog box shown in Figure 18-8 appears.

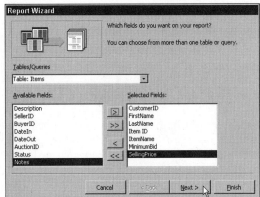

Figure 18-8:
The Report
Wizard
enables you
to add fields
from one or
more tables
or queries in
your
database.

4. **Click the down arrow in the Tables/Queries box and, from the drop-down list that appears, select the first table or query that contains the fields you need for the report.**

   The Available Fields list updates to show everything that the selected item contains. Because you didn't select a particular table or query to use back in Step 3, the wizard assumes that you want to mix and match things from all over the database.

5. **Select the fields that you want in the report by double-clicking the field names or clicking the greater than (>, >>) or less than (<, <<) buttons.**

   The greater than buttons move fields into the Selected Fields list; the less than buttons move fields out of the list.

   Although clicking the buttons is fun, the easiest way to move a field from one side to another is by double-clicking it. No matter which side the field starts on, double-clicking moves the field to the opposite list.

6. **Repeat Steps 4 and 5 for each table or query you need that contains fields for the report.**

7. **Click Next after all the fields are listed in the Selected Fields side of the dialog box.**

   The dialog box shown in Figure 18-9 appears.

   Report Wizard lets you choose the field to use when organizing your report. You also see a sample page based on the Report Wizard's extensive analysis of your data (yes, that means the wizard *guessed*). Access may or may not correctly discern how you want the data to appear (remember, it's only a program), so take a close look at each of the report-organization choices and decide which one displays the information in the most effective way. To see a different organization, click one of the *by* choices on the left side of the dialog box.

   If you don't see the dialog box shown in Figure 18-9, that's okay. It simply means that you're using only one table or query in your report.

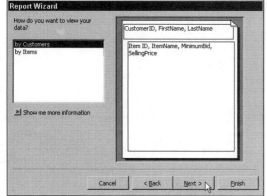

Figure 18-9:
Report
Wizard lets
you choose
how you
want your
information
grouped.

If you don't want the records sorted into groups, click the very last entry in the *by* list (in this case, the by Customers entry). For reasons beyond my comprehension (but that probably makes sense to a demented programmer somewhere), this action makes Access lump together all the records, displaying them without sorting them into groups.

Creating new groupings

Access takes organization a step further by adding more grouping options — groups based on different fields than just the one you specified in the preceding section. The dialog box shown in Figure 18-10 lists the available fields on the left side of the window. Choose as many or as few as you want. To add a new group based on a particular field, click the field name and then click the greater than (>) button. The wizard adjusts the sample page to show what your report looks like with the additional group, as shown in Figure 18-11.

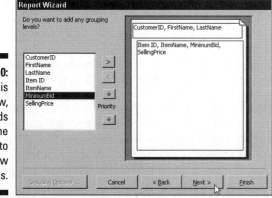

Figure 18-10:
In this
window,
drag fields
from the
left to
create new
groupings.

Figure 18-11:
Narrow
the reports
organization
by adding
more
groups.

You can rearrange the grouping if you want. For example, you can click ItemName and then click the up arrow between the two windowpanes (refer to Figure 18-11). The wizard groups the report first by ItemName and then by customer information.

Each of the fields you select to organize your report creates a new section. Each of these sections has its own header and footer area that can hold information from your database or information that you add directly to the report through design view after the wizard finishes its work.

Sorting out the details

Access calls the fields that aren't grouped as headers *detail records*. Report Wizard lets you sort those records by the remaining fields, which you can organize in either ascending or descending order, as shown in Figure 18-12. To sort records by any given field, click the down arrow and select the field from the drop-down list. Then click the button at the right to change the sorting order from ascending (with the letters going from *A* at the top to *Z* at the bottom) to descending (with the letters going from *Z* at the top to *A* at the bottom). See Chapter 10 for more details about sorting on more than one field.

Click the Summary Options button to reveal the Summary Options dialog box, as shown in Figure 18-13. (If your report doesn't include any number fields, you won't see a Summary Options button.) The Summary Options dialog box lets you tell Access to summarize your data with a number of statistical tools, including totals (Sum), averages (Avg), minimums (Min), and maximums (Max). Check the boxes next to the operations that you want performed on the fields in your report.

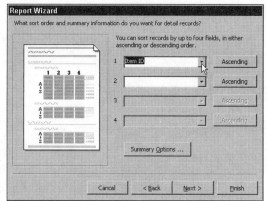

Figure 18-12:
Sort this
report by
ItemID.

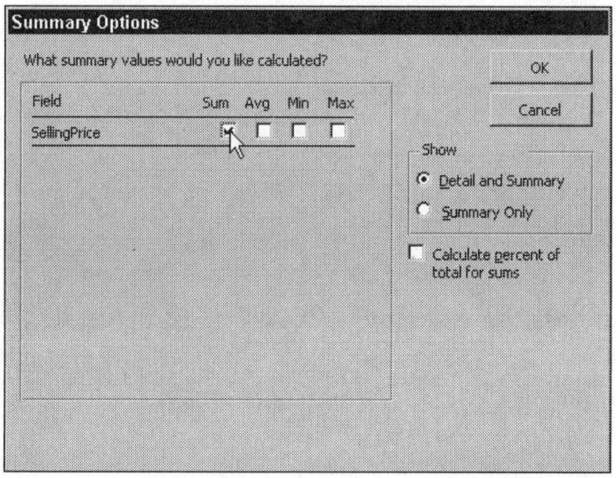

Figure 18-13:
Access
offers to add
a bunch of
summaries
and
statistics in
your report.

For example, the auction company wants Access to add all minimum bids for each group (that's what the Sum check mark does) and display the average minimum bid for each group (refer to Figure 18-13).

If you want to see both the data and the summary, click the Detail and Summary option in the Show section of the dialog box. If you need to see only the summarized information, click the Summary Only option. If you click the Calculate Percent of Total for Sums check box, Access calculates the total amount of the field and tells you the percentage of each record's contribution to that total.

Choosing a layout style

With the data selected, grouped, and sorted, the Report Wizard now takes up the task of making everything look beautiful. To save you from a lot of extra work, the wizard offers a series of ready-to-use layouts designed for clear presentation and easy reading.

Cruise through these steps to put the finishing touches on your soon-to-be-beautiful report:

1. In the Layout area, choose a style, as shown in Figure 18-14.

Access shows you a sample of the layout on the left side of the window. Your choices here vary depending on the data in your report.

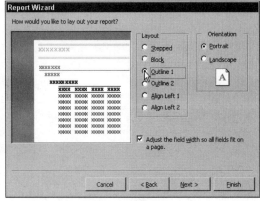

Figure 18-14:
Access
gives you
several
options for
report
layout.

2. In the Orientation section, choose how you want to lay out your report.

Generally, if you have a lot of small fields or several large fields, Landscape orientation works better. For fewer fields of any shape or size, try Portrait.

3. Check or clear the Adjust the Field Width So All Fields Fit on a Page check box.

If this box is checked (the default), Access force-fits all your fields onto one page, even if it has to squish some of them to do it. During the highly scientific squishing process, the field may end up being too small to display the data it contains. For example, a field holding the name *Harriet Isa Finkelmeier* may only display *Harriet Isa Fink* after it's squished. The rest of the name isn't lost — it just doesn't appear on the report. If you don't check the box, Access packs as many fields onto the page as it can without changing any field widths. Fields that don't fit are left off the page, but the fields that do print appear in their normal, glorious size.

4. Click Next when you're satisfied with the layout of your report.

A dialog box appears, offering you six predetermined font and color styles for your report. The left half of the window gives you a basic idea of what the style looks like.

5. **Choose the style you like the most, and then click <u>N</u>ext.**

6. **Give your report a name.**

   Your report is saved with a title. You also have the choice of previewing your report in print preview, modifying your report, or simply screaming for help.

7. **To preview your report, click Print Preview.**

8. **If you want to make changes to your report's design, click the Modify the Report's Design option.**

   Access opens the design view of your report, and you can tinker with the report to your heart's content.

9. **Click Finish.**

   Access automatically saves your new report with the other reports in your database file.

Chapter 19 explains how to modify and format your reports to create your own unique look.

Chapter 19

It's Amazing What a Little Formatting Can Do

. . . .

In This Chapter

▶ Getting into design view

▶ Working with report sections

▶ Marking text boxes and labels

▶ Previewing your stuff

▶ Putting AutoFormat to work for you

▶ Drawing lines and boxes

▶ Adding graphics to your reports

▶ Exporting reports to Microsoft Word and Excel

. . . .

*T*he Access Report Wizard is a pretty swell fellow. After a brief round of 20 compu-questions, it sets up an informative, good-looking report for you automatically. Well, at least the report's *informative* — just between you and me, I think that the Report Wizard can use a little design training.

Although the Report Wizard does the best job it can, the results aren't always exactly what you need. Those clever engineers at Microsoft foresaw this problem and left a back door open for you. That door is called *design view*. In design view, you can change anything — and I mean *anything* — about your report's design. Reorganize the text boxes, add some text, emphasize certain text boxes with boxes and lines, or do whatever else your heart desires.

This chapter guides you through some popular design view tweaking and tuning techniques. With this information in hand, your reports are sure to be the envy of the office in no time. (And there's nothing like a well-envied report to start your day off just right.)

Taking Your Report to the Design View Tune-Up Shop

The first stop in your quest for a better-looking report is design view itself. After all, you can't change *anything* in the report until it's up on the jacks in design view. Thankfully, Access offers several easy ways to tow in your report for that much-needed tune-up. Precisely how you do it depends on where you are right now in Access:

- After creating a report with the Report Wizard, the wizard asks whether you want to preview your creation or modify its design (even the wizard knows that its design skills are lacking). Click the Modify the Report's Design option to send the wizard's creation straight into design view.

- If the report is on the screen in a preview, hop into design view by clicking the Design View button on the toolbar.

- To get to design view from the database window, click the Reports button in the Objects bar and then click the name of the report you want to work on. Click the Design button (just above the report list in the database window) to open the report in design view.

No matter which method you use, Access sends you (and your report) to a design view screen that looks a lot like Figure 19-1. Now you're ready to overhaul that report!

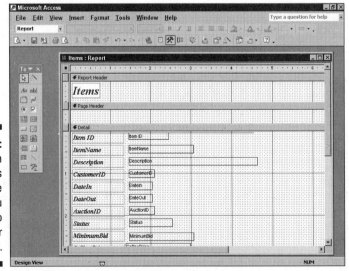

Figure 19-1:
The design view gives you all the tools you need to modify your report.

Striking Up the Bands (and the Markers, Too)

When you look at a report in design view, Access displays a slew of markers that are grouped into several *bands* (or *sections,* as they're called in Access). The *markers* show where Access plans to put the text boxes and text on your final report. They also give you an idea of how the program plans to format everything.

Access uses two kinds of markers, depending on what information the report includes:

- **Text boxes:** Boxes that display a particular field's data in the report. Every field you want to include in the final report has a text box in design view. If the report doesn't include a text box for one of the fields in your table, the data for that field won't end up in the report.

- **Labels:** Plain, simple text markers that display a text message on the report. Sometimes labels stand alone (such as "The information in this report is confidential. So there."). Often they accompany a text box to show people who read the report what data they're looking at ("Customer ID," or "Right Shoe Size," for example).

Markers are organized into sections that represent the different parts of your report. The sections govern where and how often a particular field or text message is repeated in your report. The report design in Figure 19-1 displays the three most common sections:

- Report Header
- Page Header
- Detail

Arrows to the left of the section names show you which markers each section contains.

The sections work in teams that straddle the Detail area. The teams are pretty easy to figure out (Report Header works with Report Footer, and Page Header works with Page Footer, for example). Figure 19-2 shows the mates to the sections shown in Figure 19-1. Every section adds a little something to the final report (except the Page Header and Report Footer sections, that is — they contain absolutely nothing).

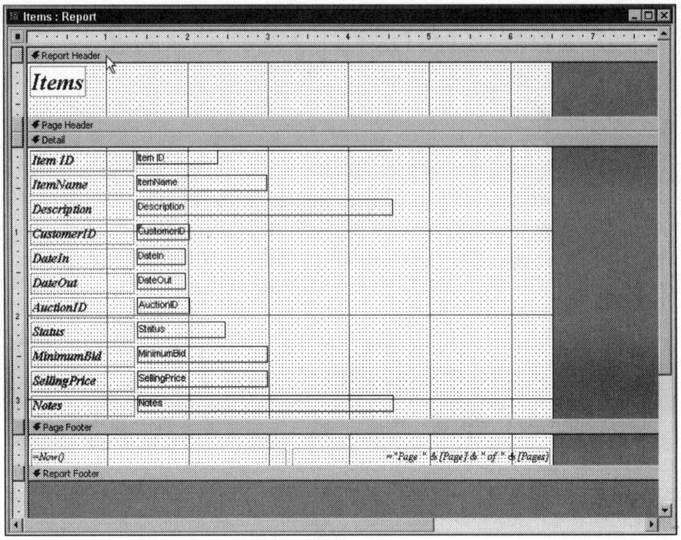

Figure 19-2:
The Page
Footer and
Report
Footer
mirror their
headers.

Here's how the most common sections work (including such important details as where and how often the sections appear in your printed report):

- ✔ **Report Header:** Anything that appears in the Report Header prints at the very start of the report. The information prints only once and appears at the top of the first page.

- ✔ **Page Header:** Information in the Page Header prints at the top of every page. The only exception is the report's first page, where Access prints the Report Header and *then* the Page Header.

- ✔ **Detail:** The meat of the report, the stuff in the Detail section fills the majority of each report page. The Detail section is repeated for every record included in the report.

- ✔ **Page Footer:** When each page is nearly full, Access finishes it off by printing the Page Footer at the bottom.

- ✔ **Report Footer:** At the bottom of the last page, immediately following the Page Footer, the Report Footer wraps up the display.

Being familiar with Glenn Miller, Claude Bolling, or John Philip Sousa won't help you when it comes to report bands in Access. (Sorry, but I just can't let the term *band* go by without making a musical note.) Because the how-to of bands (or, if you prefer, *sections*) is so important to your reports, Chapter 20 explores the topic in exhausting detail, with information on inserting and adjusting sections and convincing them to perform all kinds of automated calculations.

Formatting This, That, These, and Those

You can artfully amend almost anything in a report's design with the help of the formatting toolbar, which is shown in Figure 19-3. Whether you want to change text color, font size, or the visual effect surrounding a text box, this toolbar has the goodies you need.

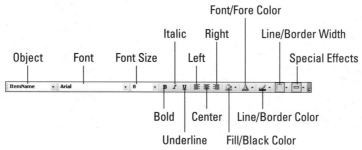

Figure 19-3:
Access provides a suite of tools to help format your report.

To adjust items in your report with the tools in the formatting toolbar, follow these steps:

1. **Click the item you want to format.**

   Any text box, label, line, or box is okay — Access is an equal opportunity formatter. When you click something, a bunch of little black boxes appear around it, much like Figure 19-4. (The little black boxes are a good sign.)

2. **Click the toolbar button for the formatting effect you want.**

   With most formatting tools, the new format immediately takes effect. Some tools (color, border, and 3-D effect) also offer a pull-down list of choices. I cover these options in more detail later in the chapter.

3. **Repeat Steps 1 and 2 for all of the text boxes you want to modify.**

   If you make a mistake while formatting, just choose Edit➪Undo Property Setting. Poof! Access removes the last formatting you applied.

The following sections step through some of the most common formatting tasks ahead of you. Just follow the instructions and your report looks like a cross between the Mona Lisa and a state tax form. (That's a compliment, I think, but I'll have to get back to you on that.)

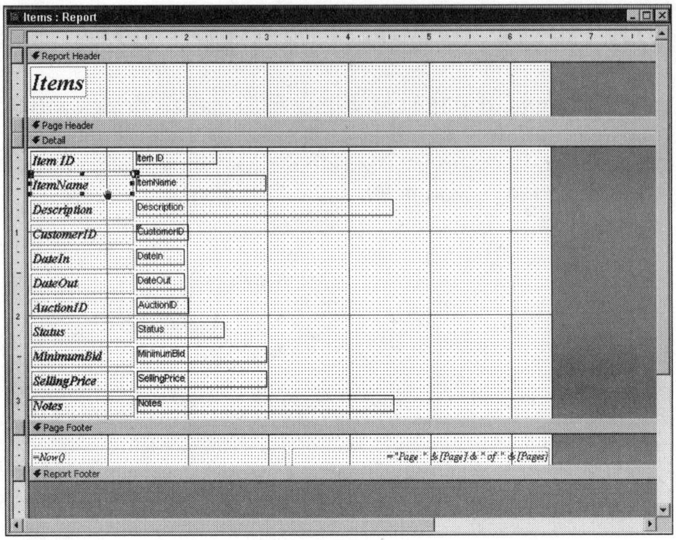

Figure 19-4:
The
ItemName
label is
selected.

Colorizing your report

Nothing brightens up a drab report like a spot of color. Access makes adding color easy with the Font/Fore Color and the Fill/Back Color buttons. These buttons are located on your friendly formatting toolbar (no surprises there).

Both buttons change the color of text markers in your report, but they differ a little in precisely how they do it:

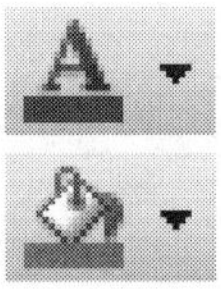

- ✔ The Font/Fore Color button changes the color of text in a text box or label marker.
- ✔ The Fill/Back Color button alters the marker's background color but leaves the text color alone.

To select a color to use, click the arrow at the right of the Font/Fore Color or Fill/Back Color button. When the menu of colors appears, click the color you want to use.

Your color choice also appears along the bottom of the toolbar button.

To change the color of a text box or label on your report, click the marker that you want to work with. To change the font color, click the Font/Fore Color button; to change the background, click Fill/Back Color, instead. The new color settings appear right away.

Taking control of your report

In addition to the normal goodies found on an everyday Access report (such as labels and text boxes), you can include all kinds of fascinating items called *controls*. You add controls to the report by using the design view toolbox (the floating island of buttons sitting somewhere around your screen).

Some controls work with specific types of fields. For example, a check box can graphically display the value of a Yes/No field. (Plus, controls look cool on the page.)

Anything this neat simply *must* be a little complicated, and the controls certainly live up to this expectation. Access includes several control wizards to take the pain out of the process. These wizards, like their brethren elsewhere in the program,

walk you through the steps for building your controls in a patient, step-by-step manner. The control wizards *usually* come to life automatically after you place a control in the report.

If you create a new control but the control wizard doesn't show up to help, make sure that the Wizard button at the top of the toolbox (the button emblazoned with a magic wand) is turned on. If it's on, the button looks as though it's pushed down a bit. If you aren't sure, click it a few times so you can see the difference.

Some of the controls (specifically the line, rectangle, page break, and image controls) are covered later in this chapter. Chapter 20 includes tips about using controls to create summaries in your report.

You can use the Font/Fore Color button also to change the color of text in a text box or any label. You can easily create special effects by choosing contrasting colors for the foreground and background, just like the white text floating on a black background in Figure 19-5.

Figure 19-5:
Set the foreground and background colors.

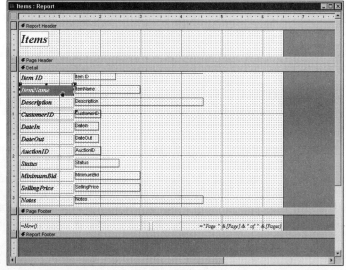

Be careful when choosing your colors — if you make the text and background colors the same, the text seems to disappear! If this happens, just choose Edit➪Undo Property Setting to bring back the original color setting.

Moving elements around

Feel like reorganizing a little bit? You can easily move just about any element (text box, label, line, and such) in a report. In fact, moving elements is *so* easy that you need to go slow and take extra care not to move elements you shouldn't.

To move a line, box, label, or text box, follow these steps:

1. **Click the item you want to move.**

   A bunch of black squares surround the item, letting you know that it's selected.

   If you have trouble selecting a line, try clicking near its ends. For some reason, Access has a tough time recognizing when you want to grab a line. Clicking right at the line's end seems to help the program figure out what you want to do.

2. **Move the mouse pointer to any edge of the selected item.**

   When you do this step, the mouse pointer turns into a little hand. Too cute, isn't it?

3. **Press and hold the left mouse button and then drag your item to a new position.**

   As you move the mouse, the little hand drags an outline of whatever object you selected. (Depending on your computer's video card, you *may* see the whole object move instead of just watching the outline box wander around the screen.)

4. **Release the mouse button when the item is hovering over its new home.**

   If something goes wrong, and you want to undo the movement, choose Edit➪Undo Property Setting or just press Ctrl+Z (the universal Undo key).

In some Access reports (specifically the ones created by the Columnar Report Wizard), the text box and label for each field in the report are attached to each other. If you move one, the other follows automatically. In this case, you have to adjust the procedure a bit if you want to move one *without* moving the other. Follow the preceding steps, but instead of moving the cursor to the edge of the marker, move it to one of the big square handles, as shown in Figure 19-6.

Label   Field

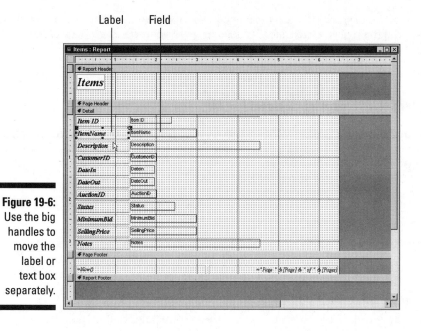

Figure 19-6:
Use the big
handles to
move the
label or
text box
separately.

Here's a summary of what the handles do:

- ✔ The handle on the far left moves the label.
- ✔ The handle in the middle of the two markers moves the text box.

As the mouse pointer enters the handle, the cursor changes to a pointing finger. That's your sign that you can proceed with Step 3 — press and hold the mouse button and then start moving. Release the mouse button when you have the text box positioned where you want it. If the mouse pointer changes to a double-ended arrow instead of a pointing hand, try moving your mouse pointer onto the big handle again. That double-ended arrow tells Access to *resize* the item, not move it.

Other types of reports, such as tabular reports or labels, don't combine the label and the text box the way columnar reports do. In such reports, either no label appears, or the label appears only once in the Page Header section. When labels aren't linked to their respective text boxes, they each appear separately — without the special large handles shown in Figure 19-6.

Use the smaller handles around the edge of a text box to resize the text box. For example, if you discover that the information in one of your text boxes is getting cut off, you can click the text box and use the small handles to make that text box longer. Or if a text box contains a lot of information, you can make the text box taller. Access wraps the information to the next line.

The amount of space between the markers controls the space between items when you print the report. Increasing that spacing gives your report a less crowded look; decreasing the space enables you to fit more information on the page.

Bordering on beautiful

Organizationally speaking, lines and marker borders are wonderful accents for your report. They draw your reader's eye to parts of the page, highlight sections of the report, and generally spruce up an other-wise drab page. The toolbar contains three buttons to put lines and borders through their paces:

- ✔ Line/Border Color
- ✔ Line/Border Width
- ✔ Special Effects

Coloring your lines and borders

The Line/Border Color button changes the color of lines that mark a text box's border and lines you draw on your report using the Line tool. This button works just like the Back Color and the Font/Fore Color buttons did for text, so you probably know a lot about using it already. (Comforting feeling, isn't it?)

To change the color of a line or a marker's border, follow these steps:

1. **Click the marker or line to select it.**

   Remember to click near the end of a line to select it; otherwise, you may end up clicking all around the line, but never highlighting it.

2. **Click the arrow next to the Line/Border Color button.**

   A drop-down display of color choices appears, as shown in Figure 19-7.

3. **Click your choice from the rainbow of options.**

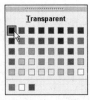

Figure 19-7:
Choose from an entire palette of colors.

Widening your lines and borders

In addition to colorizing lines and borders, you can also control their width:

1. **Click the line or text marker you want to work with.**

2. **Click the arrow next to the Line/Border Width button to display line and border width options.**

   Your choices for line and border width are represented in terms of *points* (a geeky publishing word that means ½₂ inch). The menu offers options for a hairline (half-point) line, 1 point, 2 points, 3 points,4 points, 5 points, and finally the 6-point Monster Line that Devoured Toronto. (A 6-point line is ½₂ inch thick and actually appears quite heavy on a report.)

3. **Click the line width option you want.**

   That's all there is to it! As with everything else, choosing Edit⇨Undo Property Setting repairs any accidental damage, so feel free to experiment with the options.

Adding special effects to your lines and borders

You can change the style of a marker's border by using the Special Effects button. Six choices are available under this button, as shown in Figure 19-8.

Figure 19-8: The six Special Effects border options.

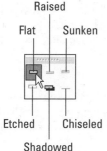

Here's a rundown of what these options do:

- ✔ The Sunken and Raised options make a text box look three-dimensional by changing the colors on two sides of the text box. Selecting a sunken border makes the label or text box appear as though it is pushed into your text; a raised border makes it seem as though your text box is rising from your text.

- ✔ The Chiseled option gives a text box the appearance of having the bottom portion of its border raised upward. The Etched option gives the effect of the border being etched into the background around the text box.

✔ The Shadow option places a shadow around the lower right of the text box.

✔ The Flat option simply puts a standard, single-line border around the entire text box.

Although the menu shows a small sample of each box, you can't really understand how they look in your report until you put them there. Try a few settings, print some reports, and see what strikes your fancy. You can always undo the changes, so why not live on the edge and try something new?

To add special effects to a marker's border, follow the same basic steps as you do for changing a border's color or width:

1. **Click the marker whose border you want to change.**

2. **Click the arrow next to the Special Effects button to display the six options.**

3. **Click the special effect you want to add.**

Tweaking your text

To change the font or the font size, simply click the arrow to the right of the Font or Font Size list box and make a selection from the drop-down list that appears. To turn on or off the bold, italic, or underline characteristics, select a block of text and click the appropriate button. If the feature is off, clicking the button turns the feature on. If the feature is on, clicking the button turns the feature off. When one of these formatting features is turned on, the button appears to be pressed into the surface of the toolbar.

You can also control the alignment of the text within labels and text boxes. To change the alignment of the text for a label or text box, simply select the marker and then click one of the three alignment buttons on the toolbar.

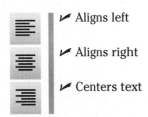

✔ Aligns left

✔ Aligns right

✔ Centers text

To make the best-looking report possible, pay attention to little details such as label and data alignment. Numeric data should be right aligned so that the numbers line up. Most other types of data should be left aligned. Headings generally should be centered. Your effort may mean the difference between a hard-to-read report and an object of informational beauty.

Taking a Peek at Your Report

After fiddling around long enough in design view, you inevitably reach a point where you want to view the actual report, rather than just look at the technical magic being used to create it. No matter how good your imagination is, it's difficult to visualize how everything will look when it all comes together in the printed report. Access provides two distinct tools for previewing your report.

- ✔ **Layout preview:** When you choose the layout preview, Access takes a portion of your data and arranges it to give you an idea of how your data will appear in the finished report. The preview shows only a sampling of your data (without performing any final calculations that you included). The idea is to see what the report *looks like,* not to review your calculations. To view layout preview, click the down-arrow next to the Report View button and then select Layout Preview from the drop-down list, as shown in Figure 19-9.

- ✔**Print preview:** If you want to see a full preview of your report, complete with the calculations and all the data, select Print Preview by clicking the Print Preview button. Or you can go the long way around and click the down arrow next to the Report View button and then select Print Preview from the drop-down list (refer to Figure 19-9).

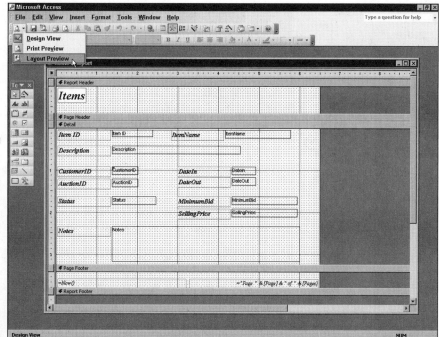

Figure 19-9:
Choose
Layout
Preview to
get a taste
for how
the report
will look;
choose Print
Preview to
see the
report in full.

Regardless of which approach you use, you see a print preview screen similar to the one shown in Figure 19-10. The various items of your report appear as they will when you print the report. You can then use the controls at the top of the print preview window to change the appearance of the screen.

See Chapter 17 for more information about using the Print Preview option.

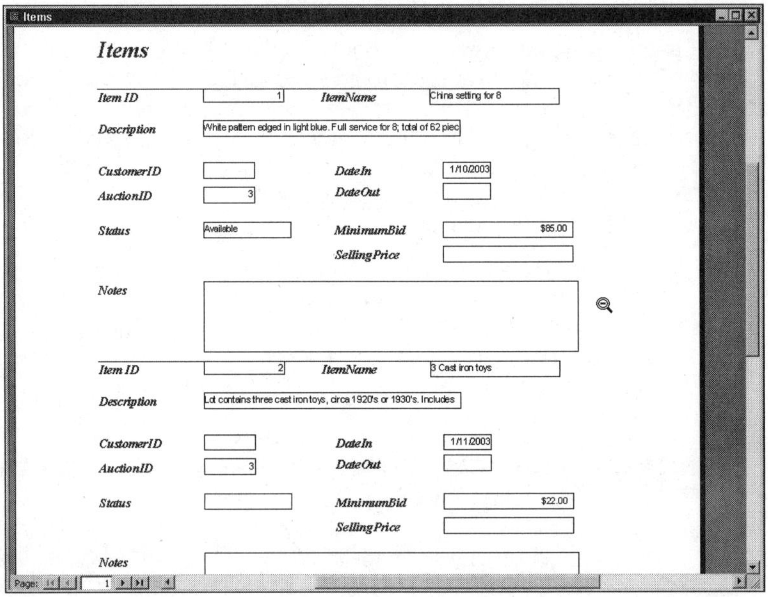

Figure 19-10:
The Print Preview option shows you exactly how the report will look.

AutoFormatting Your Way to a Beautiful Report

When you want to change the look of the entire report in one (or two) easy clicks, check out the AutoFormat button. When you click this button, Access offers several different format packages that reset everything from the headline font to the color of lines that split up items in the report.

To use AutoFormat, follow these steps:

1. **Click the empty gray area below the Report Footer band.**

   This may sound like a strange first step, but there's reason behind my peculiarity (or at least there is *this* time). Clicking in this area is the easiest way to tell Access that you don't want *any* report sections selected. If any one section is selected, AutoFormat changes the contents of only that section when you issue the AutoFormat command. Although that precision may be nice sometimes, most of the time you want AutoFormat to redo your entire report.

2. **Click the AutoFormat toolbar button.**

   A dialog box appears, listing your various package-deal formatting choices.

3. **Click the name of the format you want, as shown in Figure 19-11, and then click OK.**

   Access updates everything in your report with the newly selected look.

If just a few text boxes in one section change, but the majority of the report stays the same, go back and try that *click the empty gray area* step again. The odds are good that you had one section selected when you clicked AutoFormat.

The Customize button allows you create your own AutoFormats.

Figure 19-11: Choose the look that you like and apply it to the entire report.

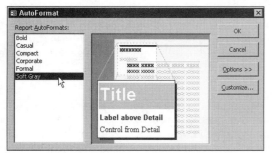

Lining Up Everything

When you start moving various items around on your report, you can easily wind up with a report that's out of alignment. For example, you may have put the column headings in the page header and the actual information farther down the page in a detail line. Of course, you want the text boxes to line up with the headers, but simply moving the items around the page by hand and eyeballing the results may not do the trick.

You can use the grid in the screen background to position screen elements by aligning them with the vertical lines or with the various dots on the design screen.

When you move an object on the report, you can choose Format⇨Snap to Grid to control whether the object stays lined up with these dots that are "snapped to the grid" or whether you can move the object freely between the dots.

When you move an object with Snap to Grid turned on, the object's upper-left corner always aligns with one of the dots on the grid. If you choose this command when you resize an object, the side of the object that you move stays aligned with the dots on the grid.

Other commands on the Format menu that you may find useful for arranging objects on your reports include the following:

- **Align:** You can choose two or more objects and align them to each other or to the grid. Selecting Left, Right, Top, or Bottom aligns the left, right, top, or bottom sides of the selected items, respectively For example, if you select three objects and then choose Format⇨Align⇨Left, the three objects move so that their left edges line up. By default, Access moves objects to line up with the object that is the farthest to the left.

- **Size:** You can change the size of a group of objects by selecting the objects and then selecting an option from the Size submenu.

  For example, you can

  - Choose Size⇨to Fit, which adjusts the size of the controls so that each one is just large enough to hold the information it contains. Choose Size⇨to Grid to adjust the controls so that all control corners are positioned on grid points.

  - Adjust the controls relative to each other. If you choose Size and then choose to Tallest, to Shortest, to Widest, or to Narrowest, each box in the selected group changes to that characteristic. If you select a group of controls and then choose Size⇨to Tallest, each of the selected controls is resized to the same height as the tallest control in the selected group.

- **Horizontal Spacing and Vertical Spacing:** These commands space a selected group of objects equally. This feature can be useful if you're trying to spread out the title items for a report. Select the items in your group and then choose Format⇨Vertical Spacing⇨Make Equal to have Access space the items equally.

Drawing Your Own Lines

An easy way to make your report a bit easier to read is to add lines that divide the various sections. To add lines to your report, follow these steps:

1. **Open the toolbox by clicking on the Toolbox toolbar button.**

2. **Click the Line tool in the toolbox.**

   Your cursor changes to a crosshair with a line trailing off to the right.

3. **Click where you want to start the line, drag to the location where you want to end the line, and release the mouse button.**

You can use the various toolbar buttons (discussed earlier in this chapter) to dress up your lines. For example, to change the line's color, thickness, and appearance, use the Line/Border Color, Line/Border Width, and Special Effects buttons, respectively.

The Box tool draws boxes around separate items on your report. Click the point that you want to be the upper-left corner of your box, and drag the box shape down to the lower-right corner. When you release the mouse button, presto, you have a box.

Inserting Page Breaks

Most of the time, page breaks aren't high on the list of report priorities. Instead, you worry about challenges such as making the summaries work, lining up the data in neat columns and rows, and selecting the proper shade of magenta (or was that more of a pinky russet?) for the lines and label borders.

Occasionally, you get the urge to tell Access precisely where a report page should end. Maybe you want to end each page with a special calculation or keep some information grouped on the same page. Regardless of the reason, inserting a page break in your report is as quick as a click.

To insert a page break in your Access report, follow these steps:

1. **Click the Page Break button in the toolbox.**

   The mouse pointer changes to a crosshair with a page next to it.

2. **Position the crosshair wherever you want the page break, and then click.**

   A few small black marks appear on the left side of the report. This is the page break marker. From now on, a new page always begins here.

If you want to remove a page break that you so carefully added, click the page break marker and then press Delete. That page break's outta there.

Sprucing Up the Place with a Few Pictures

When you click the Image or the Unbounded Object Frame tool, you get a plus-sign pointer, with the button's image at the lower right. You can use this tool to draw a box on your screen.

✔ **If you're using the Image tool:** Access opens the Insert Picture dialog box, which you can use to locate the image that you want to insert.

✔ **If you're using the Unbound Object Frame tool:** Access opens the Insert Object dialog box so you can choose the type of object to insert.

Images are great, but I strongly encourage you to add images only to the one of the headers or footers. An image in the detail section repeats many times.

If you don't have an image that you're ready to use, but rather have an image in progress, you may choose to use the Unbound Object Frame to add an OLE object. *OLE* (which stands for *object linking and embedding*) enables you to put an object onto your page, while maintaining the object's link to its original file. Any changes to the original file are reflected in the object you place in the report. You can link to an image or to any type of file that supports OLE.

Passing Your Reports around the (Microsoft) Office

You can do an awful lot with Access, but sometimes a different program can do the job better and make your life a little easier. The key to this trick is to choose Tools➪Office Links on the main menu. This menu includes three options: two for sending your report to Microsoft Word, and one for shipping it off to Excel.

Chapter 20

Headers and Footers for Groups, Pages, and Even (Egad) Entire Reports

In This Chapter

▶ Grouping and sorting your records

▶ Adjusting the size of sections

▶ Fine-tuning the layout of your report

▶ Controlling your headers and footers

▶ Putting expressions in your footers

▶ Adding page numbers and dates

*W*izards are great for creating reports, but they can only do so much for you. Even when you work with a wizard, you still need to know a little something about how to group the fields of your report to get optimum results. And someday after creating your report, you may need to alter its organization or fine-tune its components to meet your changing needs. To tweak an existing report, you need to go into design view and manually make the changes you want.

Don't despair! This chapter is designed to help you through these thorny issues. It explains the logic behind grouping your fields in a report, and shows you several options for your groups. It also walks you through the design view thicket — a thorny place if ever there was one.

Everything in Its Place

The secret to successful report organization lies in the way you position the markers (known to programmers as *controls*) for the labels and fields in the report design. Each portion of the report design is separated into *sections* (called *bands* in other database programs) that identify different portions of the report. Which parts of the report land in which section depends on the report's layout:

✔ **Columnar:** In a standard columnar report (see Figure 20-1), field descriptions print with every record's data. The layout behaves this way because both the field descriptions and data area are in the report's Detail section. Because the report title is in the Report Header section, it prints only once, at the very beginning of the report.

✔ **Tabular:** The setup is quite different in a standard tabular report, as shown in Figure 20-2. The title prints at the top of the report, just as in the columnar report, but the similarity ends there. Instead of hanging out with the data, the field descriptions move to the Page Header section. Here, they print once per page instead of once per record. The data areas are by themselves in the Detail section.

Understanding the section concept is a prerequisite for performing any serious surgery on your report or for running off to build a report from scratch. Otherwise, your report groupings don't work right, fields are out of place, and life with Access is less fulfilling than it can be.

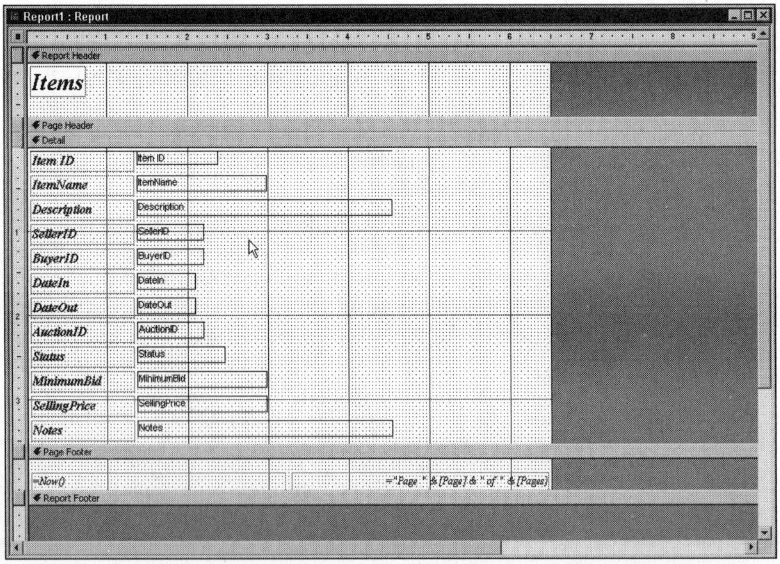

Figure 20-1: In a columnar report, labels are to the left of the fields and repeat for each record.

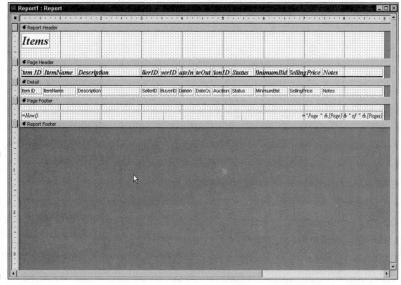

Figure 20-2: In a tabular report, the labels become column headings.

The most important point to understand about sections is that the contents of each section are printed *only* when certain events occur. For example, the information in the Page Header is repeated at the top of each page, but the Report Header prints on only the first page.

Getting a grip on sections is easy when you look at the *innermost section* of your report first and work your way outward, like so:

✓ **Detail:** Access prints items in this section each time it moves to a new record. Your report includes a copy of the Detail section for each record in the table.

✓ **Group headers and footers:** You may have markers for one or more *group sections*. In Figure 20-3, information in the report is grouped by AuctionID, and then by LastName (you can tell by the section bars labeled AuctionID Header and LastName Header — the section bars identify which field is used for grouping).

Group sections always come in pairs: the group header and the group footer. The *group header* section is above the Detail section in the report design; the *group footer* is always below Detail. Information in these sections repeats for every unique value in the group's field. For example, the report shown in Figure 20-3 reprints everything in the AuctionID Header for each unique auction number. Within the section for each auction, Access repeats the information in the LastName Header for each customer.

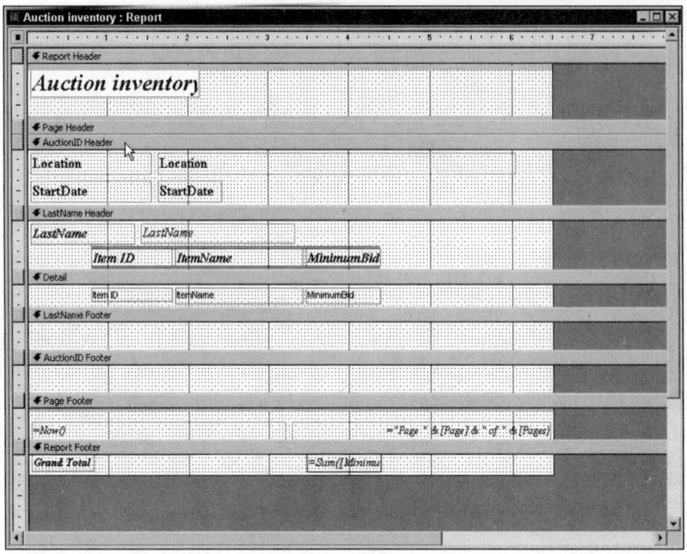

Figure 20-3:
Grouping
records by
AuctionID
and then by
LastName.

✔ **Page Header and Page Footer:** These sections appear at the top and bottom of every page. They're among the few sections not controlled by the contents of your records. Use the information in the Page Header and Footer sections to mark the pages of your report.

✔ **Report Header and Footer:** These sections appear at the start and end of your report. They make only one appearance in your report — unlike the other sections, which pop up many times.

So when Access produces a report, what does it do with all these sections? The process goes this way:

1. Access begins by printing the Report Header at the top of the first page.

2. Next, it prints the Page Header, if you choose to have the Page Header appear on the first page. (Otherwise, Access reprints this header at the top of every page except the first one.)

3. If your report has groups, the Group Headers for the first set of records appear next.

4. When the headers are in place, Access finally prints the Detail lines for each record in the first group.

5. After it's finished with all the Detail lines for the first group, Access prints that group's Group Footer.

6. If you have more than one group, Access starts the process over again by printing the next Group Header, and then that group's Detail lines, and then that group's Group Footer.

7. At the end of each page, Access prints the Page Footer.

8. When it finishes with the last group, Access prints the Report Footer — which, like the Report Header, appears only once in a given report.

Here's what you can do with headers and footers:

- ✔ The Report Header provides general information about the report. This is a good place to add the report title, printing date, and version information.

- ✔ The Page Header contains any information you want to appear at the top of each page (such as the date or your company logo).

- ✔ The headers for each group usually identify the contents of that group and the field names.

- ✔ The footers for each group generally contain summary information, such as counts and calculations. For example, the footer section of the AuctionID group may hold a calculation that totals the minimum bids.

- ✔ The Page Footer, which appears at the bottom of every page, traditionally holds the page number and report date fields.

  If keeping the information in your report private is critical, consider typing something like *Company Confidential* in the footer. (Won't your corporate lawyers be proud!)

- ✔ By the time the Report Footer prints, about the only information left is a master summary of what happened during the report. You may also include contact information (whom to call with questions about the report) if you plan to distribute the report widely throughout the company.

Grouping your records

If you're designing a report from scratch, you can use the Sorting and Grouping dialog box to create your groups and control how they behave. Perhaps more importantly, if you use a wizard to create a report for you, you can still use this dialog box to control how that report behaves and where information appears.

When the Report Wizard creates a report for you, it includes a header and footer section for each group you want. If you tell the Report Wizard to group by the AuctionID field, for example, it automatically creates both the AuctionID Header and the AuctionID Footer sections. You aren't limited to what the wizard does, though. If you're a little adventuresome, you can augment the wizard's work with your own grouping sections.

The key to creating your own grouping sections is the Sorting and Grouping dialog box, as shown in Figure 20-4. This dialog box controls how Access organizes the records in your report. Each grouping section in your report is included in the sorting and grouping list automatically (regardless of whether you or the wizard created the section). You can also have additional entries that sort the records, although these entries don't generate their own section headers.

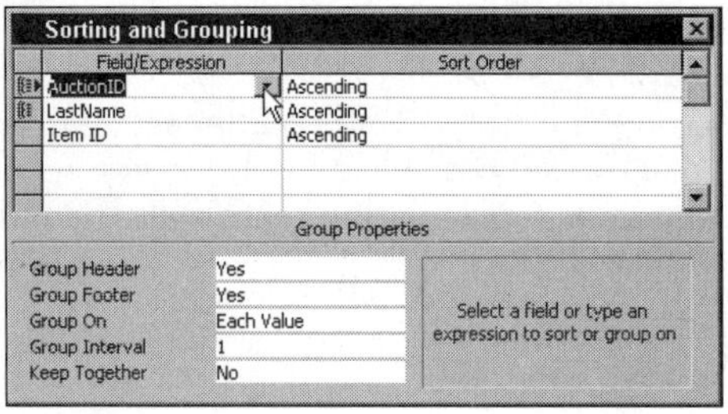

Figure 20-4:
The Sorting and Grouping dialog box enables you to adjust the organization of your report.

To build your own groupings, follow these steps:

1. Choose View⇨Sorting and Grouping.

   The Sorting and Grouping dialog box appears.

2. Click a blank field under Field/Expression.

   The blinking toothpick cursor appears, along with a down arrow.

3. Click the down arrow, and then select a field.

   Access adds a new line for that field to the list in the Sorting and Grouping dialog box. By default, Access plans to do an ascending sort (smallest to largest) with the data in that field.

4. Click the Group Header area at the bottom of the dialog box.

   You're telling Access that you want the entry to be a full-fledged group.

Group on, dude!

Groups are one of the too-cool-for-words features that make Access reports so flexible. But wait — groups have still *more* untapped power, thanks to the Group On setting in the Sorting and Grouping dialog box. This setting tells Access when to begin a new group of records in a report. The dialog box contains two settings for your grouping pleasure:

✔ **Each Value** tells Access to group identical entries together. If any difference exists between values in the grouping field, Access puts them into different groups. Each Value is a great setting if you're grouping by customer numbers, vendor numbers, or government identification numbers. It's not such a great choice if you're working with names, because every little variation (Kaufield instead of Kaufeld, for example) ends up in its own group.

✔ **Interval** tells Access that you're interested in organizing by a range of entries. Exactly how Access interprets the Interval setting depends on whether you're grouping with a number or text field.

If you're grouping a number field with the Interval setting, Access counts by the Interval setting when making the groups. For example, if your Interval is 10, then Access groups records that have values from 0 to 9, 10 to 19, 20 to 29, and so on.

With text fields, Access works a little differently. Suppose you specify an Interval of 1 — Access then groups records by the first character of the text field. In other words, all the *A*s form one group, followed by all the *B*s, and so on. If you set an Interval of 2, Access groups the records by the first two characters in the text field, so Maine and Massachusetts group together (both begin with *Ma*) but Maine and Mississippi are in separate groups.

5. **Click the down arrow that appears and then select Yes from the drop-down menu.**

   Behind the scenes, Access adds a new group section to your report design. To include a footer for your new group as well, repeat this step in the Group Footer entry of the dialog box.

6. **Close the dialog box after you finish.**

   That's it — your new group is in place.

To remove a group, click the gray button to the left of the Field/Expression line for the group and then press Delete. Access asks whether you really want to delete the group. Click Yes.

If you want to change the order of the various groups, just dash back to the Sorting and Grouping dialog box (choose View➪Sorting and Grouping). Click the gray button next to the group you want to move. Then click and drag the group to its new location. Access automatically adjusts your report design accordingly.

Be careful when changing the grouping order! It's easy to make an innocent-looking change and then discover that nothing in your report is organized correctly anymore. Before making any big adjustments to the report, take a minute to save the report (choose File➪Save). That way, if something goes wrong and the report becomes horribly disfigured, just close it (File➪Close) without saving your changes. Ahhh. Your original report is safe and sound.

The properties for the currently selected group appear at the bottom of the Sorting and Grouping dialog box.

✔ **Group Header and Group Footer:** Specifies whether the group will include a section for a Group Header, a section for a Group Footer, or both in your report.

✔ **Group On:** Determines how Access creates the groups for that value — check out the "Group on, dude!" sidebar.

✔ **Group Interval:** You probably won't ever touch this strange, geek-level setting. (In fact, I highly recommend *not* touching it.) The Group Interval tells Access how many characters it should look at in each field when it's deciding how to group your records. The default setting (a Group Interval of 1) tells Access to group the records alphabetically by looking only at the first letter of the field. Shifting that setting from 1 to 3 makes Access group everything by the first three characters of every record (putting Smith, Smithers, and Smizotsky together into the same group).

✔ **Keep Together:** Controls whether all the information in a group must be printed on the same page, whether the first Detail line and the headings for that group must be printed on the same page, and whether Access can split the information any way it wants as long as it all gets printed on one page or another. You have three choices under the Keep Together property:

- **No:** Access does whatever it pleases.

- **Whole group:** Access prints the entire group, from Header to Footer, on the same page.

- **With first detail:** Access prints all the information from the Header for the group through the Detail section for the first entry in that group on the same page. Choose this option to ensure that each page starts with a set of headings.

Changing a section's size

One problem you may have with designing your own report is controlling how much space appears in a section. When you print a section — be it a Page Header, a Section Header, or a Detail line — it normally takes up the same amount of space as shown on the design screen. You generally want to tighten the space within the group so that little space is wasted on your page, but your section needs to be large enough to contain all the markers and such that go into it. To change the size of a section, put your cursor on the edge of the bar immediately below a section, and then drag up to decrease the size or drag down to increase it.

You can avoid all this manual effort by telling Access to automatically resize the sections based on how much information lands in them. Discover the details in the next section, "Fine-Tuning the Layout."

Fine-Tuning the Layout

With the right fields in the correct header, footer, and detail sections, you've successfully finished the biggest step in building your report. Now you're down to the little things — tweaking, adjusting, and touching up the details of how your report presents itself. The properties described in the following sections govern the visual aspect — the look and feel — of your report.

Some of the stuff in the coming paragraphs looks kinda technical at first glance because these settings dig deep into the machinery of report making. Don't let the high-tech look scare you. By organizing your headers, footers, and detail rows, you already conquered the hard part of building the report. This stuff's just the icing.

Playing with the properties

In an amazing stroke of usability, Access keeps all properties settings for your report in a single dialog box. To start adjusting the details of anything in the entire report, just double-click the item you want modify. To display the controls over the entire report, double-click the little box in the upper-left part of the window (shown in Figure 20-5). No matter where you double-click, up pops a very useful dialog box.

The title of the box identifies the piece of the report that you double-clicked. Depending on what you clicked, the title might say *Report*, *Section*, *Text Box*, or *Label*, along with a specific item name. As an extra bonus, Access highlights the item in your report so you know exactly which piece you're working with right then. For example, Figure 20-5 shows the properties dialog box for the Page Header section of the report. You can tell because the dialog box title reads *Section:Page Header*, the drop-down menu (discussed shortly) says *Page Header*, and Access highlighted the Page Header section bar in the design window.

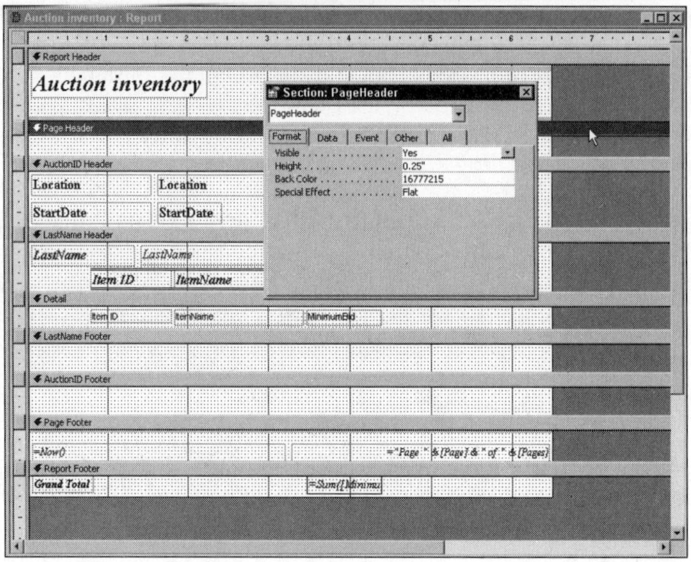

Figure 20-5:
Double-click
any piece
of the report
to see that
item's
properties.

This dialog box itself includes two things: a drop-down list across the top of the dialog box that catalogs the sections of your report, and an ever-changing selection of tabbed section settings that fills the rest of the dialog box. The drop-down list covers absolutely *every* area of your report, starting with the entire report and then drilling down to the headers, fields, labels, and even blank lines inside the report. Every section has a slightly different group of tabbed options, so make sure you choose the right report section from the drop-down list before changing a whole slew of settings.

Five tabbed areas (Format, Data, Event, Other, and All) appear in the dialog box. The only tab you really care about is Format. It handles 99 percent of the details that you'll ever want to change. The rest of the tabs in the dialog box (Data, Event, Other, and All) appeal only to hard-core Access programmers — and even programmers care about them only a little.

If you can't find a particular setting in the bottom area of the dialog box, check to see which report section is named at the top of the box. If the wrong section name appears, the settings won't look right either.

Directing the report and page headings

To adjust when various headings appear in your report, start with the Report properties dialog box. Because you can't double-click the entire report

(Access always thinks you're double-clicking *inside* the report somewhere) double-click the odd little box identified in Figure 20-6. That displays the Report properties dialog box.

After the box appears, try these settings:

- ✓ The default setting for the Page Header and Page Footer is All Pages, meaning that Access prints a header and footer on every page in the report.

- ✓ Choose Not with Rpt Hdr (or Not with Rpt Ftr for the footer) to tell Access to skip the first and last pages (where the Report Header and Report Footer are printed), but print the Page Header on all the others.

- ✓ The Keep Together option affects the Keep Together entry, which you set in the Sorting and Grouping dialog box (see "Grouping your records," earlier in this chapter). Choose Per Page to apply the Keep Together setting to pages. Or, in a report with multiple columns, choose Per Column to apply the Keep Together setting to columns.

The Page Header section comes with a bunch of options, too. Double-click the Page Header to display the Section:PageHeader dialog box, shown back in Figure 20-5.

Double-click here

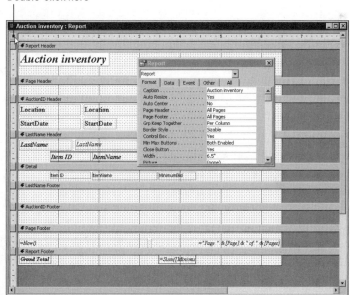

Figure 20-6: To adjust settings for the entire report, double-click this unlikely looking box.

Click the Format tab on the Page Header dialog box for the following options:

✓ **Visible:** You can use this property to control whether the Page Header appears at all.

✓ **Height:** Access automatically sets this property as you click and drag the section header up and down on the screen. To specify an exact size (for example, if you want the header area to be *precisely* 4 centimeters tall), type the size in this section. (Access automatically uses the units of measurement you chose for Windows itself.)

✓ **Back Color:** If you want to adjust the section's color, click this box and then click the small gray button that appears to the right of the entry. This button displays a color palette. Click your choice and then let Access worry about the obnoxious color number that goes into the Back Color box.

Although you can control the color of your Page Header's background from the Report dialog box, an easier method is to click the section in design view and use the drop-down lists on the formatting toolbar.

✓ **Special Effect:** This property adjusts the visual effect for the section heading, much as the Special Effect button does for the markers in the report itself. Your choices are somewhat limited here, though. Click the Special Effect box and then click the down arrow to list what's available. Choose Flat (the default setting), Raised, or Sunken.

Adjusting individual sections

What if you want to change the format of not the entire report but just one section — for example, the header for one group? Simple. In design view, double-click GroupHeader to call upon the dialog box shown in Figure 20-7.

Figure 20-7: Double-clicking a group header lets you specify how Access handles the group.

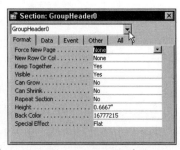

With the Force New Page option, you can control whether the change for that group automatically forces the information to start on a new page. When you set this option, you can determine whether this page break occurs only before the header, only after the footer, or in both places. Similarly, you can control the way in which section starts and endings are handled for multiple column reports (such as having the group always start in a separate column). As with the previous dialog boxes, you can control whether the group is kept together and whether the section is visible.

Take particular note of Can Grow, Can Shrink, and Repeat Section. Here's what happens when you enable these settings:

- **Can Grow:** The section expands as necessary, based on the data in it. Can Grow is particularly useful when you're printing a report that contains a Memo field. You set the width of the field so that it's as wide as you want. Then you can use the Can Grow property to enable Access to adjust the height available for the information.

- **Can Shrink:** The section can become smaller if, for example, some of the fields are empty. To use the Can Grow and Can Shrink properties, you need to set them for both the section and the items in the section that can grow or shrink.

- **Repeat Section:** Controls whether Access repeats the heading on the new page (or pages, if the section is so big that it covers more than two pages when a group is split across pages or columns).

Taking it one item at a time

Double-clicking doesn't just work for sections. When you want to adjust the formatting of any item of your report — a field, a label, or something you've drawn on your report — just double-click that item in design view. Access leads you to a marvelous dialog box from which you can perform all manner of technical nitpicking.

Filling in Those Sections

Although Access includes several default settings for headers and footers, those settings aren't personalized or imaginative. You can do much more with headers and footers than simply display labels for your data. You can build expressions in these sections or insert text that introduces or summarizes your data. Now those are the kinds of headers and footers that impress your friends, influence your coworkers, and win over your boss.

At the head of the class

How you place the labels in the report's header sections controls how the final report both looks and works, so you really oughta put some thought into those headers. You want to make sure that all your headings are easy to understand and that they add useful information to the report.

When you're setting up a report, feel free to play around with the header layouts. Experiment with your options and see what you can come up with — the way the information repeats through the report may surprise you.

For example, when you use a wizard to create a grouped report, Access puts labels for your records into the page header by default. Figure 20-8 shows such a report in action. Notice that the column headings are printed above the site name. The descriptions for the column headings appear at the top of each and every page because they're in the Page Header section. This example is certainly not a bad layout, but you can accomplish the same goal in other ways.

Figure 20-9 shows an alternate arrangement. In this case, the Start, ItemName, and Min Bid headings repeat every time the last name is printed because I moved them from the Page Header to the LastName Header section of the report. This arrangement reads a little easier than the version shown in Figure 20-8 because the column descriptions sit directly above their matching columns.

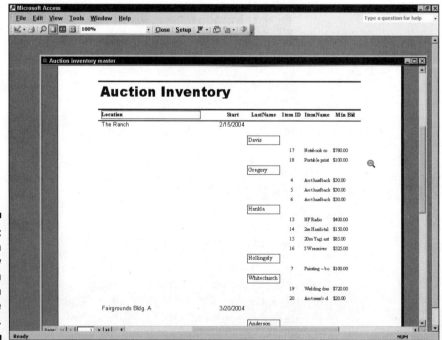

Figure 20-8:
The Auction Inventory Report with the labels in the page header.

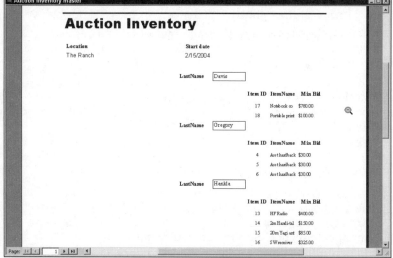

Figures 20-8 and 20-9 show some of the labels (such as LastName) moved from where the wizard placed them and various sections resized to make the reports more aesthetically pleasing. In addition, the pair of lines used to mark the top and bottom of the Page Header was removed to close that space.

Page numbers and dates

Access can insert certain types of information for you in either the Header or the Footer. Most notably, Access can insert page numbers or dates, using the Page Number command and the Date and Time command in the Insert menu.

Hey, what page is this?

Choosing Insert⇨Page Numbers displays the Page Numbers dialog box. From this dialog box, you have several options for your page-numbering pleasure:

✔ **Format:** Choose Page N to print the word *Page* followed by the appropriate page number. Or choose Page N of M to count the total number of pages in the report and print that number in addition to the current page (as in *Page 2 of 15*).

✔ **Position:** Tell Access whether to print the page number in the Page Header or the Page Footer.

- ✔ **Alignment:** Set the position of the page number on the page. Click the arrow at the right edge of the list box to scroll through your options.

- ✔ **Show Number on First Page:** Select this option to include a page number on the first page of your report. Deselect it to keep your first page unnumbered.

To change the way that the page numbers work on your report, first manually delete the existing page number field by clicking it and pressing the Delete key. After the number is gone, choose Insert➪Page Numbers to build the new page numbers.

When did you print this report, anyway?

Choose Insert➪Date and Time to display the Date and Time dialog box. The most important options are Include Date and Include Time. Select the exact format from a set of choices. The dialog box displays a sample of your settings in the section cleverly marked *Sample*.

Including the date and time might not seem useful today, but it makes a *huge* difference with information that changes regularly. By printing the information automatically at the bottom of your report pages, Access automatically documents for certain when the report came out. Even if you don't think you need to know that stuff, do it anyway. It never hurts to build a date stamp or a time *and* date stamp into your report footers.

Part V
Wizards, Forms, and Other Mystical Stuff

The 5th Wave   By Rich Tennant

"You ever get the feeling this project could just up and die at any moment?"

In this part . . .

*P*art V defies rational explanation. (How's *that* for a compelling lead?) It introduces a wide range of stuff that's useful individually, but unrelated. When you get down to it, the only thing tying these topics together is the fact that they're not related to anything else.

Chapter 21 (appropriately enough) takes you and your databases into the 21st century with Internet integration — one of the much-heralded features of Access.

Also, be sure to check out Chapter 22 to find out all about forms in Access. (Uh-oh — my inner nerd is starting to get excited. . . .) Forms are powerful and flexible . . . and they're fun to make — that's right, I said *fun*.

Chapter 23 delves into the wonderful world of importing and exporting data. Chapter 24 shows you how to analyze the heck out of your tables. (Perhaps you should just go ahead and read the part while I try to get the nerd back under control.)

And, for something completely different, Chapter 25 describes how, by adding just a bit of geeky technology to your life, you can actually tell Access what to do without touching your keyboard. (No, it responds only to vocal commands. Gesturing still doesn't help.)

Chapter 21

Spinning Your Data onto the Web

. . . .

. . . .

Access is a powerhouse of Internet and intranet information. If you're itching to join the online revolution or yearn for fun and profit on the electronic superhighway, Access (and the rest of the Office suite, for that matter) is ready to get you started.

In this chapter, you take a quick look at the online capabilities of Access and uncover some of the details of hyperlinks and online database publishing. The chapter closes with some advanced topics for your further research pleasure. (These topics are just too high on the technonerd scale for this book.)

Access and the Internet: A Match Made in Redmond

These days, it seems that all software makers are touting their products' cozy linkage with the Internet. Whether it's a natural fit or the marketing equivalent of a shotgun wedding, everyone's joining the rush to cyberspace.

Thankfully, Internet integration with Access is on the *natural fit* end of the scale. Databases are a perfect complement to the Net's popular Web information system. The Web offers lots of interactivity and a flexible presentation medium. But until now, publishing a database on the Web was a complex process requiring time, effort, and a willingness to cheerfully rip your hair out by the roots.

To make the data-publishing process much easier and less hair-intensive, Microsoft came up with a way to bring the Net right into Access. The key to the behind-the-scenes magic is Microsoft's ActiveX technology.

You sometimes hear terms such as OLE (Object Linking and Embedding), COM (Component Object Model), and even DNA (Distributed interNet Architecture). Believe it or not, these terms are essentially synonymous with ActiveX. (Microsoft has an unfortunate habit of periodically giving its technology a new name for somewhat dubious marketing purposes.) Basically, ActiveX (or OLE or COM or whatever) is the technology that allows different programs to share information. Don't stress out about the technology — you don't need to know *anything* technical about ActiveX to make Access sing duets with the Internet or your company's intranet.

The Internet power of Access comes directly from the Microsoft Web browser, Internet Explorer, through a cool ActiveX pipeline. When you work with hyperlinks, browse the Net from a form, or search your company's intranet, Internet Explorer does all the work behind the scenes. Even when it looks as though Access is in charge, the Internet information is coming directly from Internet Explorer. ActiveX technology makes everything appear seamless.

To make Access do its Internet tricks, you must be running Internet Explorer 5.0 or above. In addition, you need a connection to the Internet (or to your company's intranet).

Building Hyperlinks in Your Table

Sitting right in the center of the Internet discussion is the term *hyperlink,* or the more commonly heard versions, *links* or *tags*. Although *hyperlink* sounds vaguely like a frenzied game show host, it's actually a special storage compartment for storing the address of a resource on either the Internet or your local corporate network. Hyperlinks start with a special identification code that explains to the computer what kind of resource it's pointing to (the geeks call this the *protocol)*. Table 21-1 lists the most common protocol codes you'll find, along with an explanation of the kind of resource the code refers to.

Table 21-1	Types of Hyperlinks in Access
Protocol Code	*What It Does*
file://	Opens a local or network-based file
ftp://	File Transfer Protocol; links to an FTP server
http://	Hypertext Transfer Protocol; links to a Web page
mailto:	Sends e-mail to a network or Internet address
news://	Opens an Internet newsgroup

For a complete list of hyperlinks that Access understands, press F1 to open the Access Help system and then search for the term *hyperlink*.

If you surf the Web regularly, many of these terms should look familiar. Although most of them are geared toward Internet or intranet applications, Access can use hyperlinks also to identify locally stored Microsoft Office documents (that's what `file://` does). This technology is so flexible that the sky's the limit.

Adding a hyperlink field to your table

You can't let hyperlinks just stand around without a permanent home, so Access sports a field type specifically for this special data. As you probably guessed, this type is called the hyperlink field. Figure 21-1 shows a table design containing a hyperlink field.

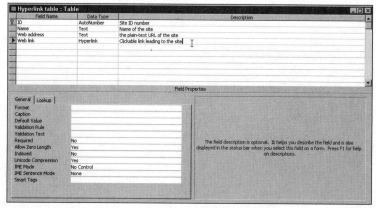

Figure 21-1: Adding a hyperlink field to a table.

Adding a hyperlink field to a table doesn't require any special steps. Just use the same steps for adding *any* field to a table. The hyperlink field is no different than the other mundane fields surrounding it.

Typing and using hyperlinks

Hyperlinks in Access can have up to four parts, all separated by pound signs. In order, they look like this:

```
display text#address#subaddress#screen tip
```

Table 21-2 lists these four parts individually and tells a little about what each one does. Most of the parts are optional, as the table shows.

Table 21-2	Formatting Hyperlinks in Access
Hyperlink Part	*What It Is*
Display text	Optional. The text that's displayed. If omitted, the URL is displayed.
Address	Required. The URL (Uniform Resource Locator) such as a Web page.
Subaddress	Optional. A link on the same page or document.
Screen tip	Optional. Text that pops up if the user pauses his or her mouse cursor over the address.

Figure 21-2 shows a formatted hyperlink entered into a table and as it appears on an Access form. Sometimes it takes a bit of trial and error to make a link appear exactly as you want it, so don't worry if things don't quite work on the first try.

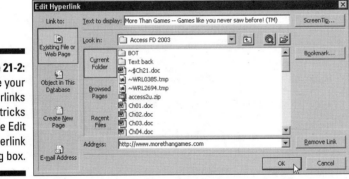

Figure 21-2:
Make your hyperlinks do tricks with the Edit Hyperlink dialog box.

Here are some examples of formatted hyperlinks and the obscure commands required to create them. (For an easier way to make complex hyperlinks, peek at the upcoming Tip.)

✔ www.microsoft.com displays the URL http://www.microsoft.com.

✔ Microsoft Corporation# http://www.microsoft.com# displays the words *Microsoft Corporation* in your Access table instead of showing the hyperlink itself.

✔ Microsoft Corporation# http://www.microsoft.com# Information# displays *Microsoft Corporation* and links to a topic called *Information* on that page.

✔ Microsoft Corporation# http://www.microsoft.com# Information#Redmond# displays *Microsoft Corporation* and links to a topic called *Information* on that page. When the user pauses the mouse pointer over the link, the word *Redmond* pops up. This trick works well when referring to documentation on an in-house Web site.

✔ Microsoft Corporation# http://www.microsoft.com##Redmond# displays *Microsoft Corporation*. When the user pauses the mouse pointer over the link, the word *Redmond* pops up. Because this one doesn't include a subaddress, it uses two pound signs between the URL and the tip, *Redmond*.

If all of those pound signs give you flashbacks to your last trip past the grocery store meat counter, format your hyperlinks the easy way with the Edit Hyperlink menu. To use this, right-click the hyperlink field you want to change in your table, and choose Hyperlink⇨Edit Hyperlink from the pop-up menu. The nifty little dialog box shown in Figure 21-2 appears. You can set the site address, the text that's displayed (if you want the link to say *Microsoft Corporation*), and the screen tip (the little text that pops up when your mouse hovers over a Web address). This dialog box also helps you include links for documents, spreadsheets, graphics, or even e-mail addresses right in an Access table. Pretty neat, eh? (Okay, it's a bit geeky, too.) Experiment with the dialog box a little to find out how everything works. It takes only a moment.

Although most hyperlinks store Web or other Internet addresses, they can point to just about anything in the known world. Thanks to their flexible tags, hyperlinks understand Web pages, intranet servers, database objects (reports, forms, and such), and even plain Microsoft Office documents on your computer or another networked PC.

Hyperlinks in your table work just like the ones you find on the Web — just point and click:

1. **Either log on to your network or start your Internet connection.**

   Internet Explorer needs everything up and running before it consents to make an appearance.

2. **Open the Access database you want to use, and then open the table containing those wonderful hyperlinks.**

   The fun is about to begin!

3. **Click the hyperlink of your choice.**

   If the hyperlink is to a Web page, Internet Explorer leaps on the screen, displaying the Web site from the link. If the link leads to something other than a Web site, Windows automatically fires up the right program to handle whatever the link has to offer.

Pushing Your Data onto the Web

Now that Access contains your coolest information, why not share your stuff with others in your company — or even publish it for the world? Whether you're building a commercial site geared toward fame and online fortune or a cross-department intranet to supercharge your company, Access contains all the tools you need to whip your data into Web-ready shape in no time.

Although you don't need to know anything about HTML to build Web pages with Access, you probably need to know some HTML before your project is finished. For a painless introduction to HTML, check out *HTML 4 For Dummies,* 4th Edition, by Ed Tittel and Natanya Pitts (published by Wiley Publishing, Inc.).

Access helps you publish data in two ways: static and dynamic. The method for your project depends on the equipment, goals, and expertise available in your immediate surroundings. Here's a quick comparison of the options:

✔ **Static:** This option is a straight conversion from Access to HTML. Its name reflects the fact that the stuff you convert doesn't change over time — it's a lot like taking a picture of your data. If you add more records to your table and want to include them in your Web-based stuff, you need to re-create the Web pages.

Static conversion is a great option for address lists and catalogs that don't change very often. It's also a good place to start when you're exploring the possibilities of the Web. You can convert almost any Access object — including tables, queries, forms, and reports — into a static Web page with the File➪Export option. (I show you how to do just that in the next section.)

✔ **Dynamic:** Instead of creating a simple HTML page that contains all your data, the Dynamic option builds a special goodie that Access calls a *data access page.* This is an HTML page that gives people access to your data, so they can see (and even change) your information through the corporate network or the Web. Data access pages work only with Access tables and queries.

Thanks to the Data Access Page Wizard, building a data access page isn't tough. But because all this technical magic requires some serious cooperation among the Web server, Access, and your database, *implementing* the finished data access page isn't necessarily a task for beginners. If your page will be viewed by more than a few people outside your company, you probably need to enlist the aid of a Web pro.

TIP

A few words about the Web (and why you care)

Although hyperlinks may seem like just so much technohype, they really are important. Nearly all businesses have a Web presence and many (if not most) are moving information to the Web. Companies are also creating in-house *intranets* (custom Web servers offering information to networked employees).

The capabilities of Access put it in the middle of the Web and intranet excitement — and that presents a cool opportunity for you. Duties that used to belong exclusively to *those computer* *people* are landing in graphic arts, marketing, and almost everywhere else. New jobs are born overnight as companies wrestle with the Web's powerful communication features.

If you're looking for a new career path in your corporate life, knowledge of the Web may be just the ticket. Whether you move into Web site development, information management, or even your own Web-oriented consulting business, this is an exciting time full of new possibilities. Dive in and discover what's waiting for you!

Although the details of making a data access page work may require some help from a trained computer professional, anyone can create a data access page by using the wizard. The process works a lot like the Form or Report Wizard. Here are the step-by-step details:

1. **Open the database containing the data destined for your intranet or the Web.**

   The database window hops to the screen.

2. **On the left side of the window, click the Pages button.**

   The database window changes, displaying three options dealing with data access pages.

3. **Double-click the Create Data Access Page by Using the Wizard option.**

   After a gratuitous amount of hard drive activity, the Data Access Page Wizard ambles forth, as shown in Figure 21-3.

4. **In the T̲ables/Queries box, click the down arrow, and then click the table or query you want on the data access page.**

   The Available Fields window lists all the fields in the selected table or query.

5. **For each field you want in the data access page, click the field name and then click the > button (greater than symbol).**

   The highlighted field hops into the Selected Fields list.

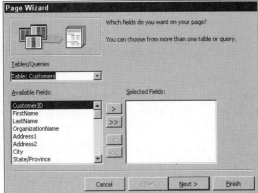

Figure 21-3:
The Data
Access
Page
Wizard
looks a lot
like the
Report
Wizard.

To copy all possible fields to the Selected Fields list, click the >> button (double greater than symbol). To remove a field, click its entry in the Selected Fields list, and then click the < button (less than symbol). To clear out the entire list and start over, click the << button (double less than symbol).

6. **Repeat Steps 4 and 5 for each table or query that you want to include. When all the fields are ready, click Next.**

   Data access pages understand how related tables work together, so you can include fields from several tables in one data access page. (Chapter 5 covers everything you ever wanted to know about relationships. For tips about other relationships, consult a good counselor.)

7. **To show your data in groups on your new data access page, click the fields you want to use to subtotal your records and then click the > button (greater than symbol) to add the new groups. After you finish, click Next.**

   With grouping complete, Access moves along to sorting and summary information.

   Groups in a data access page work just like groups in a report.

8. **To sort the detail records even further, select a field on the Sort Order and Summary Information page. Click Next after you're finished.**

   Most of the time, you won't need yet *another* layer of organization for your data. By this time, the data is sliced and diced a couple of times, thanks to the grouping options. However, if you *do* need more layers, feel free to add up to four more levels of sorting and summarizing.

9. **Type the page title you want, and then click Finish.**

The Wizard clunks, shimmies, and generally ambles around for a bit. After making you wait just long enough to prove that the process is woefully complex, the wizard delivers your finished data access page, as shown in Figure 21-4.

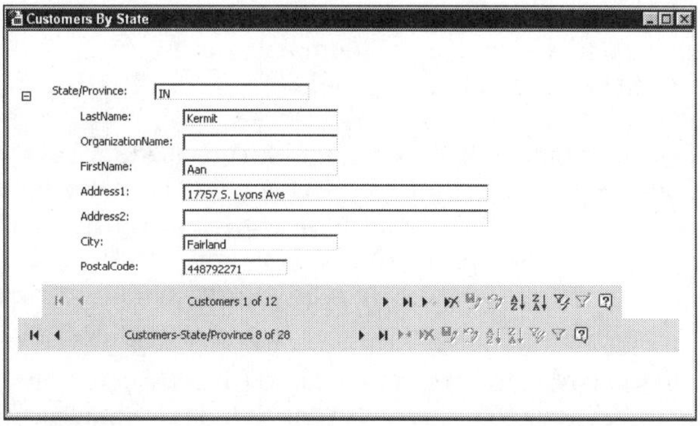

Figure 21-4: The finished data access page — looking good!

10. **Test your new page by running your Web browser and loading the page for a quick look, as shown in Figure 21-5.**

You may not be able to deploy your data access page on a big commercial Web site. Just as ActiveX technology makes it easy to create the page, it also restricts where it can be displayed. As of this writing, only Internet Explorer (Version 5.0 and above) can display data access pages.

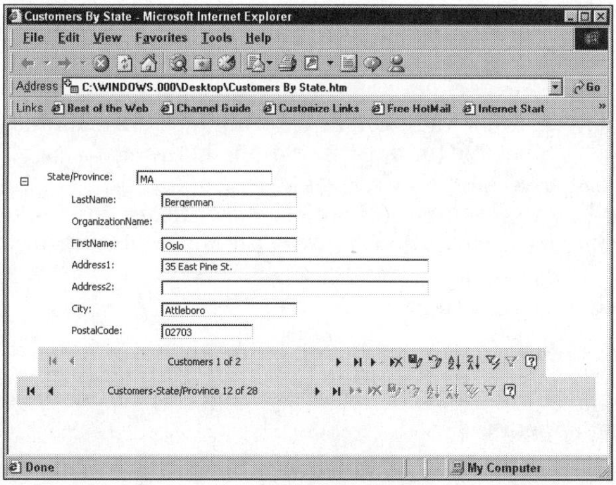

Figure 21-5: The data access page displayed in Internet Explorer.

Advanced Topics for Your Copious Nerd Time

If all the stuff in this chapter doesn't quell your technological impulses, don't worry — there's plenty more where this came from. Here are a few ideas to keep your mind active, your Web pages sharp, and your Access forms looking truly cool. Each item includes a brief summary plus a term to give to Office Assistant if you want all the details.

- ✔ Directly export datasheets, reports, and forms as static HTML pages with the File⇨Export menu selection. One or two quick clicks is all it takes to convert your data into a simple, unchanging Web page. This option is great when you're fluent in HTML and want to quickly generate a few pages of information that are ready for manual tweaking. Search for **export to HTML**.

- ✔ Put hyperlinks right into your reports and forms. Access lets you attach hyperlinks directly to command buttons, labels, or images. Search for **add hyperlink to form**.

- ✔ Build HTML template files to make your exported tables look, act, and dress the same. If you're building the mother of all database Web sites, template files are a big time-saver. Plus, they give your site a consistent, professional feel. Search for **HTML template files**.

- ✔ Add a Web browser to any Access form. Navigate through Web documents directly from a form — no need to switch between Access and your Web browser! This feature has great possibilities for corporate intranets, plus a lot of promise on the Internet, too. Search for **Web page on a form**.

These features just scratch the surface of all the special capabilities of Access. In addition to working with the Net, Access also works closely with the other members of the Microsoft Office suite. There's so much to know about how the programs interact that Microsoft created a huge informational file on the subject. The file is available for free through the Internet. To get all the details, view the Office Resource Kit by visiting www.microsoft.com/office/ork. However, in life, there are three certainties: death, taxes, and broken hyperlinks. If the preceding address doesn't work for you, follow these steps:

1. **Type** www.microsoft.com.

   A Support option appears at the top of the window.

2. **Click Support, and then choose Knowledge Base from the drop-down menu that appears.**

3. **In the Knowledge Base window, type the search term** Office Resource Kit.

   The search engine should return a link to the correct location.

Chapter 22

Making Forms that Look Cool and Work Great

. . . .

In This Chapter

▶ Taking a look at forms in Access

▶ Building a form with the Form Wizard

▶ Making simple forms with the AutoForm Wizard

▶ Improving on the Form Wizard's creation

. . . .

Paper forms make up the lifeblood of almost every enterprise. If they didn't, life would probably be simpler, and we'd have more trees, but that's beside the point. Because real life is the mirror that software engineers peer into when they design programs, Access includes the ever-cherished capability of viewing and working with forms.

Electronic forms are infinitely friendlier than their old-fashioned counterparts, the dreaded PBFs *(paper-based forms).* In fact, you may even discover that you *like* messing around with forms in Access. (If that happens to you, don't tell anyone.) This chapter looks at what forms can do for you, explores a few ways to make forms, and tosses out some tips for customizing forms so that they're exactly what you need.

Tax Forms and Data Forms Are Different Animals

All forms are not created equal. Paper forms make cool airplanes, are hard to update, take up physical space, and (depending on the number of forms involved) occasionally constitute a safety hazard when stacked. Access forms, on the other hand, are simple to update, easy to store, and are rarely a safety risk (although designing a form *can* be hazardous to your productivity because it's kinda fun).

Access forms have all kinds of advantages over old-fashioned paper forms — and they'll spoil you if you're used to wandering through your data in datasheet view. Here's a sampling of how forms in Access make viewing your data easier. You can

- ✔ **Escape the clutches of datasheet view:** Instead of scrolling back and forth through a datasheet, you focus on one record at a time, with all the data pleasantly laid out on a single screen.

- ✔ **Modify at will:** When your needs change, update the form in design view. And you don't have to worry about recycling 10,000 leftover copies of the old form.

- ✔ **See your data any way you want:** Access lets you take one set of data and present it in as many different forms as you want — all without re-entering a bit of data for the new form. Create a special form for the data-entry folks, another for your analysts, and a third for yourself. Well-designed forms give the right information to the right people without revealing unnecessary data.

- ✔ **View the entries in a table or the results of a query:** Forms pull information from tables or queries with equal ease. Forms based on queries are especially flexible because they always display the latest information.

- ✔ **Combine data from linked tables:** One form can display data from several related tables. Forms automatically use the relationships built into your database.

Like reports and queries, forms are stored in the database file under their own button, as shown in Figure 22-1. Forms are full-fledged Access objects, so you can do all kinds of cool tricks with them.

Depending on your needs, you can make forms in three ways:

- ✔ The Form Wizard walks you through a series of questions and proudly produces a rather bland-looking form.

- ✔ The three AutoForm tools make the same forms as the Form Wizard but don't ask any questions.

- ✔ Access sets up a blank form, drops off a toolbox full of form-related goodies, shakes your hand, and then wanders off to do something fun while you make a form from scratch.

I believe in keeping systems as simple as possible because simple things just work better. In keeping with that philosophy, this chapter explains how to enlist the Form Wizard and the AutoForm tools to build basic forms *for* you. The chapter closes with tips and tricks for manually turning these Masterpieces of Vanilla into Truly Cool Forms.

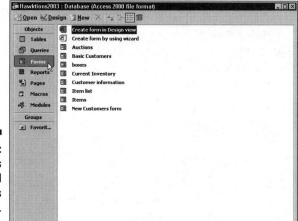

Figure 22-1:
Click Forms
to see all
your Access
forms.

Creating a Form at the Wave of a Wand

The easiest way to create the best in computer-designed forms (not stunning forms or incredibly useful forms) is by using the Form Wizard. As with all other Access wizards, the Form Wizard steps you through the creation process.

To get the Form Wizard up and running, follow these steps:

1. **Open your database file.**

2. **In the Objects bar, click the Forms button.**

   Access displays a list of the forms currently in your database. Don't fret if the current list looks empty — you're about to change that.

3. **Near the top of the of the database window, click the <u>N</u>ew button.**

   The New Form dialog box appears.

   The next time you want to create a form, you also can double-click the Create Form by Using the Wizard option instead of using New. Think of this option as a shortcut to the wizard's lair.

4. **Double-click Form Wizard, as shown in Figure 22-2.**

   At this point, the computer's hard disk usually sounds like it's having a massive fight with itself. When the noise dies down, the Form Wizard poofs into action.

Figure 22-2:
Invoking the
Form Wizard.

5. **In the Tables/Queries box, click the down arrow to list the tables and queries in your database, and then select the one that contains the fields you want to view with this form.**

   The Form Wizard lists the available fields.

6. **In the Available Fields list, double-click a field name to include the field in your form. Repeat this step for each field destined for the form (see Figure 22-3).**

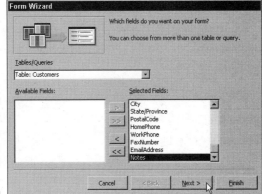

Figure 22-3:
Select the
fields you
want to see
on the form.

   If you want to see all the fields, click the >> button in the middle of the screen. To remove a field that you accidentally chose, double-click its name in the Selected Fields list. The field jumps back to the Available Fields side of the dialog box.

7. **When you're finished, click Next.**

   If you selected fields from more than one table, the Form Wizard takes a moment to ask how you want to organize the data in your form.

8. **If the wizard asks you about sorting the data, click your choice in the list on the left side of the dialog box, and then click N̲ext.**

9. **When the wizard asks about the form layout, leave the option set to C̲olumnar (for a single-table form) or D̲atasheet (for forms containing data from more than one table), and then click N̲ext.**

   For more information about the other options, check out the "Giving the Form Just the Right Look" section, later in this chapter.

10. **Choose the color and background styles for displaying your data, as shown in Figure 22-4, and then click N̲ext.**

    Although the colorful forms look neat, some of them slow down the performance of your forms. Experiment a little to find the right combination for your needs.

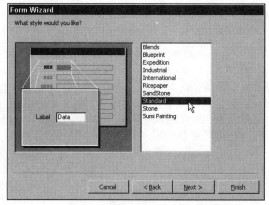

Figure 22-4: It's tempting to be fancy, but for now keep it simple.

11. **In the What Title Do You Want for Your Form? box at the top of the Form Wizard screen, type a descriptive title.**

    By default, the Form Wizard offers you the name of the table that you used to feed the form, but *please* use something more descriptive than that.

12. **Click F̲inish.**

    Your new form appears on the screen, ready for action, as shown in Figure 22-5.

    The Form Wizard automatically saves the form as part of the creation process, so you don't need to manually save and name it.

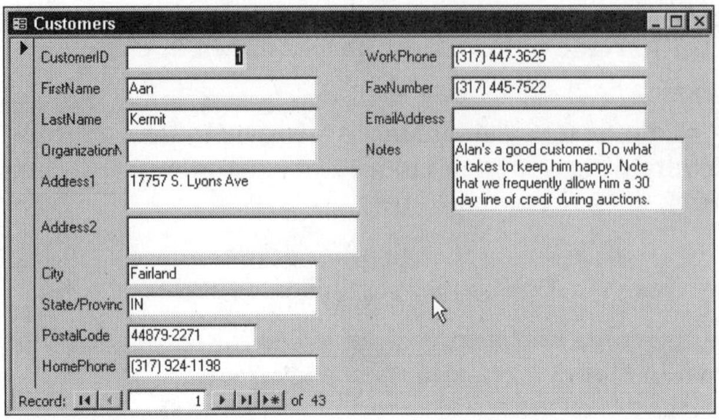

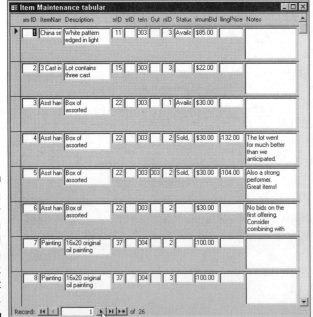

Figure 22-5:
The new
form's not
pretty, but
it's a place
to start.

Giving the Form Just the Right Look

Depending on the data you select for your form (for example, whether you use more than one table), you have different options for displaying your data:

- ✔ **Columnar:** A classic, one-record-per-page form. Most data entry forms use Columnar.
- ✔ **Tabular:** A multiple-records-per-page form (see Figure 22-6). Be ready for some cosmetic surgery (rearranging and resizing to make the form more attractive) to grind away the rough edges and make the form truly useful. This type of layout is good for reports.

Figure 22-6:
This Tabular
form is
functional
but needs a
little work
to make it
prettier.

✔ **Datasheet:** A spreadsheet-like grid. Essentially, this is an Access datasheet view embedded in a form and is appropriate when an Excel-style presentation suits your needs.

✔ **Justified:** The data is laid out across the whole form over multiple rows (see Figure 22-7). This is an interesting layout and may be especially useful where you have memo fields.

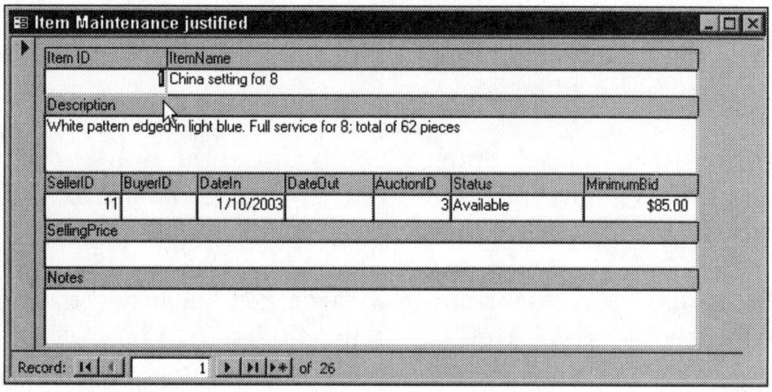

Figure 22-7: The Justified form layout.

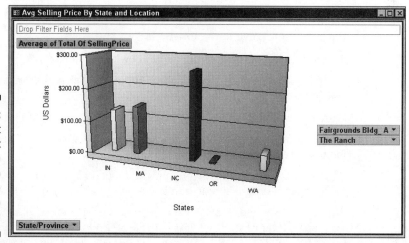

✔ **Pivot Table:** Summarizes data, allows you to interactively play with — er, analyze — data on the screen, plus displays or hides details depending on your whims.

✔ **Pivot Chart:** A graphical analysis of data (see Figure 22-8) that lets you drag items you want to analyze.

Figure 22-8: The Pivot Chart layout allows the viewer to choose the data to analyze.

Mass Production at Its Best: Forms from the Auto Factory

When I was a kid, I became fascinated with business and how it worked. Reading about the move from hand-built products to Henry Ford's automated assembly line particularly amazed me. (Yes, I *was* a little different. Why do you ask?) The assembly line had its good and bad points, but the quote that always defined the Ford assembly line for me was, "You can have any color you want, as long as it's black."

With that thought in mind, let me welcome you to the AutoForm Factory. Our motto: "You can have any form you want, as long as it's one of the three we make." Ah, the joys of flexible production management.

Access claims that the AutoForms are wizards, but because they're so limited — er, I mean *focused* — I don't think of them as full-fledged purveyors of the magical arts. Semantics aside, you can use AutoForms to build any of the form types mentioned in the preceding section.

Using AutoForms is a quick process. Despite their alleged *wizard* status, AutoForms are more like office temps: Just point them at data, stand back, and before you know it, the form is finished. Follow these steps to use AutoForms:

1. **With your database open, click the Forms button (in the Objects bar on the left side of the database window).**

2. **Click New.**

   The New Form dialog box hops onto the screen, ready to help.

3. **Click the AutoForm entry for the layout you want.**

   Access highlights the appropriate mini-wizard name.

4. **Click the down arrow next to the Choose the Table text box (below the Wizard list).**

   A drop-down list of tables and queries in the current database appears.

5. **Click the table or query that you want to provide information for this form, and then click OK.**

   The appropriate mini-wizard begins its focused little job, and your new form appears on the screen in a few moments.

The AutoForm items work with any one table or query. To include fields from more than one table in an AutoForm, build the AutoForm from a query that pulls the fields together on its own. That part of the process goes *way* beyond the AutoForm's limited brain power.

6. **To save your form, choose File⇨Save or click the Save button on the toolbar. Type a name for the form in the dialog box that appears.**

   After a few moments of hard drive chugging, your form finds a home somewhere inside the computer.

7. **Click OK.**

   Unlike the Form Wizard, AutoForms *don't* automatically save the form they create, so you have to save the form manually. The form is added to your database on the Forms button.

Ultimate Beauty through Cosmetic Surgery

Tell me the brutal truth, okay? I want your honest opinion on this. Ready? Would you rather slavishly toil away in the data-entry sweatshop of Figure 22-5 or casually pop a few records into Figure 22-9 between tennis sets? Take your time to answer.

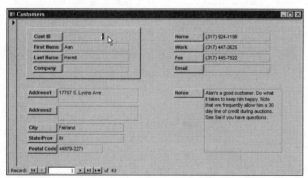

Figure 22-9: This is the same form as Figure 22-5 (honest!) after five or six minutes of surgery.

Believe it or not, those images are the *same kind of form.* Yup, it's true. The *Before* image in Figure 22-5 is a standard columnar form straight from the AutoForm Factory of the preceding section. The *After* image is also a standard columnar form, but I transformed it by moving some fields around, adding some graphics to segment the form, and changing the tab order to make data entry more intuitive.

In the next section, I show how you too can make your forms more, well, sexy. (And if you find these forms sexy, you're probably breaking some law.) Access gives you the basic tool kit used by top form surgeons around the country. In no time at all, your frumpy forms are sleek data-entry machines, both functionally useful and visually appealing.

Taking a form into Design view

Before you can make *any* of these changes, the form has to be in design view. Access provides two easy ways to get there:

- ✔ **From the database window:** Click the Forms button on the Objects bar to list the available forms. Click the form you want to change, and then click Design.

- ✔ **From a form window:** Click the Design button on the toolbar or choose View➪Design from the menu.

Don't let design view stress you out. If something goes wrong and you accidentally mess up your form, just choose File➪Close from the menu. When Access asks about saving your changes, politely click No. This step throws out all the horrible changes you just made to the form. Take a few deep breaths to calm your nerves and start the design process over again.

Moving fields

To move a field around in design view, follow these steps:

1. **Put the mouse pointer anywhere on the field that you want to move.**

   You can point to the field name or the box where the field value goes. Either place is equally fine for what you're doing.

   If the field is already selected (the name has a box around it that's decorated with small, filled-in squares), click any blank spot of your form to deselect the field; then start with Step 1. Otherwise, Access gets confused and thinks you want to do something *other* than just move the field.

2. **Press and hold down the left mouse button.**

   The mouse pointer turns into a hand, which is how Access tells you that it's ready to move something. Strange response, isn't it?

3. **Drag the field to its new location.**

   As you move the field, a pair of white boxes moves along with the cursor to show you precisely where the field goes.

4. **When the field is in position, release the mouse button.**

   The field drops smoothly into place.

   If you don't like where the field landed, either move it again or press Ctrl+Z to undo the move and start over from scratch.

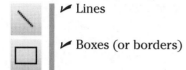

Adding lines and boxes

Two buttons near the bottom of design view enable you to create the following on your form:

✔ Lines

✔ Boxes (or borders)

Here's how to use these tools:

1. **Click the tool of your choice.**

   The tool appears pushed in, just like a toggle button.

2. **Put the mouse pointer where you want to start the line or place the corner of a box; then press and hold down the left mouse button.**

   Aim is important, but you can always undo or move the graphic if the project doesn't work out quite right.

3. **Move the cursor to the spot where the line ends or to the opposite corner of your box and then release the mouse button.**

   The line or box appears on the screen.

You can apply special effects to your line or box graphics:

✔ Lines can be flat or raised. Even though the other options seem to be available, they don't look any different from raised when you're working with a line.

✔ Boxes have six special effects: flat, etched, raised, shadowed, sunken, and chiseled.

To use these special effects, draw a line or box and then right-click it (if it's a line, right-click one end). Choose Special Effects from the pop-up menu and then click the particular effect you like best.

If you want to further customize your line or box, give the following Border settings a try. In the Special Effects dialog box, click the Format button and then click one of the following:

✔ **Border Style:** Adjusts how the line looks, with options ranging from solid to dotted.

✔ **Border Color:** Changes the line's color.

✔ **Border Width:** Makes the line anything from a wispy hairline to a bold 6-point behemoth.

Experiment with the settings to come up with the best combination. As with the special effects settings, click the X button at the top-right corner to close the dialog box when you're finished.

Changing the field tab order

When you have a window open inside any program and press the Tab key, the cursor moves around the screen from item to item in a predefined order. Access allows you to create a tab order so that the cursor moves through your forms in a rational manner (such as going from the First Name field to the Last Name field). You accomplish this by changing the Tab Index property of each control as follows:

1. **With the form open in design view, choose View⇨Tab Order.**

   The Tab Order dialog box opens, listing the fields in their current tab order.

2. **Click the small square to the left of the field you want to work with (as shown in Figure 22-10).**

   The field becomes highlighted.

To have Access automatically set the tab order for all the fields in the form, click the Auto Order button at the bottom of the Tab Order dialog box. Access sets the order according to where the field is in the form. It starts at the upper-left side of the form and goes across, moves down one line, and then repeats the process. Fields end up in order horizontally (fields on line one, fields on line two, and so on).

Figure 22-10: In the Tab Order dialog box, you can rearrange the order that the cursor moves through your fields.

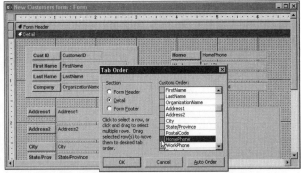

3. **Click and drag the field to its new position in the tab order.**

   As you drag the field, a dark gray bar moves with it, showing where the field goes in the tab order. When the bar is in the right place, release the button. Access moves the field to its new position in the tab order.

4. Repeat Steps 2 and 3 for any other fields you want to change.

Access doesn't care how much you work with the tab order, so play to your heart's content.

5. Click OK after you finish adjusting the tab order.

The Tab Order dialog box runs off to wherever dialog boxes hang out when they're not on the screen.

6. Click the Form View button on the toolbar and test your work.

If any fields are still out of order, note them and then work through these steps to correct the order.

Chapter 23

If Love Is Universal, Why Can't I Export to It?

*T*o achieve true success these days, speaking only the tongue of the country that bore you isn't enough. You need to be comfortable with several languages before the pinnacle of achievement is within your grasp. I, for example, am fluent in American English, a language that the British view as a poor substitute for grunting and knocking rocks together. For work, I also studied several variants of the geek vernacular, including Windows, Unix, the pictorial troubleshooting tongue *$%@&#!*, and the esoteric dialect Macintosh (a particularly challenging idiom where all the words look and act alike).

Access is multilingual as well, because its electronic world is filled with more disagreeing tongues than the United Nations in general session. To simplify your life, Access understands a few spreadsheets, several competing databases, and even plain old text files. Because of this capability, you can exchange data with almost any source out there. Access is one of the most flexible programs I've ever seen (and I've seen a *bunch* of programs).

This chapter looks at the import and export capabilities of Access, how they work, and what you can do with them. If you work with Access and almost any other program, you need this chapter, because sometime soon, some data will be in the wrong place — and guess whose job it will be to move it.

Importing Only the Best Information for Your Databases

Access includes two ways of sucking data into its greedy clutches. *Importing* involves translating the data from a foreign format into the Access database file format (which, according to Microsoft, all the world's data should be stored in). The other method is *linking*, where you build a temporary bridge between the external data and Access.

If you worked with older versions of Access, linking used to be called *attaching*. The concept is the same; only the name has been changed to confuse the innocent.

Translating file formats

Regardless of whether you import or link the data, Access understands only certain data formats. Table 23-1 lists the most common file types that Access interacts with. Believe it or not, the entries in this table cover the majority of data stored on PCs around the world.

Table 23-1	Access Language Fluencies		
Program	*File Extension*	*Versions*	*Comments*
Access	.MDB	2.0, 7.0/95, 8.0/97, 9.0/2000, 10.0/2002	Although they share the same name, these versions use slightly different file formats than Access.
ODBC	n/a	n/a	Use ODBC (Open Database Connectivity) to connect to other databases such as Oracle.
Exchange/ Outlook	n/a	n/a	Link your Outlook Contacts folder straight to an Access database.
dBASE	.DBF	III, IV, 5	One of the most popular formats out there; many programs use the dBASE format.

Program	File Extension	Versions	Comments
FoxPro	.DBF	2.x, 3.0, 5.0, 6.x	The other desktop database program of Microsoft; not directly compatible with dBASE in some cases.
Paradox	.DB	3.x, 4.x, 5.0	A competing database from Borland.
Excel	.XLS	3.0, 4.0, 5.0, 7.0/95, 8.0/97, 9.0/2000, 10.0/2002	Although Excel is a spreadsheet, many people use it as a simple flat file database manager.
Lotus 1-2-3	.WKS, .WK1, .WK31, .WK4	All	At one time, the most popular spreadsheet.
Text	.TXT	n/a	The "if all else fails" format; Access understands both delimited and fixed-width text files.
XML	.XML	All	XML (eXtensible Markup Language) stores and describes your data.
HTML	.HTM, .HTML	1.0 (lists), 2.0 (tables), 3.x (tables)	The Web page codes that make a Web page a Web page.

Although Access is pretty intelligent about the translation process, you need to watch out for some quirks. Here are some specific tips to keep in mind as you play The Great Data Liberator and set imperiled information free to enjoy a new life in Access:

✔ Double-check information coming from any spreadsheet program to be sure that it's *consistent* and *complete*. Above all, make sure that all entries in each column (field) are the same type (all numbers, text, or whatever). Otherwise, the import won't work correctly (and you know how forgiving software is of such "little" problems).

✔ When working with dBASE and FoxPro files, keep careful track of the index files that go along with the database files. Access needs the index to work with the table. If Access can't find the index or if it's corrupt, try canceling the prompt that requests the index file and see whether the import worked.

✔ If a Paradox table doesn't have a primary key, Access can't write changes to it. To correct the problem, use Paradox to create a primary key in the table and *then* link the table to Access.

✔ If you have difficulty importing a given format, try opening the file with the old database product and using that program's exporting tools to shove your data into a text file (the data techies use its formal name, ASCII). Text may be cumbersome to manage, but it's the most widely recognized form of data known to man (or computer).

Always back up your data before importing, exporting, or even leaving the office for a short vacation. The computer person's advice always begins, "Well, nothing should go wrong," but wise folks prepare for the worst. Make copies of your databases *before* trying the techniques in this chapter.

Importing or linking your files

The precise details of importing and linking depend greatly on the type of file you're importing, but here are the general steps to get you started in the right direction. Although the instructions are written mainly for importing, they include supporting notes about linking as well.

Ready to take a spin at the *Data Import Polka?* Here goes:

1. **Open the Access database that you're pulling data into.**

   If you're not familiar with this step, *stop* — don't go any further. Flip to Chapter 1 and spend some time getting comfy with Access before attempting to import.

2. **Choose File⇨Get External Data⇨Import.**

   The dialog box shown in Figure 23-1 appears.

To import or to link — the answer is, it depends

Because Access offers two ways to get data in, a logical question comes up: Which method should I use? Because this question involves a computer, the simple answer is that it depends.

The answer mainly depends on the other program and its fate in your organization. Are you still using the other program to update the data? Do other people use the program to access the data? If so, use a link with Access. This option

lets you play with the data while keeping it in the original format so that everyone else can use it as well.

On the other hand, if the other application was mothballed and you're rescuing data, import the data permanently and give it a comfortable new home. Preserving a data format that nobody cares about anymore makes no sense.

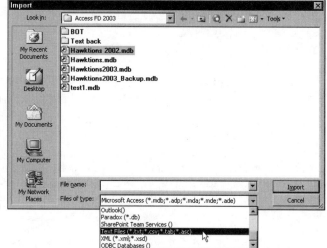

Figure 23-1:
Make sure
that you
choose the
correct file
type.

3. **In the Files of Type box (at the bottom of the window), click the down arrow, and then click the kind of data you're importing. (If necessary, use the Look In list box to navigate your way to the files.)**

   The dialog box displays the matching files for your selection pleasure. Make sure that you choose the correct file type. Otherwise, Access doesn't list the file you're looking for in the dialog box!

   If your database file has a strange, nonstandard extension on the end of the file name (such as .FOO, .DTA, or .XXX), Access may not be able to make heads or tails of the file. In that case, seek help from your technical support people or local computer jockey.

4. **Double-click the file that you want to import.**

   Here's where the process takes off in wildly different directions depending on the file format you're importing and whether you're linking or importing. The only sage advice I can give is to cross your fingers, follow the on-screen instructions carefully, refer to the preceding tips, hope for the best, and take comfort in the knowledge that you made backup copies of your databases before starting this sordid process. (You *did* make those backups, right?)

If you're importing and the process is taking forever, Access is probably struggling with errors in the inbound data. Press Ctrl+Break to stop the import process and check the data that's being imported for obvious errors (bad or corrupt data, badly organized spreadsheet data, invalid index, and so on).

Sending Your Data on a Long, One-Way Trip

In the interest of keeping you awake, I'll keep this explanation short: Exporting is just like importing, except where it's different.

Hmm . . . perhaps that explanation was a little *too* short.

Exporting a table involves reorganizing the data it contains into a different format. As with importing, Access can translate the data into a variety of languages, depending on your needs. The master list of export formats is the same one governing imports, described earlier in the chapter.

The main problem to keep an eye out for when exporting is *data loss*. Not all storage formats are created equal (after all, Microsoft didn't come up with them *all*, which is arguably a good situation). Just because the data looked glorious in your Access table doesn't mean a suitable home is waiting when you ship the information off to, say, Paradox or FoxPro. Special Access data types such as AutoNumber, Yes/No, Memo, and OLE are almost sure to cause problems. Be ready for some creative problem-solving to make the data work just the way you want it to work.

Likewise, field names can be trouble. Access is generous about what you can put into a field name. dBASE, on the other hand, is downright totalitarian about field names. This attitude can lead to multiple fields with the same name — a frustrating (if slightly humorous) problem. If you export an Access table with fields called Projected2000Sales, Projected2000Net, and Projected2000Overhead, ending up with three fields named Projected1 is distinctly possible — *not* a pleasant thought. Be ready to spend some time tuning the export so that it works just the way you want.

The steps to exporting a table are much simpler than they are for importing. Here goes:

1. **With the database open, click the table that you want to export.**

   As you may expect, the table name is highlighted for the world to see.

2. **Choose File⇨Export from the main menu.**

   The Export Table dialog box bounds merrily onto the screen.

3. **In the Save As Type box, click the down arrow to list the available exporting formats; then select the one you want (as shown in Figure 23-2).**

If the format you're looking for is in Table 23-1 but is not in your list on the screen, run the Access setup program again (oh joy, oh rapture!) and install that format on your system.

Figure 23-2:
I chose to
export a
table as
HTML.

4. **Brace yourself and click Export.**

   Depending on the file type you export to, you may get absolutely no feedback that the export was successful other than the lack of an error message. You should be able to go to the other program and see your table there.

If you export to HTML or to XML, you can click the Autostart check box (shown in Figure 23-2). That option saves you a little time by telling Access to fire up Internet Explorer automatically and display your data. Figure 23-3 shows the final results of the export, proudly presented by Microsoft's favorite Web browser.

When exporting to HTML or XML, perfectionist developers use the file that Access created as a starting point. From there, they manually add all the delightful HTML tags that format, color, indent, and visually fluff up the data on the screen. Whether you want to do this is entirely up to you. Creating the Web page in Figure 23-3 took only a few steps, but the results don't look particularly beautiful. If you feel the need, open the finished HTML or XML file with your favorite Web page editor (such as Microsoft FrontPage) and add appropriate formatting, colors, and so on.

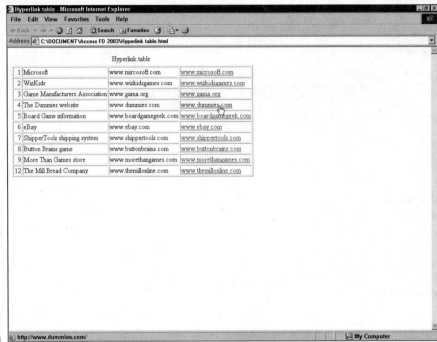

Figure 23-3:
Internet
Explorer
proudly
displays
my table.

Chapter 24

The Analyzer: Your Data's Dr. Freud, Dr. Watson, and Dr. Jekyll

In This Chapter

▶ Becoming relational with the Table Analyzer

▶ Making the database document

▶ Steering clear of the Performance Analyzer

*1*f I didn't know better, I'd file this chapter under the heading *Oh Sure, That's What It Does* (said with heavy sarcasm). After all, the Analyzer promises to do the three tasks nearest to a database person's heart:

✔ Convert flat files into relational databases automatically

✔ Document the database and all its sundry parts (including tables, queries, forms, and reports)

✔ Analyze the structure of your tables to make sure that everything is set up in the best possible way

Although technology has come a long way in recent years, it's not as advanced as you may expect. That caveat is true of the Analyzer, too — it promises more than it delivers. On the bright side, it delivers a great deal, so the Analyzer gets a chapter of its own, a place to extol its two virtues and reveal its shortcoming. (I guess one out of three isn't bad.)

It Slices, It Dices, It Builds Relational Databases!

Arguably, the Analyzer's biggest promise is hiding under Tools⇨Analyze⇨Table. This piece of software claims it can turn a flat file table into a relational database with minimal human intervention *and* check for spelling errors in the data at the same time.

Truth be told, the Analyzer tries awfully hard to convert the flat file into a relational database. But, like most software, sometimes it gets confused and vaults off in the wrong direction. I still recommend giving the Analyzer a try, simply because it *may* work on your table, and if it does, you just saved a ton of time and effort.

The Analyzer works best with a flat file table that contains plenty of duplicate information. For example, imagine a flat file table for a video rental store. Each record in the table contains customer and movie data. If the same customer rents six movies, the table contains six separate records with the customer's name, address, and other information duplicated in every one. Multiply that by 1000 customers, and you have precisely the kind of flat file mess that the Analyzer loves to solve.

With that thought in mind, here's how to invoke the Table Analyzer Wizard:

1. **Open your database and choose Tools➪Analyze➪Table.**

   After a period of thought punctuated by hard disk activity, the Table Analyzer Wizard dialog box appears, as shown in Figure 24-1.

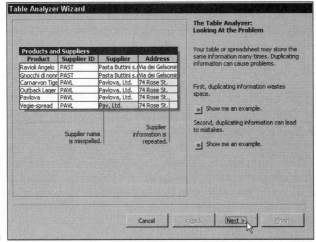

Figure 24-1: Introducing the Table Analyzer.

2. **Read the first two screens if you want (they're strictly educational); click Next after each one.**

   Another Table Analyzer Wizard screen appears, as shown in Figure 24-2.

3. **Click the name of the table on which you want to do relational magic, and then click Next.**

   In the dialog box that appears, the wizard asks whether you want to decide which fields go where or just let the wizard do its thing.

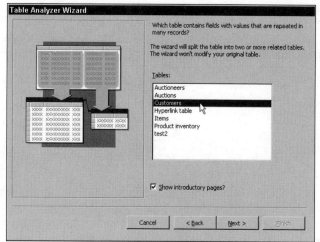

Figure 24-2:
Select a
table to
analyze.

4. **Click the Yes option (if it's not already selected) to give the wizard a free hand in massaging your table, and then click Next.**

   This step starts the analysis process. The wizard leaps into the task, displaying a few horizontal bar charts to show how the project is progressing. When the Analysis Stages bar gets all the way to the end, the wizard is finished. The results look like those shown in Figure 24-3.

5. **If you like what the wizard came up with, name the tables by clicking each table and then clicking the Name Table button (the one that looks like a pencil doodling on a table). Or you can use your mouse to drag and drop fields from table to table and rename the tables. When you're finished, click Next.**

   If the wizard recommends that you don't split your table, carefully click the Cancel button and pat yourself on the head for a job well done. That's the wizard's way of saying that it thinks your table is fine just as it is.

6. **Designate a key field by clicking a field in the table and then clicking the Key button. (The Key button replaced the Name Table button from Step 5 in the upper-right side of the dialog box.)**

   This step lets you replace many of the Generated Unique ID entries that the wizard put in the tables. Make sure that each table has a key field before continuing!

   Now that the structure is basically complete, the wizard turns its attention to typographical errors in the database. Essentially, the wizard acts as a spell-checker by searching for fields that *seem* to be the same except for minor differences.

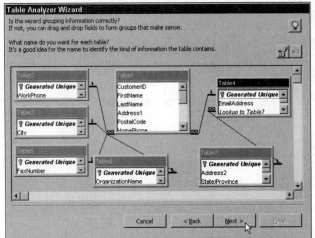

Figure 24-3:
Unfortunately,
Access
didn't do a
good job of
analyzing
the
database.

You don't have to do anything to make the typo-checker kick in. Typo-checking happens automatically after Access analyzes the database structure. Depending on the condition of your data, you may have many records to correct. Be patient — the wizard really *is* helping!

After the wizard makes corrections, it offers to create a query that looks and acts like your original table. If you have reports and forms that work with the flat file, they'll work with the new table(s).

7. **Click the No option if you've changed your mind and want to forget the whole thing. Otherwise, click Finish to exit the wizard.**

If you click Finish, Access creates a query that runs against your original table. The query looks and acts like a "real" table. The original table is renamed, and any reports and forms automatically use the query instead of the original table.

The Table Analyzer is highly unlikely to correctly split a flat file database into a properly designed relational database. You're much better off bringing the database to a qualified human and letting him or her properly redesign it.

Documentation: What to Give the Nerd in Your Life

Pardon me while I put on my technoweenie hat and taped-together glasses for a moment. The world needs more *documentation* (can't ever have enough, in fact). If life were better documented, it would be easier.

In truth, documentation is probably the task furthest from your mind right now, but it's still important, especially if you're creating something for your business. I know that you barely have time to get the database running and tested, but you absolutely need to document what you're creating.

Like many problems, documenting your work is a tradeoff between a dire need and a lack of time. What's a person to do? Call the Documenter!

This second piece of the Analyzer puzzle browses through everything in your database (and I do mean everything) and documents the living daylights out of it all. The Documenter collects information so obscure that I'm not even sure the programmers know what some of it means.

The neat part of the Documenter is that it works by itself. Really. You start it, sic it on a database, and nip off for a spot of lunch. When you come back, the Documenter's report is finished and waiting. Poof! Instant documentation.

Here's how to put the Documenter to work on your database:

1. **Open the database file and choose <u>T</u>ools⇨Analyze⇨<u>D</u>ocumenter.**

2. **In the Documenter dialog box, click the All Object Types tab, as shown in Figure 24-4.**

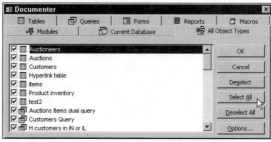

Figure 24-4:
Click the
All Object
Types
tab and
then click
Select All.

3. **Click the Select <u>A</u>ll button to document your entire database, and then click OK to start the process.**

    The Documenter begins by examining all the objects in your database, starting with the tables and moving on to the queries, forms, reports, and so on. During the process, your forms appear on the screen for a moment — that's normal.

    The process often takes a while, so use this time for lunch or a coffee break. When the Documenter finishes, it leaves a report packed with information about your database, as shown in Figure 24-5.

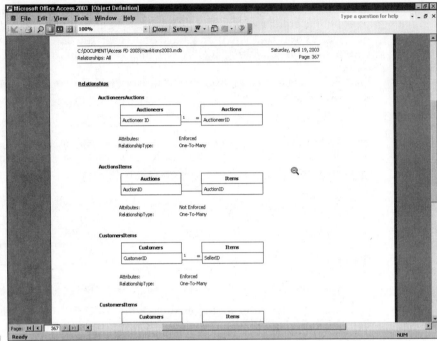

Figure 24-5:
Page 367
shows some
of the table
relationships.

4. **Click the Print button on the toolbar or choose File⇨Print to get a paper copy.**

Access doesn't care a whit about trees or how much paper costs, so it gleefully generates hundreds of documentation pages about your database. If you don't want a ream of paper describing your database, consider saving the report and then referring back to it later. To store the report for posterity, choose File⇨Save As Table and then give the table a name.

Performance: Toward a Better Database

Like the Design Analyzer, the Performance Analyzer is far from perfect. When you run it (and you should), take the suggestions with a grain of salt. Goodness knows that it tries, but it's just a machine.

To use the Performance Analyzer, follow these steps:

1. **Open the database file and choose Tools⇨Analyze⇨Performance.**

The Database Performance Analyzer appears.

2. **Choose the objects that you want to analyze, and then click Next.**

   I recommend clicking the All Object Types tab and then clicking the Select All button, as you did for the Documentation tool. The screen is identical to the one shown in Figure 24-4.

3. **Select each result (as shown in Figure 24-6) and review the comments.**

   If Access can make the changes for you, the Optimize button will be enabled. Otherwise, use a pencil and paper and jot down any good thoughts that Access may offer.

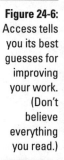

Figure 24-6:
Access tells
you its best
guesses for
improving
your work.
(Don't
believe
everything
you read.)

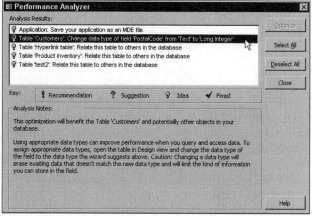

Ask your local computer guru for his or her opinion before implementing any of Access's recommended changes.

Chapter 25

Talking to Your Computer

*I*t wasn't long ago that talking to your computer marked you as a disturbed person or a Trekkie. Perceptions have changed. The entire Office suite, including Access, has the Lernout & Hauspie (L & H) speech recognition engine built in. That means you can pretty much tell Access what to do and have a reasonable expectation that it won't talk back. (Did you ever wish your significant other would do the same?)

Most people find speech recognition in Access to be of limited usefulness unless their database contains a lot of lengthy text fields where dictation may come in handy. But if you're among the many thousands who have trouble using the keyboard, voice recognition may well be a savior.

This chapter provides an overview of how speech recognition works in Access (which pretty much covers the other Office applications, too), how to use it, and why you might care.

What Is Speech Recognition (and What Can I Do with It)?

Speech recognition is an amazing technology. The computer "listens" to what you say by breaking electronic signals from a microphone into individual *tokens* and then combining those tokens into words based on a predefined vocabulary that the software understands. (So, if you said "gastroenterologist," the software would likely be confused unless you previously bought and installed a medical vocabulary.) However, it gets more complicated than that.

Consider the phrase "Two bee oar knot too be." It doesn't look like much when you read it, but if you read it out loud, you probably recognize Hamlet's famous quote from the Shakespeare play. The connected sounds called up the solution from your memory, and suddenly the gobbledy-gook made sense.

When the computer listens to that same phrase, it hears only letter combinations. It needs some other tools and rules to assemble those sounds into a classic theater reference. It has to discern among several — sometimes *many* — possibilities for each word, and then choose the right one. Then it repeats the process over and over to finally build a sentence. And then it assembles the sentences into a paragraph. And if it messes up *anywhere,* things start going *very* badly. To overcome these problems, the computer applies some grammatical rules to discern among the myriad words, and organize the words into music — er, text.

Further complicating the process of speech recognition is the fact that we all talk differently, and we may be in a noisy environment. Accurate speech recognition is nothing short of a miracle, but as good as today's technology is, it's still far from perfect. Even with its problems, people with repetitive strain injuries or other disabilities may find speech recognition a boon.

You can use the speech recognition feature in two ways:

- **Dictation:** If you place the cursor in the customer last name field and say "Smith," for example, Access responds by typing the word *Smith* for you. You can use dictation pretty much anywhere you can type text.
- **Command:** If you dictate the command "Print," for example, Access prints the document.

Installing Speech Recognition

Microsoft recommends the following *minimum* configuration for your computer if you want to use speech recognition:

- ✔ A high-quality, headset-based microphone with gain adjustment (built-in amplifier). Microsoft recommends a USB microphone, but I think it's some kind of plot.

- ✔ A 400 MHz or faster CPU.

- ✔ 128MB memory.

- ✔ Windows 98 or later or Windows NT 4.0 or later.

- ✔ Microsoft Internet Explorer 5.0 or later.

The key requirement in this list is memory. I performed some informal testing, with the following results: On a 350-MHz PC with 256MB of memory, speech recognition worked well; on a 733-MHz PC with 128MB, performance was not great; and on a 400-MHz PC with 128MB, performance was dismal. Your results may not match these. Running a lot of software simultaneously increases the amount of processing power your computer needs overall, which affects the system's speech recognition capabilities, too.

As you may expect, before you can use speech recognition, you have to install it. What you probably *didn't* expect, though, is that you install speech recognition for Access by firing up Microsoft Word. Yes, for goodness-only-knows what reason, Microsoft shoved the speech recognition tool into Word. To install everything, flip over to Word 2003, and choose Tools⇨Speech from the main menu. Follow the step-by-step installation process, and before long, your computer should understand all those colorful things you often say to it.

All Office applications share the speech recognition feature. Thank goodness you need to install it only once.

Sending Access to Voice Training School

Before you can use speech recognition effectively, you need to train it to recognize your speech patterns. Bostonians, with their rapid speech and refusal to sound out the letter *R*, sound very different than residents of Biloxi and New Orleans with their slow, Southern drawls. The training process helps the computer to understand how *you* say "hello" and "good-bye."

Access enters training mode automatically the first time you try to use speech recognition. If you find that the computer isn't doing a good job of understanding you, you can give it more training by selecting Training on the speech toolbar (which opens any time you invoke speech recognition).

To train Access to recognize your speech patterns, follow these steps:

1. **Put on the headset and place the microphone about an inch from your mouth.**

   Avoid putting the microphone directly in front of your mouth, where it will detect breathing sounds. Try to position the microphone the same way every time you use the speech recognition feature.

2. **Choose Tools⇨Speech.**

   Access displays the Welcome box, as shown in Figure 25-1.

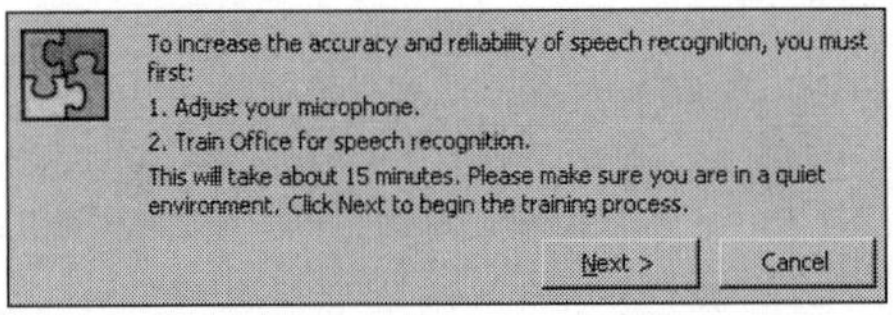

Figure 25-1:
Welcome
to speech
recognition.

3. **Follow the prompts on the next few screens to set up the optimal volume on your microphone.**

   Office adjusts your volume settings behind the scenes as you read a few sentences. You're ready to train the computer to recognize your voice!

4. **Follow the prompts to read displayed text into the microphone, as shown in Figure 25-2.**

   Access keeps track of your progress and highlights words as it understands them. If it doesn't recognize a word, Access leaves that word unhighlighted. Simply repeat the word or phrase. You're finished!

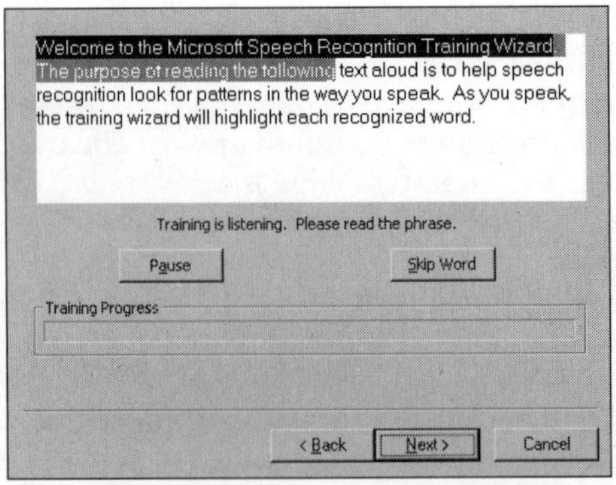

Figure 25-2:
Access
highlights
words as it
understands
them.

When you finish speech recognition training, you see the window shown in Figure 25-3. Note that Access promises only about 85 percent accuracy at first. The more you use speech recognition, the better it understands you.

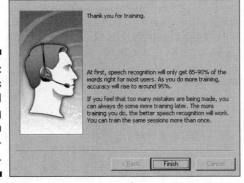

Figure 25-3: Access has completed the training course on understanding *you*.

If recognition accuracy is too low, you can return to training mode for additional reading exercises. Retraining is a quick way to improve accuracy.

Speaking to Access

To turn on speech recognition, choose Tools➪Speech. The language toolbar appears, as shown in Figure 25-4. Turn the microphone on or off by clicking the Microphone icon.

Figure 25-4: The language toolbar is your access to the world of speech recognition.

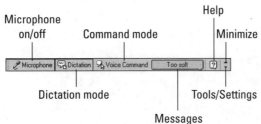

Microphone on/off — Command mode — Help — Minimize

Dictation mode — Messages — Tools/Settings

The first time you choose Speech, you launch into training mode automatically.

The language toolbar gives you access to several alternative input methods besides speech recognition. For example, if you have a graphics tablet attached to your PC, you can write on the tablet with a stylus and use Office's handwriting feature to turn your writing into text.

You can use speech recognition in dictation mode or command mode. Understanding the difference between the two modes is important. Suppose, for example, you say the word "open." In dictation mode, Access types the word; in command mode, it displays the File Open dialog box.

The next sections cover each mode in turn.

"Access, take a letter please"

Dictation mode works just like it sounds — you speak into the microphone, and Access types what you say (or at least what it *thinks* you said). To go into dictation mode, follow these steps:

1. **If you're in command mode, click the Dictation button on the language toolbar or say "dictation."**

   The speech toolbar always displays the current mode: dictation or command.

2. **Click the box where you want Access to type, and start speaking.**

   Speak in a normal voice, enunciating each word, but not pausing between words. Watch the language toolbar for any prompts. (For example, in Figure 25-4, Access tells me that I'm speaking too softly.)

Figure 25-5 shows the result of my dictating to Access. In the first record, Access recognized what I said with no errors. In the second record, I said, "This is record number three. I have already deleted record number two." Figure 25-5 shows what Access *thought* I said. See the next section, "Correcting dictation errors," for details about smoothing out the misunderstandings.

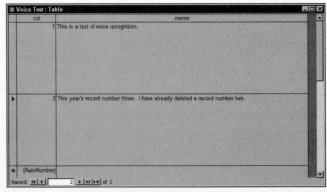

Figure 25-5:
The results of dictating three sentences — one is perfect, one is close, and one is pretty well mangled.

To get out of dictation mode, click the Voice Command button on the language toolbar or say "voice command." Alternatively, you can turn off the microphone by clicking the Microphone button.

When dictating, you can spell out any word by saying "spelling mode," pausing a moment, and then saying the letters.

Built into dictation mode are a number of special things you can say. Table 25-1 lists some of the more common commands.

Table 25-1	Some Dictation-Mode Commands
What You Say	*What's Inserted*
"Dot" or "period"	.
"At sign"	@
"Comma"	,
"Backslash"	\
"Slash"	/
"Equals"	=
"Plus" or "plus sign"	+
"New line"	Enter keystroke
"New paragraph"	Two Enter keystrokes
"1"	One (numbers less than 20 are spelled out)
"21"	21 (numbers 20 or greater are inserted as digits)

For a complete list of dictation mode commands, search the Help file for "Things you can do and say with speech recognition."

Correcting dictation errors

You can correct errors anytime during dictation. Microsoft recommends that you wait until you finish dictating so that you don't interrupt your train of thought. I tried dictating several pages of text and then went back to correct errors. I couldn't even recall what I was trying to say. It's up to you how and when you correct errors — experiment to see which method suits you.

You can correct errors in three ways:

- ✔ **Retype the errors:** Select the text in error and simply retype it. This method is often the easiest.

- ✔ **Dictate over the errors:** Highlight the incorrect text by using your mouse or keyboard and re-dictate.

    If you decide to dictate over an error, you're best off highlighting a whole phrase. For example, in Figure 25-5 I said, "This is record number three" but the computer heard "This year's record number three." I could have highlighted the word "year's" and re-dictated "is." But speech recognition is more accurate with phrases. Selecting and re-dictating "This is record" or perhaps even the whole sentence serves you better.

- ✔ **Spell over the errors:** Select an error by using the mouse or keyboard, say "spelling mode," pause a moment, and then say each letter of the word, pausing between letters. Say "dictation mode" when you're finished.

Using command mode

Command mode lets you tell Access what to do. For example, if you open a datasheet and say "print," Access sends the datasheet to the printer immediately.

If you're in dictation mode, you can go into command mode by saying "voice command." (You can also click the Voice Command button on the language toolbar.) Here are some guidelines for using command mode:

- ✔ **To select toolbar items,** say the name of the toolbar button, such as Save or Spelling. If you don't know the name of a toolbar item, pause the mouse cursor over it to display the screen tip.

- ✔ **To open a menu,** say its name. For example, saying "file" prompts the File menu to drop down. If you then say "insert," the Insert menu drops down.

- ✔ **To select a menu item,** say its name while the menu is open. For example, to display the About box, say "help" to open the Help menu and then say "about Microsoft Access."

- ✔ **To "click" a button,** say its name. For example, saying "okay" activates the OK button.

- ✔ **To work with windows and dialog boxes,** say the caption of the control that you want to work with. For example, Figure 25-6 shows the Options dialog box in Access. To move to the Spelling tab, say its name. To add a check mark to the top option, say "suggest from main dictionary only." Saying "suggest from main dictionary only" a second time causes the option to be unchecked. To access the drop-down list of languages, say "dictionary language."

Figure 25-6:
While in command mode, you can work in any window or dialog box without touching the mouse or keyboard.

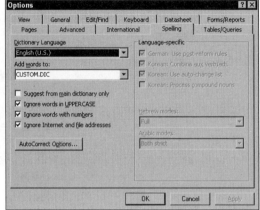

As with dictation mode, command mode recognizes some specific commands. Table 25-2 lists these commands and their actions.

Table 25-2	Some Command-Mode Commands
What You Say	*What Happens*
"Left" or "go left"	Cursor moves to the left
"Right" or "go right"	Cursor moves to the right
"Page down"	Page down
"Page up"	Page up
"Tab"	Tab
"Delete"	Delete
"Right click"	Open context menu
"Escape"	Press Esc
"Return" or "Enter"	Press Enter
"Space"	Press Spacebar

Improving Speech Recognition

The following are some tips on increasing speech recognition accuracy in Access. For more tips, consult the Help file and also check out the Microsoft Office Web site by clicking Office on the Web on the Access Help menu.

- ✔ Work in a quiet environment. If you work in a noisy office, Access tries to detect what everyone else around you is saying.

- ✔ Use a high-quality microphone. Make sure it provides signal boost and that it's unidirectional (that is, it "listens" in only one direction).

- ✔ Wear the headset and microphone in the same position each time you dictate. Make sure the microphone is about an inch from your lips but not right in front of your lips (it's best if the microphone is just below or to the side of your mouth).

- ✔ Use a high-quality sound card. If you detect hissing through your head-set, so does Access. Try moving the sound card as far away from the power supply as possible.

- ✔ Speak in phrases rather than pausing between words. Enunciate clearly.

- ✔ Turn off the microphone when you're not dictating.

- ✔ Train your computer by reading prepared texts in the Training Wizard.

- ✔ Add new words to the dictionary by choosing Tools⇨Add/Delete words. Type the new word and then pronounce it.

Part VI
The Part of Tens

The 5th Wave   By Rich Tennant

"This isn't a quantitative or a qualitative estimate of the job. This is a wish-upon-a-star estimate of the project."

In this part . . .

All hail the traditional Part of Tens, purveyor of numerically organized information, keeper of the sacred decimal count, and upholder of the proud *For Dummies* tradition.

Every *For Dummies* book closes with a Part of Tens. Think of it as the *For Dummies* version of denouement. Anyway, this book's final part includes stuff you can use today, stuff you may need tomorrow, and stuff for *way* on down the road. I tried to include a little something for everyone, so read every chapter *very* closely and see whether you can find the stuff that I put in just for you.

By the way, no animals were harmed, exploited, or even consulted in the quest to bring you this information (although the kids did remember to feed the gerbils periodically throughout the project). One technoweenie got slightly miffed, but I'm sure he'll get over it.

Chapter 26

Ten Timesaving
Keyboard Shortcuts

• •

In This Chapter

▶ Select an entire field: F2

▶ Insert the current date: Ctrl+; (semicolon)

▶ Insert the current time: Ctrl+: (colon)

▶ Insert the same field value as in the last record: Ctrl+' (apostrophe)

▶ Insert a line break: Ctrl+Enter

▶ Add a record: Ctrl++(plus sign)

▶ Delete the current record: Ctrl+– (minus sign)

▶ Save the record: Shift+Enter

▶ Undo your last changes: Ctrl+Z

▶ Open the selected object in design view: Ctrl+Enter

• •

*J*ust because Windows is supposed to be the ultimate graphical user environment doesn't mean that you won't need the keyboard anymore. In fact, Access has some cool shortcuts up its sleeve. This chapter highlights ten keystroke combinations that enter data automatically, make editing quicker, and generally simplify your life.

Select an Entire Field: F2

The F2 shortcut is handy when you're replacing a lengthy address or description field. Instead of wrestling with the mouse to make sure that you highlighted everything in the field, simply press F2. The keystroke works in both datasheet view and form view.

Insert the Current Date: Ctrl+; (Semicolon)

The Ctrl+; (semicolon) keystroke combination not only saves time but also increases accuracy. Ever mistype a date because you were in a hurry (or because the keyboard can't spell)? Ctrl+; resolves the issue by doing the work for you. To execute this command, press and hold down the Ctrl key and then press the semicolon key. The keystroke works in datasheet view and form view.

Insert the Current Time: Ctrl+: (Colon)

The Ctrl+: (colon) shortcut is another nod to accuracy. To insert the current time, you press and hold down the Ctrl button and Shift keys, and then press the semicolon key. The keystroke works in datasheet view and form view.

Insert the Same Field Value as in the Last Record: Ctrl+' (Apostrophe)

While entering data, you often come across a whole bunch of records containing similar information — for example, people from the same city and state. Instead of manually typing the duplicate information in every record, the Ctrl+' (apostrophe) keystroke quickly enters it for you in datasheet view and form view.

Ctrl+' (apostrophe) isn't psychic, though. Instead, it merely says, "Well, I see that you're in the City field. In the last record, the city was Tucumcari, so I bet that's what you want in this record, too." And then it promptly copies the value from the preceding record into the current one. (Of course, this works for any field, not just address information.)

Insert a Line Break: Ctrl+Enter

When a long entry in a memo or large text field feels like it's never going to quit, end the monotony with a line break. Well-placed line breaks make your data more legible, too. The keystroke is available in datasheet view and form view.

Add a Record: Ctrl++ (Plus Sign)

Although Ctrl++ looks funny (just how *do* you write *plus* + without spelling it out?), this keyboard shortcut keeps you on the go when you're in a hot-and-heavy edit mode. Because you don't have to keep switching between the keyboard and the mouse to insert new records, your speed increases, as does your accuracy.

Unlike the Ctrl+: (colon) keystroke covered earlier in the chapter, you don't need to press the Shift key to make Ctrl++ work. Go figure.

Delete the Current Record: Ctrl+ – (Minus Sign)

Do you suffer from pesky, unsightly, or unneeded records in your tables? Ctrl+– painlessly excises the records that you want to delete. And just like this shortcut's cousin, Ctrl++, this shortcut works in both datasheet view and form view.

Save the Record: Shift+Enter

After a long, hard edit, make sure that the record is saved with a quick Shift+Enter. This keystroke signals Access that you've truly finished working on the record and are ready to store it for posterity. The software takes the cue and saves your changes immediately. Use this key combo in datasheet view or form view. It's a real time-saver!

Undo Your Last Changes: Ctrl+Z

Everyone should have the Undo keystroke memorized. With the propensity of Access to automatically save changes every time you turn around, it can really save your bacon. When something goes wrong, don't panic — try Ctrl+Z instead. This keystroke combination works almost everywhere in Access and even beyond in many Windows applications.

Open the Selected Object in Design View: Ctrl+Enter

Hey, what's this? Ctrl+Enter does *two* functions in Access? You're right:

- ✔ When you're editing a table in datasheet view or form view, Ctrl+Enter inserts a line break.
- ✔ When you're in database view, use Ctrl+Enter to whip open something in design view.

Let the ordinary folks use the mouse — be different and do it from the keyboard!

Chapter 27

Ten Common Crises and How to Survive Them

In This Chapter

▶ You type 73.725, but it changes to 74

▶ Your run a query but the results look screwy

▶ And when you looked again, the record was gone

▶ The validation that never was

▶ The sometimes-there, sometimes-gone menus

▶ You can't link to a dBASE table

▶ You can't update a linked dBASE or Paradox table

▶ You get a key violation when importing a table

▶ Try as you may, the program won't start

▶ The wizard won't come out of his keep

*W*here there are computers, so also is there software, because a computer is nothing without its software. Where there is software, so also are there problems, because software without problems is obviously outdated and in need of replacement.

Problems are a part of life. When the problems strike in or around your precious data, they seem all the more fearsome. This chapter touches on ten problems you may encounter while using Access. If your problem is covered here, try the solution I outline. If your particular trouble isn't on the list, refer to Chapter 3 for some other spots to seek help.

And good luck.

You Type 73.725, but It Changes to 74

Automatic rounding can frustrate the living daylights out of you, but correcting it is easy. By default, Access sets all number fields to accept *long integers* — numbers without decimal places. You need to change the setting to *single*, which is short for *single-precision number,* not *hey you swinging text field, let's go party with the forms.*

Open the table in design view and then click the field that's giving you fits. On the General tab of the Properties area at the bottom of the screen, click the Field Size box. Click the down arrow on the end of the box, and then select Single from the drop-down menu that appears. Save the table, and your automatic rounding problem is over.

You Run a Query but the Results Look Screwy

Everybody — even the experts — get weird results from a query every now and then. Take heart! These things almost always happen because something small went wrong in the query. To make things right again, open your query and check it for the following problems:

 ✔ **A few stray characters wandered into your criteria:** A single misplaced keystroke sends Access on a wild data chase. Tidy things up (review your criteria and dubble-chick your speeling), and then try the query again.

 ✔ **The selection logic needs some help:** Juggling a bunch of AND and OR connections in a query quickly messes up even the hardiest of database designers. Look through Chapters 11 and 13 for tips on fortifying your query's thought processes.

 ✔ **The tables didn't join correctly (or didn't join at all):** If your query results show *way* too many records and the query uses two or more tables, improper joining is the likely cause. Flip back to Chapter 12 for more about joining one table to another.

 ✔ **The tables joined correctly, but Access can't find a legitimate match between the tables:** If your query involves two or more tables and you get fewer records than you expected, this is the likely cause. For example, if you have an order entry database and run a query listing all customers and their orders, by default you would see only those customers who have placed an order. To see all customers whether or not they have placed an order:

1. **In the design view, right-click the join (the line connecting the two tables) and choose Join Properties.**

   For a quick refresher about joining tables in the design view, check out Chapter 12.

2. **Examine the types of joins offered and choose the one that says something like "Include ALL records from 'Customers' and only those records from 'Orders' where the joined fields are equal."**

   The actual text you see differs according to the names of your tables. In technical mumbo-jumbo, this is called an *outer join.* Very cool.

3. **Click OK and run the query.**

   You should now have all records from the Customers table whether or not there are corresponding records in the Orders table.

✔ If your query involves several criteria, some calculated fields, and a tangled bunch of various joins, try breaking the task into several smaller steps instead of trying to subdue the beast in a single massive blow. The step-by-step approach lets you focus on each piece, one at a time, making sure each works perfectly before moving on to the next one. See Chapter 15 for more on that approach.

Don't forget that you can always use the Expression Builder to help you put together particularly tricky questions.

If your query still won't work no matter what you do, ask someone else to take a quick peek at it. After staring at the query, fiddling with it, and generally beating on it for so long, it's easy to overlook the simplest of problems. Getting a fresh pair of eyes on the problem often solves things fast.

And When You Looked Again, the Record Was Gone

"The record was there — right there!" The key word in that sentence is the verb, because it indicates that the record *isn't* there now. Precisely *where* the record went only the computer knows, and machines have a code of silence about these details. (It's a subset of the rules that make all the copiers break at the same time.)

Don't panic. Panicky people make strange changes, and you need your wits about you for the next few minutes. You can panic later after the dust settles.

Before doing anything technical with Access (or hitting the computer with a baseball bat), press Ctrl+Z. That's the Undo command. If the record comes back, you're in luck.

If the Undo command didn't accomplish anything, you're in slightly more trouble. The next best solution is to copy the record from a backup of the database file. This solution works only if you backed up your database at some point since the record was originally added. If you have a paper copy of the data, you could manually re-enter it into the database. If that record was your only copy of the information, raise your hand, look at the computer, and wave good-bye, because it's gone now (you have my deepest sympathy).

Please, oh *please,* keep current backups of your information. You never know when bad things will happen (insert eerie organ music here).

The Validation That Never Was

Validations are one of my favorite features in Access. But like anything, validations can cause problems if they're not used properly.

The biggest concern is a validation rule that *can't* be valid. For example, suppose someone wants to limit a particular field so that it accepts entries between 0 and 100. To accomplish this feat, the person creates a validation that says <0 AND >100. Unfortunately, that rule won't work — ever! The person mixed up the symbols and created a rule that accepts only a number that's less than 0 *and* greater than 100. According to my college math professor, not too many numbers like that are running loose in the world.

Don't let this problem happen to your validations. To avoid such crises, write your rule on paper and then test it with some sample data. Be sure to include examples of both good and bad entries to make sure that the rule works just like it's supposed to.

The Sometimes-There, Sometimes-Gone Menus

Thanks to someone in the *Conceptually Cool, but Functionally Frustrating New Feature Division* of Microsoft, the menus in Access (and all its brethren in the latest episode of *Microsoft Office: the Beast That Ate Your Hard Drive*) don't automatically show all of the possible menu items available. Instead, they show only the most commonly used menu items, plus a little down-pointing chevron at the bottom of the menu. (Yes, this is *supposed* to make your life easier. Isn't that nice to know?)

That little chevron is your key to the full menu. When you click the chevron, the menu magically expands to its full size, proudly displaying all of the options available on it. At this point, click whichever menu item you want.

After you click the chevron and select an item from the full menu, Access automatically adds that item to the *short* version of the menu.

You Can't Link to a dBASE Table

If you can't link to a dBASE table, tell Access that the table came from a different version of dBASE. If you chose dBASE 5 initially but it didn't work, try dBASE IV or dBASE III.

You Can't Update a Linked dBASE or Paradox Table

If you can't update a dBASE or Paradox table to which you have linked, you probably need to get the techies involved. The default drivers delivered with Access allow read-only access to dBASE and Paradox tables; you need to have the Borland Database Engine (BDE) installed on your computer. As of this writing, your best bet for information is the community-operated BDE Support page at www.bdesupport.com. You can download the engine files there, get some excellent help documents, and hook up with other developers. If you need more information about connecting Access and Paradox, go to the Microsoft Knowledge Base (http://search.support.microsoft.com) and search for Borland Database Engine.

You Get a Key Violation While Importing a Table

When you get a key violation while importing a table, the data you're importing contains a duplicate key value. Because Access can't arbitrarily change the data in question, you need to make the repair. Go back to the master program, find the offending record, and build a good key to replace the duplicated one. After you're sure that the key values are unique, try, try again.

Try as You May, the Program Won't Start

After choosing Access from the Start menu, the oh-so-cool Access splash screen (the pretty picture that keeps you entertained while the program takes too long to load) flows smoothly onto the screen. Suddenly, the serene moment shatters as a small warning box bursts in, shouting that Windows can't find ODD_ESOTERIC_FILE.MDB. The Access splash screen fades, and you're left facing the Windows desktop.

This sequence really does happen from time to time. Honestly, such events are just part of life with computers. I teach my troubleshooting classes a simple mantra to cover precisely this problem: *It's a file. Files go bad.*

Because the error message was kind enough to give you a file name (not all errors are so generous), use Explorer to look for the file. If it's there, odds are that the file is corrupt. If the file isn't there, well, at least you know why Access didn't find it.

Either way, you need to replace the file with a healthy version from your original Access program disks. If you have a CD-ROM copy of Access, this process is easy. Just point Explorer at the installation CD-ROM, find the file, and copy it to the Access subdirectory.

If Access lives on your company's network, contact your friendly Information Systems support folks for guidance. In that case, the problem is very likely out of your hands. Wish the computer gurus luck, and then take a coffee break while they work on the problem.

The Wizard Won't Come Out of His Keep

A wizard that won't start is a more focused version of the preceding problem, in which Access won't start. Now the problem is localized to a particular wizard. The solution is the same: Look for the missing file, replace it from the master disks, and then see whether that solves the problem.

If all else fails (which may happen), pick up a bag of nacho chips and call in your favorite nerd for some assistance.

By default, the Access menus and other dialog boxes show all possible options — not just the options currently installed on your computer. This means that as you use Access, it may periodically say that a menu option you select doesn't exist on your computer. In that case, whip out the Access CD-ROM and install it. If your computer is part of a network in a business, contact your computer support folks because they probably need (or want) to handle the installation themselves.

Chapter 28

Ten Tips from Database Nerds

*L*ike 'em or loathe 'em, the technical experts are always with you. In their more lucid moments, they possess nuggets of wisdom. This chapter is a distillation of good advice that I picked up over the years. Some of it is focused; other parts are downright philosophical. Such is life with the technical experts (but you knew that already).

Document As if Your Life Depends on It

Yes, documenting is a pain. Yes, it's a bother. Yes, I document everything myself (kinda scary when a guy actually listens to his own advice). If you build a database, make sure that you document every little detail about it.

What should your documentation include? Well, everything! Here's a list of items to start you on your documentation journey:

 ✔ **General information about the database:** Include file locations (with specific network paths, not just drive letters such as *G:*), an explanation of what the database does, and information on how it works.

- **Table layouts, including field names, sizes, contents, and sample contents:** If some of the data comes from esoteric or temporary sources (like the shipping report that you shred right after data entry), note that fact in the documentation.

- **Report names, an explanation of the information on the report, and a list of who gets a copy of the report when it's printed:** If you need to run some queries before creating a report, document the process. (Better, get a nerd to help you automate the work.) Documenting who receives the report is particularly important. Jot down the job title and department in the documentation as well as the current person in the position.

- **Queries and logic:** For every query, provide a detailed explanation of how the query works, especially if it involves multiple tables or data sources outside Access (such as SQL tables or other big-time information storage areas).

- **Answer the question "Why?":** As you document your database, focus on *why* your design works the way that it works. Why do the queries use those particular tables? Why do the reports go to those people? Granted, if you work in a corporate environment, you may not *know* why the system works the way it does, but it never hurts to inquire.

- **Miscellaneous details:** Provide information such as the backup process and schedule, where backup tapes are located (you *are* making backups, right?), and what to do if the computer isn't working. If your database runs an important business function, such as accounting, inventory, point-of-sale, or order entry, make sure that a manual process is in place to keep the business going if the computer breaks down — and remember to document the process!

If you need help with any of these items, *ask someone!* Whether you borrow someone from your Information Systems department or rent a computer geek, get the help you need. Treat your documentation like insurance — no business should run without it.

Every 6 to 12 months, review your documentation to see whether updates are needed. Documentation is only useful if it's up-to-date and if someone other than yourself can understand it. Likewise, make sure you (or your counterparts in the department) know where the documentation is located. If you have an electronic version, keep it backed up and have a printout handy.

Don't Make Your Fields Too Big

As you build tables, take a moment to make your text fields the appropriate size for the data you keep there. By default, Access sets up text fields to hold 50 characters — a pretty generous setting, particularly if the field holds two-letter state abbreviations. Granted, 48 characters of space aren't anything to write home about, but multiply that space across a table with 100,000 customer addresses in it, and you get 4.8MB of storage space that's very busy holding nothing.

Adjust the field size with the Field Size setting on the General tab in design view.

Use Number Fields for Real Numbers

Use number fields for numbers, not for text pretending to be a number. Computers perceive a huge difference between the postal code 47999 and the number 47,999. The computer views a postal code as a series of characters that all happen to be digits, but the number is treated as an actual number that you can use for math and all kinds of other fun numeric stuff.

When choosing the type for a new field with numbers in it, ask yourself a simple question: Are you *ever* going to make a calculation or do anything math related with the field? If so, use a number type. If not, store the field as text and go on with your life.

Validate Data

Validations work hand in hand with masks to prevent bad data from getting close to your tables. Validations are easy to make, quick to set up, and ever vigilant (even when you're so tired you can't see straight). If you aren't using validations to protect the integrity of your database, you really should start. Flip to Chapter 7 and have a look at the topic.

Use Understandable Names

When building a table or creating a database, think about the names you use. Will you remember what they mean three months from now? Six months from now? Are they intuitive enough so that someone else can look at the table and figure out what it does, long after your knowledge of Access puts your career on the fast track? Windows allows long file names; please use them. You don't need to get carried away, but now you have no excuse for a file called *03Q1bdg5*. Using *2003 Q1 Budget Rev 5* makes much more sense to everyone involved.

Take Great Care When Deleting

Whenever you're deleting field values from a table, make sure that you're killing the values in the right record, check again, and then — only when you're sure — delete the original. Even then, you can still do a quick Ctrl+Z and recover the little bugger.

Why all the checking and double-checking? Because after you delete a field value *and do anything else in the table,* Access completely forgets about your old value. It's gone, just as if it never existed. If you delete a record from a table, the record is really gone because there is no Undo available for an entire record. If that record happened to be important and you don't have a current backup file, you're out of luck. Sorry!

Keep Backups

There's no substitute for a current backup of your data, particularly if the data is vital to your company. Effective strategies often include maintaining backup copies at another location in case a disaster destroys your work facility. Don't believe me? Let the phrase *no receivables* float through your mind for a while. How do you feel about backups now? I thought you'd see it my way.

Think First and Then Think Again

Apply the "think first and then think again" rule to any Access step that contains the word *delete* or *redesign.* Think about what you're doing. Then think again. Software makes handling large amounts of data easier than ever before, but it also offers the tools to screw up your data on a scale not seen since the time of P.T. Barnum.

Get Organized and Keep It Simple

Although the advice to get organized and keep it simple may seem different at first blush, they work together to promote classic nerd values such as *a place for every gadget* and *my query ran faster than yours, so there.* By keeping your computer orderly and organizing your entire workspace, you have everything you need at hand. Get yourself a recliner and a remote control, and you never need to leave the office again.

Yes, you can get *too* organized. In fact, overorganizing is altogether too easy. Temper your desire to organize with a passion for working with as few steps as possible. On your computer, limit the number of folders and subfolders you use — a maximum of five levels of folders is more than enough for just about anybody. If you go much beyond five levels, your organization starts bumping into your productivity (and nobody likes a productivity loss, least of all the people who come up with those silly little slogans for corporate feel-good posters).

Know When to Ask for Help

If you're having trouble with something, swallow your ego and ask for help. Saying "I don't know" and then trying to find out holds no shame. This rule is especially important when you're riding herd on thousands of records in a database. Small missteps quickly magnify and multiply a small problem into a huge crisis. Ask for help before the situation becomes dire.

Index

• G •

• U •

• V •

FOR DUMMIES®

The easy way to get more done and have more fun

PERSONAL FINANCE

0-7645-5231-7

0-7645-2431-3

0-7645-5331-3

Also available:

Estate Planning For Dummies
(0-7645-5501-4)

401(k)s For Dummies
(0-7645-5468-9)

Frugal Living For Dummies
(0-7645-5403-4)

Microsoft Money "X" For Dummies
(0-7645-1689-2)

Mutual Funds For Dummies
(0-7645-5329-1)

Personal Bankruptcy For Dummies
(0-7645-5498-0)

Quicken "X" For Dummies
(0-7645-1666-3)

Stock Investing For Dummies
(0-7645-5411-5)

Taxes For Dummies 2003
(0-7645-5475-1)

BUSINESS & CAREERS

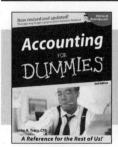

0-7645-5314-3

0-7645-5307-0

0-7645-5471-9

Also available:

Business Plans Kit For Dummies
(0-7645-5365-8)

Consulting For Dummies
(0-7645-5034-9)

Cool Careers For Dummies
(0-7645-5345-3)

Human Resources Kit For Dummies
(0-7645-5131-0)

Managing For Dummies
(1-5688-4858-7)

QuickBooks All-in-One Desk Reference For Dummies
(0-7645-1963-8)

Selling For Dummies
(0-7645-5363-1)

Small Business Kit For Dummies
(0-7645-5093-4)

Starting an eBay Business For Dummies
(0-7645-1547-0)

HEALTH, SPORTS & FITNESS

0-7645-5167-1

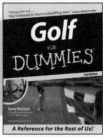

0-7645-5146-9

0-7645-5154-X

Also available:

Controlling Cholesterol For Dummies
(0-7645-5440-9)

Dieting For Dummies
(0-7645-5126-4)

High Blood Pressure For Dummies
(0-7645-5424-7)

Martial Arts For Dummies
(0-7645-5358-5)

Menopause For Dummies
(0-7645-5458-1)

Nutrition For Dummies
(0-7645-5180-9)

Power Yoga For Dummies
(0-7645-5342-9)

Thyroid For Dummies
(0-7645-5385-2)

Weight Training For Dummies
(0-7645-5168-X)

Yoga For Dummies
(0-7645-5117-5)

Available wherever books are sold.
Go to www.dummies.com or call 1-877-762-2974 to order direct.

FOR DUMMIES®

A world of resources to help you grow

HOME, GARDEN & HOBBIES

0-7645-5295-3

0-7645-5130-2

0-7645-5106-X

Also available:

Auto Repair For Dummies
(0-7645-5089-6)

Chess For Dummies
(0-7645-5003-9)

Home Maintenance For
Dummies
(0-7645-5215-5)

Organizing For Dummies
(0-7645-5300-3)

Piano For Dummies
(0-7645-5105-1)

Poker For Dummies
(0-7645-5232-5)

Quilting For Dummies
(0-7645-5118-3)

Rock Guitar For Dummies
(0-7645-5356-9)

Roses For Dummies
(0-7645-5202-3)

Sewing For Dummies
(0-7645-5137-X)

FOOD & WINE

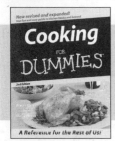

0-7645-5250-3

0-7645-5390-9

0-7645-5114-0

Also available:

Bartending For Dummies
(0-7645-5051-9)

Chinese Cooking For
Dummies
(0-7645-5247-3)

Christmas Cooking For
Dummies
(0-7645-5407-7)

Diabetes Cookbook For
Dummies
(0-7645-5230-9)

Grilling For Dummies
(0-7645-5076-4)

Low-Fat Cooking For
Dummies
(0-7645-5035-7)

Slow Cookers For Dummies
(0-7645-5240-6)

TRAVEL

0-7645-5453-0

0-7645-5438-7

0-7645-5448-4

Also available:

America's National Parks For
Dummies
(0-7645-6204-5)

Caribbean For Dummies
(0-7645-5445-X)

Cruise Vacations For
Dummies 2003
(0-7645-5459-X)

Europe For Dummies
(0-7645-5456-5)

Ireland For Dummies
(0-7645-6199-5)

France For Dummies
(0-7645-6292-4)

London For Dummies
(0-7645-5416-6)

Mexico's Beach Resorts For
Dummies
(0-7645-6262-2)

Paris For Dummies
(0-7645-5494-8)

RV Vacations For Dummies
(0-7645-5443-3)

Walt Disney World & Orlando
For Dummies
(0-7645-5444-1)

Available wherever books are sold. Go to www.dummies.com or call 1-877-762-2974 to order direct.

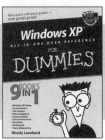
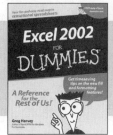

FOR DUMMIES®

Helping you expand your horizons and realize your potential

INTERNET

0-7645-0894-6

0-7645-1659-0

0-7645-1642-6

Also available:

America Online 7.0 For Dummies
(0-7645-1624-8)

Genealogy Online For Dummies
(0-7645-0807-5)

The Internet All-in-One Desk Reference For Dummies
(0-7645-1659-0)

Internet Explorer 6 For Dummies
(0-7645-1344-3)

The Internet For Dummies Quick Reference
(0-7645-1645-0)

Internet Privacy For Dummies
(0-7645-0846-6)

Researching Online For Dummies
(0-7645-0546-7)

Starting an Online Business For Dummies
(0-7645-1655-8)

DIGITAL MEDIA

0-7645-1664-7

0-7645-1675-2

0-7645-0806-7

Also available:

CD and DVD Recording For Dummies
(0-7645-1627-2)

Digital Photography All-in-One Desk Reference For Dummies
(0-7645-1800-3)

Digital Photography For Dummies Quick Reference
(0-7645-0750-8)

Home Recording for Musicians For Dummies
(0-7645-1634-5)

MP3 For Dummies
(0-7645-0858-X)

Paint Shop Pro "X" For Dummies
(0-7645-2440-2)

Photo Retouching & Restoration For Dummies
(0-7645-1662-0)

Scanners For Dummies
(0-7645-0783-4)

GRAPHICS

0-7645-0817-2

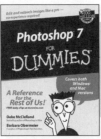

0-7645-1651-5

0-7645-0895-4

Also available:

Adobe Acrobat 5 PDF For Dummies
(0-7645-1652-3)

Fireworks 4 For Dummies
(0-7645-0804-0)

Illustrator 10 For Dummies
(0-7645-3636-2)

QuarkXPress 5 For Dummies
(0-7645-0643-9)

Visio 2000 For Dummies
(0-7645-0635-8)

Available wherever books are sold. Go to www.dummies.com or call 1-877-762-2974 to order direct.

FOR DUMMIES®

The advice and explanations you need to succeed

SELF-HELP, SPIRITUALITY & RELIGION

0-7645-5302-X

0-7645-5418-2

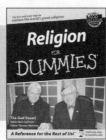
0-7645-5264-3

Also available:

The Bible For Dummies
(0-7645-5296-1)

Buddhism For Dummies
(0-7645-5359-3)

Christian Prayer For Dummies
(0-7645-5500-6)

Dating For Dummies
(0-7645-5072-1)

Judaism For Dummies
(0-7645-5299-6)

Potty Training For Dummies
(0-7645-5417-4)

Pregnancy For Dummies
(0-7645-5074-8)

Rekindling Romance For Dummies
(0-7645-5303-8)

Spirituality For Dummies
(0-7645-5298-8)

Weddings For Dummies
(0-7645-5055-1)

PETS

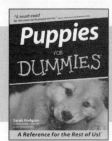
0-7645-5255-4

0-7645-5286-4

0-7645-5275-9

Also available:

Labrador Retrievers For Dummies
(0-7645-5281-3)

Aquariums For Dummies
(0-7645-5156-6)

Birds For Dummies
(0-7645-5139-6)

Dogs For Dummies
(0-7645-5274-0)

Ferrets For Dummies
(0-7645-5259-7)

German Shepherds For Dummies
(0-7645-5280-5)

Golden Retrievers For Dummies
(0-7645-5267-8)

Horses For Dummies
(0-7645-5138-8)

Jack Russell Terriers For Dummies
(0-7645-5268-6)

Puppies Raising & Training Diary For Dummies
(0-7645-0876-8)

EDUCATION & TEST PREPARATION

0-7645-5194-9

0-7645-5325-9

0-7645-5210-4

Also available:

Chemistry For Dummies
(0-7645-5430-1)

English Grammar For Dummies
(0-7645-5322-4)

French For Dummies
(0-7645-5193-0)

The GMAT For Dummies
(0-7645-5251-1)

Inglés Para Dummies
(0-7645-5427-1)

Italian For Dummies
(0-7645-5196-5)

Research Papers For Dummies
(0-7645-5426-3)

The SAT I For Dummies
(0-7645-5472-7)

U.S. History For Dummies
(0-7645-5249-X)

World History For Dummies
(0-7645-5242-2)

Available wherever books are sold. Go to www.dummies.com or call 1-877-762-2974 to order direct.

FOR DUMMIES®

We take the mystery out of complicated subjects

WEB DEVELOPMENT

0-7645-1643-4

0-7645-0723-0

0-7645-1630-2

Also available:

ASP.NET For Dummies
(0-7645-0866-0)

Building a Web Site For
Dummies
(0-7645-0720-6)

ColdFusion "MX" For
Dummies (0-7645-1672-8)

Creating Web Pages
All-in-One Desk Reference
For Dummies
(0-7645-1542-X)

FrontPage 2002 For Dummies
(0-7645-0821-0)

HTML 4 For Dummies Quick
Reference
(0-7645-0721-4)

Macromedia Studio "MX"
All-in-One Desk Reference
For Dummies
(0-7645-1799-6)

Web Design For Dummies
(0-7645-0823-7)

PROGRAMMING & DATABASES

0-7645-0746-X

0-7645-1657-4

0-7645-0818-0

Also available:

Beginning Programming For
Dummies
(0-7645-0835-0)

Crystal Reports "X"
For Dummies
(0-7645-1641-8)

Java & XML For Dummies
(0-7645-1658-2)

Java 2 For Dummies
(0-7645-0765-6)

JavaScript For Dummies
(0-7645-0633-1)

Oracle9i For Dummies
(0-7645-0880-6)

Perl For Dummies
(0-7645-0776-1)

PHP and MySQL For
Dummies
(0-7645-1650-7)

SQL For Dummies
(0-7645-0737-0)

VisualBasic .NET For
Dummies
(0-7645-0867-9)

Visual Studio .NET All-in-One
Desk Reference For Dummies
(0-7645-1626-4)

LINUX, NETWORKING & CERTIFICATION

0-7645-1545-4

0-7645-0772-9

0-7645-0812-1

Also available:

CCNP All-in-One Certification
For Dummies
(0-7645-1648-5)

Cisco Networking For
Dummies
(0-7645-1668-X)

CISSP For Dummies
(0-7645-1670-1)

CIW Foundations For
Dummies with CD-ROM
(0-7645-1635-3)

Firewalls For Dummies
(0-7645-0884-9)

Home Networking For
Dummies
(0-7645-0857-1)

Red Hat Linux All-in-One
Desk Reference For Dummies
(0-7645-2442-9)

TCP/IP For Dummies
(0-7645-1760-0)

UNIX For Dummies
(0-7645-0419-3)